This book is affectionately dedicated to
Srikar, Surabhi and Praveen

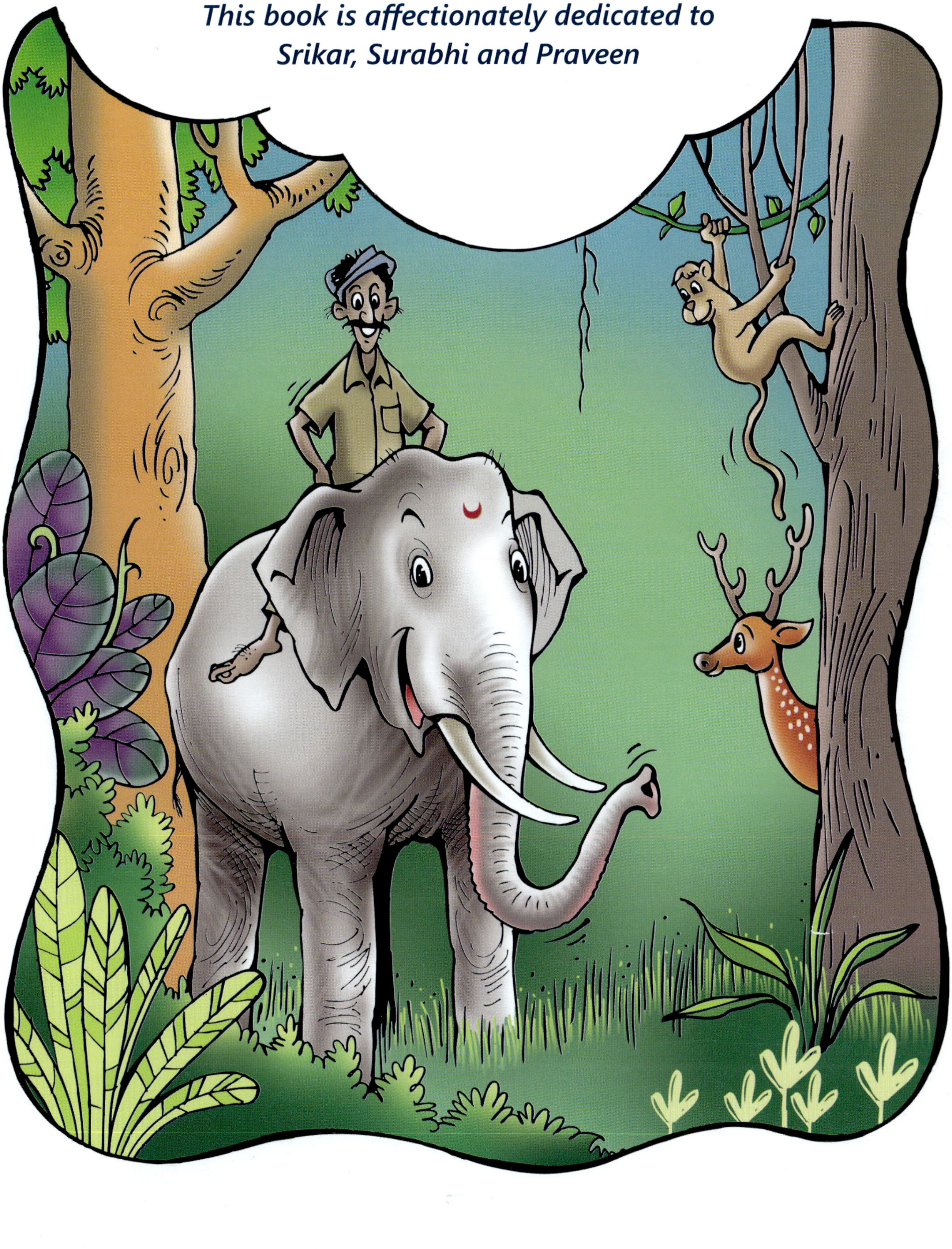

The book is a result of the ongoing collaboration between CLIC Abroad Foundation and Abraham Baldwin Agricultural College.

Idea, Story and Conceptualization: **D.K. Bhaskar**

Story and Script: **Alladi Jayasri**

Design and illustrations: **Yathi Siddakatte**

Write to:

Bangalore Environment Trust
A1, Chartered Cottage,
#8, Langford Road, Bengaluru - 560025
Karnataka, India
Tel: +91 80 22225515

Price: 949/-

Printed by:
Parishree Printers
#38/2, 2nd Cross, Nagappa Street,
Srirampuram, Bengaluru - 560021
email: info@parishree.com
www.parishree.com

About the book

Elephants in India are an important part of the religion, culture and the natural environment. Elephants were an essential part of royalty and all royal activities, including war, celebrations, and entertainment. Many mythological stories and folk tales surround the majestic species. Elephants have long been revered in world culture as the elephant headed god Ganesha, Ganapati or Vinayaka. The celestial elephant Iravata, which became the mount of Indra, the Kings of Gods, is a familiar story around the world. One tale told by our elders says that when gods found a treasured white elephant in the ocean, they celebrated it through a heavy downpour that signified the end of drought. But in modern times, such bedtime stories, fables and spirituals about the wisdom, strength and inspiration of elephants are slowly being replaced by time with gadgets. There is a real danger that children may never learn how elephants and the natural world have been critically important to the planet for thousands of years — much longer and much greater than their mere presence in the forest might imply to a child today.

This book is a small way to preserve our cultural relevance and understanding of elephants. It is based on the real-life story of Balarama, an elephant who was captured from the forests of the Western Ghats in the prime of life and trained in captivity to be the lead elephant in the world famous Dasara festival of Mysore. This book follows the journey of Balarama from the jungle to the city, and is intended to help young and all enthusiastic readers understand the complex relationship between man and elephant that forms one great foundation of Indian culture.

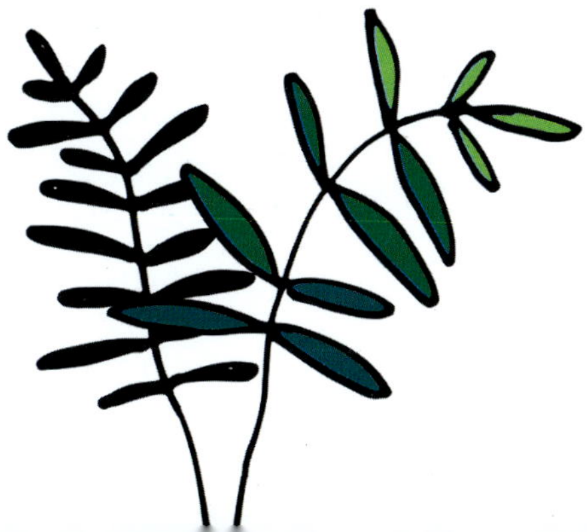

Prologue

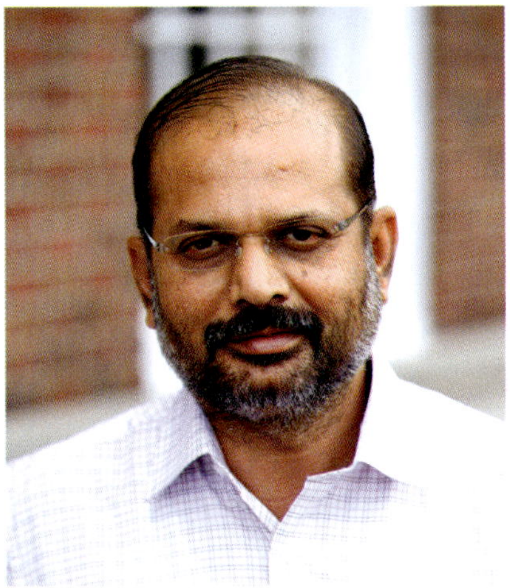

C. Jayaram *IFS*
Principal Chief Conservator of Forests (Wildlife) and The Chief Wildlife Warden, Karnataka

This book titled 'Balarama Story' is not a folklore and is a biography of an elephant Balarama, one among a few hundred elephants of Mysore Landscape participated in Mysore Nada Habba – the world famous Mysore Dasara. The Kings of Mourya Dynasty and ruler Ashoka used elephants in their regiment to wage wars unlike the Wadiyars of Mysore who revered the mighty animal as a symbol of nobility. An inevitable Khedda operation to capture the wild elephants could have momentarily hurt these giants. The humane approach of the Maharajas to nurture the elephants as a part of his palace speaks volumes of his benevolence. The grandeur of Dasara is mainly due to the presence of elephants in the procession which made the Nada Habba world famous. Presently the Karnataka Forest Department is responsible for the care and upkeep of elephants participating in the Dasara procession. Annually these elephants are brought from various elephant camps of the state to Mysore Palace two months in advance to acclimatize and prepare them to participate in the procession apart from training the main elephant carrying the Golden Howdah. Balarama has its record in the history for having carried Goddess Chamundeshwari in Golden Howdah weighing about 800 kgs for more than a decade. Balarama was inducted

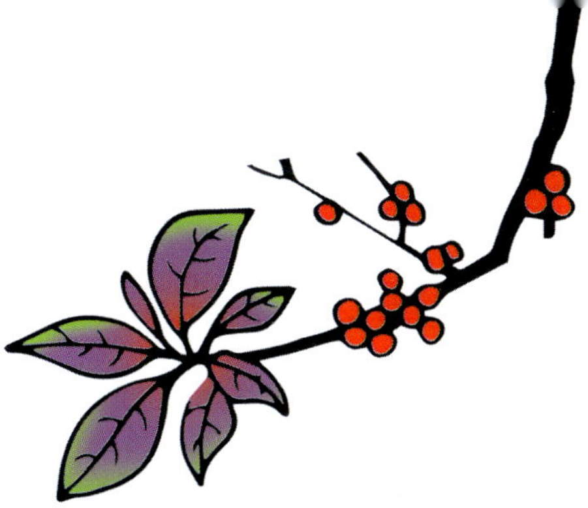

to the elephant regiment of Karnataka Forest Department during 1987 and joined the Dasara procession team during 1994. Balarama, the lead elephant, was popular among the people watching procession for its majestic look with soft temperament. Presently aged about 60 years is leading the retired life in Mattigodu elephant camp of Rajiv Gandhi National Park, Nagarahole.

The authors of the Book 'Balarama Story' have explained the life and times of Balarama in a lucid way that will have lasting impression on young minds. The book is as captivating as a story being told by a grandmother to the children. This is a great endeavor by the authors to bring the true story of an unsung hero from the nature. Hope to see more such stories from the nooks of the wilderness.

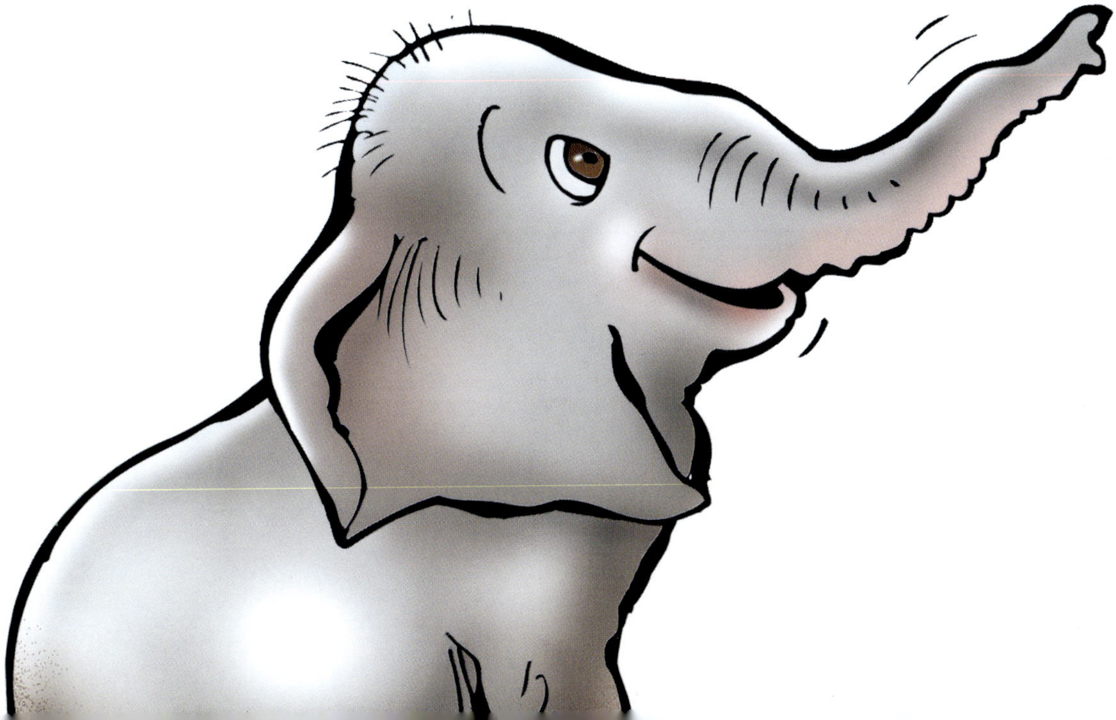

Foreword

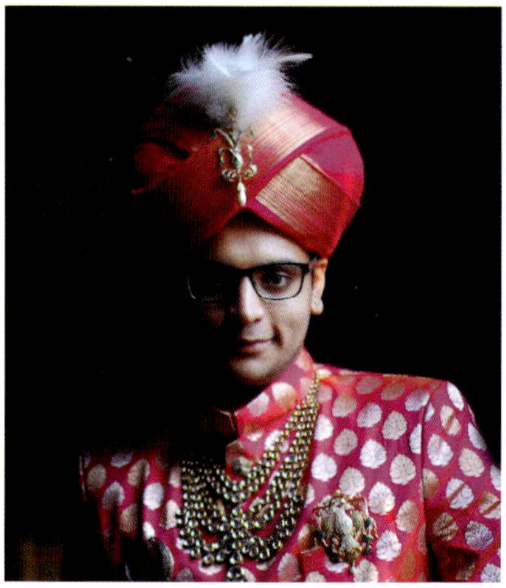

Sri Yaduveer Krishnadatta Chamaraja Wadiyar,
Maharaja of Mysore

The Elephant has long been the symbol of Royal Tradition in India. Indeed, we can trace the history of our relationship with the elephant from our mythical times. Our scriptures, in particular the Rig-Veda, reference Airavata, the magnificent white elephant of Lord Indra, with his ten tusks and five trunks, symbolizing the grandeur of Indra and his magnanimity as a ruler.

The Elephant, has an inextricable link to the narrative of the subcontinent and, in many cases, has shaped the fortunes of our country. It was on the subcontinent that the Asian Elephant was first tamed for agricultural use and later for war. The rise and fall of many a dynasty in our recorded history was predicated on the elephant. One of the factors that dissuaded Alexander's Army from making inroads into India, was the fact that the Nanda rulers would be able to muster an army with over 2000 elephants. Later, Chandragupta Maurya had a Elephantry with over 7000 elephants, which allowed him to be successful in his military campaigns and build the Mauryan Empire, perhaps one of the greatest empires the subcontinent has witnessed.

The icon of the Mysore Dasara, has always been that of the Maharajas of Yore, seated in the Golden Ambari, atop their magnificent elephants. This image is synonymous with the festival, and is central to our tradition and its vibrancy. The Maharaja seated in the Ambari, on his Elephant, or in modern times, the idol of Goddess Chamundeshwari, which is placed in the Ambari, is the central attraction of the festivities and marks the victory of good over evil. The elephant is accorded the greatest of respect in its act of symbolizing the victory of good.

Balarama's Story: An Elephant's Journey, in essence looks to highlight, through its unique narration, the importance of the Elephant to the history of the subcontinent, and also in traditions, that are still prevalent. It also brings to the forefront important aspects of the tradition that may need revisiting. Tradition is meant to honor the past, but it is molded alongside the needs and aspirations of the present, so that it is built to sustain itself in the future, and we need to keep this concept in mind so as to look into how we can give back, to the Elephants, who have given us so much.

Human-elephant conflict is a major issue, and one that is becoming more and more acute with the shrinking of the Elephants habitats. The Elephant is facing a dire threat and it is the need of the hour to highlight their plight. Indeed, we must find a means to protect their natural home in the forests of India, but also realize their importance in the culture and tradition of our great country. This dilemma, of balancing an ancient tradition with the constraints of modern perspectives, speaks to the larger picture of the problems within Indian society in general, that of being the most ancient of civilizations, yet still catching up to modernity.

The challenge will be in ensuring we maintain a balance between modernity and our ancient heritage, and the way we view the Elephant, and its bond to our society will dictate their fortunes in the future narrative of India.

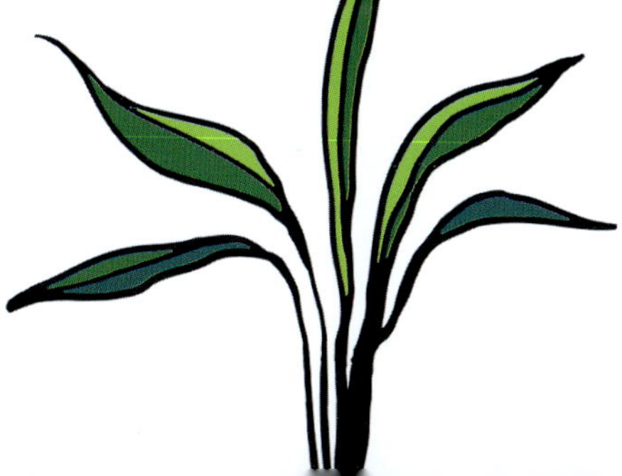

Foreword

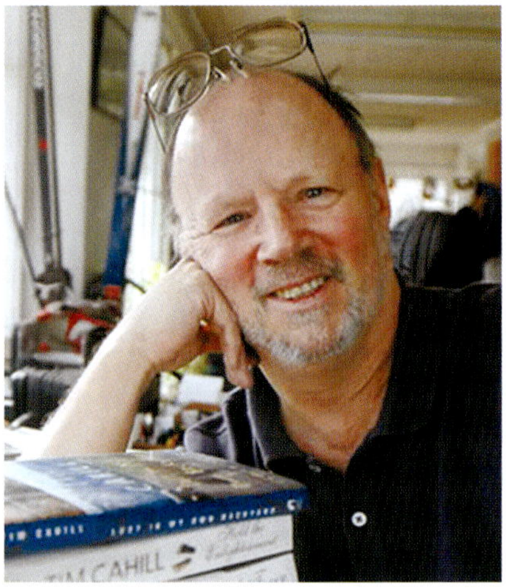

Tim Cahill
Author & Founding Editor,
Outside Magazine

I am a writer and folks often ask me about my latest project. "I'm writing a foreword for a book about elephants," I said at a recent dinner party. Three of four people turned to me. One woman said, "I love elephants. Can I read it?"

"Well," I said, "it's a book for children. I mean, the elephants can talk."

"But you don't do children's books."

"I know, but I think this one is important. And I like it. It's delightful."

Of course, I had to explain this, and it's a story with a curve or two in it.

Several years ago, I was in Namibia where I had a chance to study desert elephants. The animals were making a comeback. They lived along the course of a seasonal river, a green oasis in the sand. This was not a National Park and our group was able to camp out and follow the elephants on foot. A separate group was doing the same, and we chatted with them now and again. This is where I met Bhaskar Krisnamurthy, an Indian fellow who mainly studied Indian elephants and currently lives in Kansas City.

Bhaskar and I talked about Indian elephants and how those great creatures could co-exist with local farmers and not tear up their crops. He had a lot of practical ideas and had collaborated on a film, "Elephants in the Coffee," which is about resolving the conflict between elephants and farmers.

The man was passionate about these magnificent animals. Once, in India, working with the elephants, he was kidnapped by poachers and held for several days until he escaped through the forest. This seemed to me a remarkable story but Bhaskar told it almost in passing as he discussed poaching in India.

Bhaskar was full of ideas and, I quickly learned, was a man who got things done. So, I wasn't surprised when he sent me this book, for children, written from an elephant's point of view.

The elephants here do indeed talk, but what is remarkable is that, aside from that, everything is spot on accurate. Elephants are, indeed, maternal. Young elephants do have to learn how to use their trunks. They form strong bonds with one another and they do seem to mourn their dead.

The scenes of capture are accurate. These elephants are trained by a single trainer, a mahout. And in Bhaskar's experience, the mahout and elephant do form a deep friendship.

Many of the words, like mahout, will be unfamiliar to non-Indian readers. There is a glossary in the back that older readers will want to consult. I think kids would enjoy it without knowing all the words, but it is a book they could keep coming back to and find a deeper meaning with each reading. A child who has seen the world through an elephant's eyes will grow up concerned about elephant conservation. That's why I think it is important.

And that was the story I told at the dinner party. We were an older group, all of us grandparents. The woman who loved elephants said, "I want to read that." So did everyone else at the table. They wanted to read it to their grand kids. They wanted to read it themselves. And that's the kind of book this is: it will please children and even those children's grandparents will learn something from it.

It is, as I said, both delightful and important.

Contents

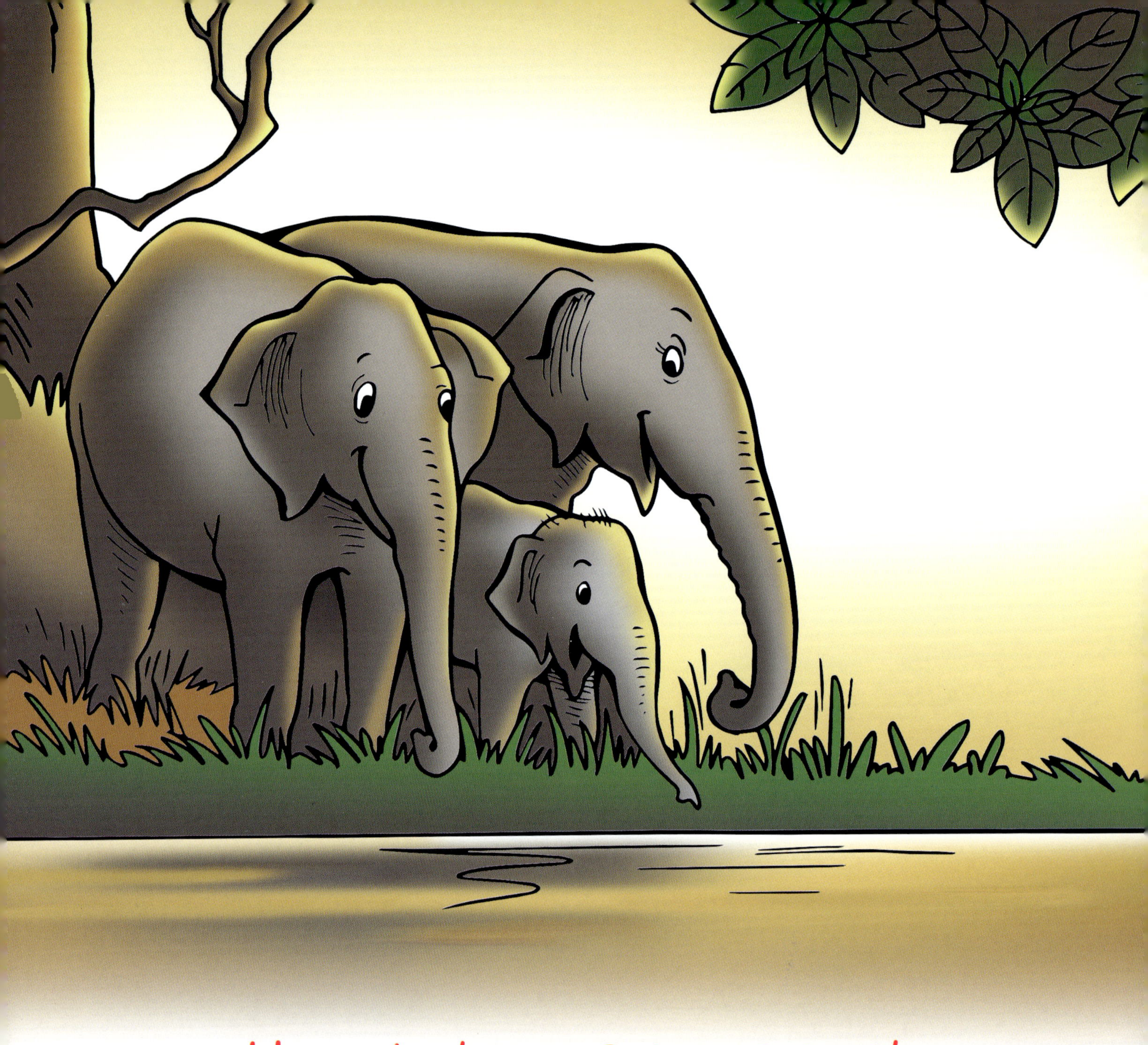

How elephants came to earth

One chilly morning in Nagarahole forest, Baby Balarama followed his aunt out of their watering hole. Auntie Aaney was headed for their favorite spot in the cool waters of the Kabini. The stream gurgled merrily and ripples of gold and silver danced as they caught the sunbeam.

Baby Balarama the elephant watched a lone osprey flit about dipping into the water and posing on the wooden stumps, as he shuffled along to keep up with Auntie Aaney. The other babies, Arjuna, Bhima, Nakula, and Mohini, were already there. Balarama, the naughtiest one of all, was always last.

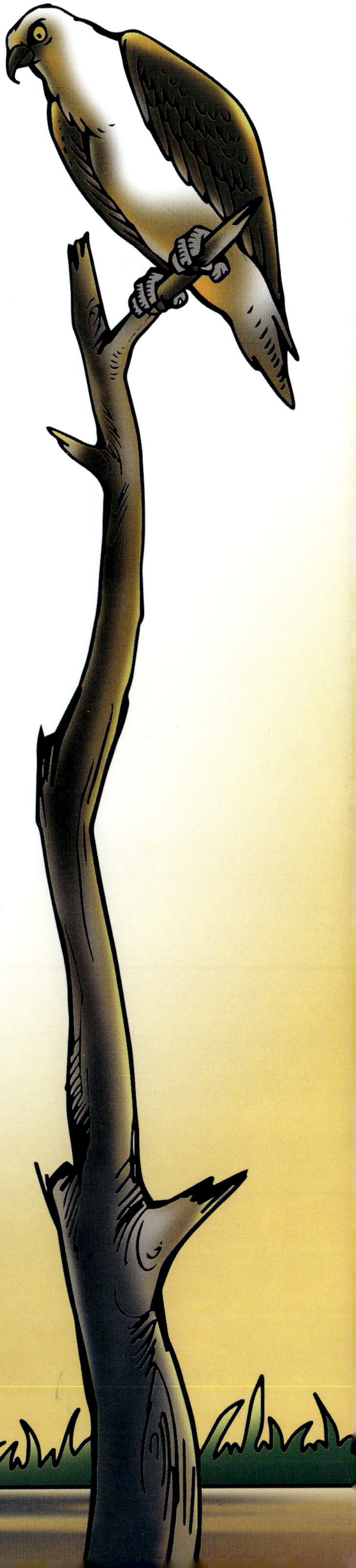

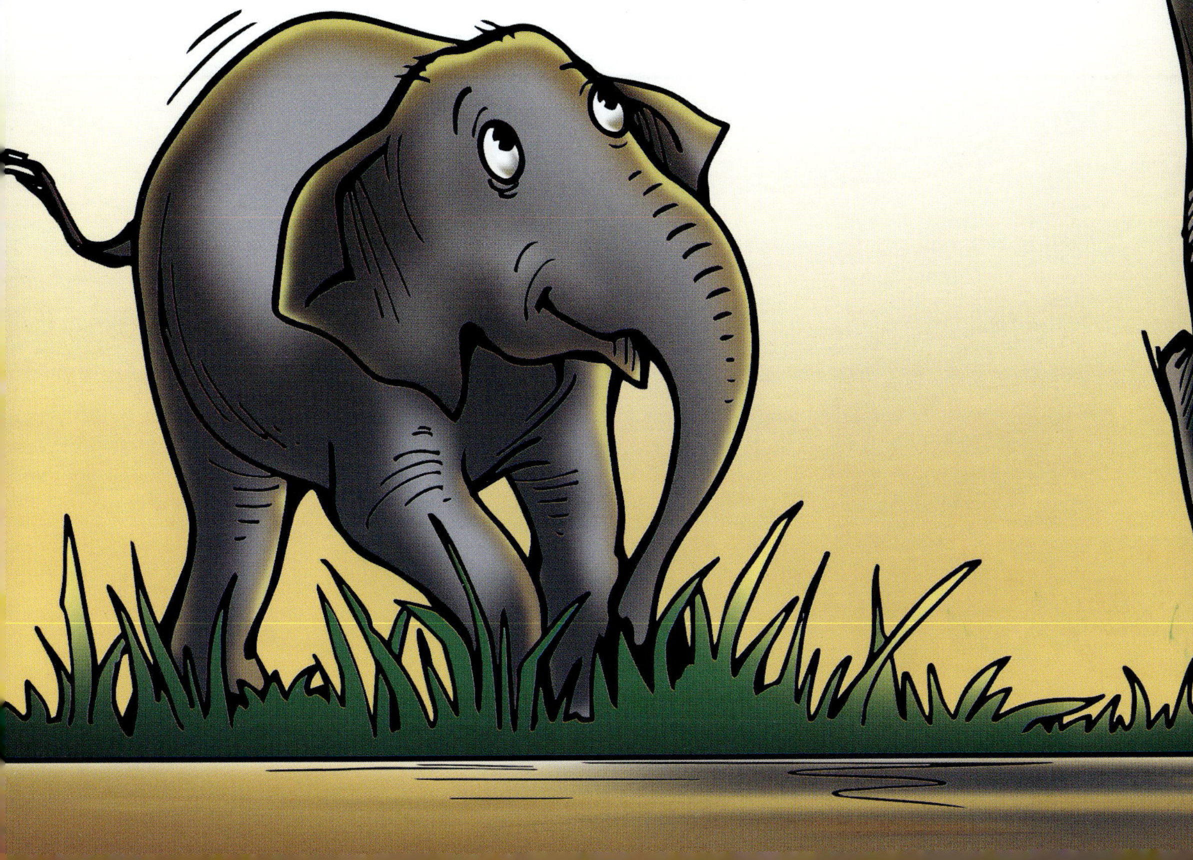

"Come here, little ones," Auntie said, when they had reached the water's edge. Balarama fell into water, raising his trunk and trumpeting joyfully as he felt the first tingle of the cold water on his back.

He turned back as Auntie said again, "come here, everyone. I'm going to tell you a story"

Balarama forgot about playing in the water, and rushed to nuzzle Auntie Aaney. "Do you know how we elephants came to be here on Earth?"

Balarama was surprised. "Earth? I know we are here, Auntie, In Nagarahole, by the Kabini... What are you saying?" he said.

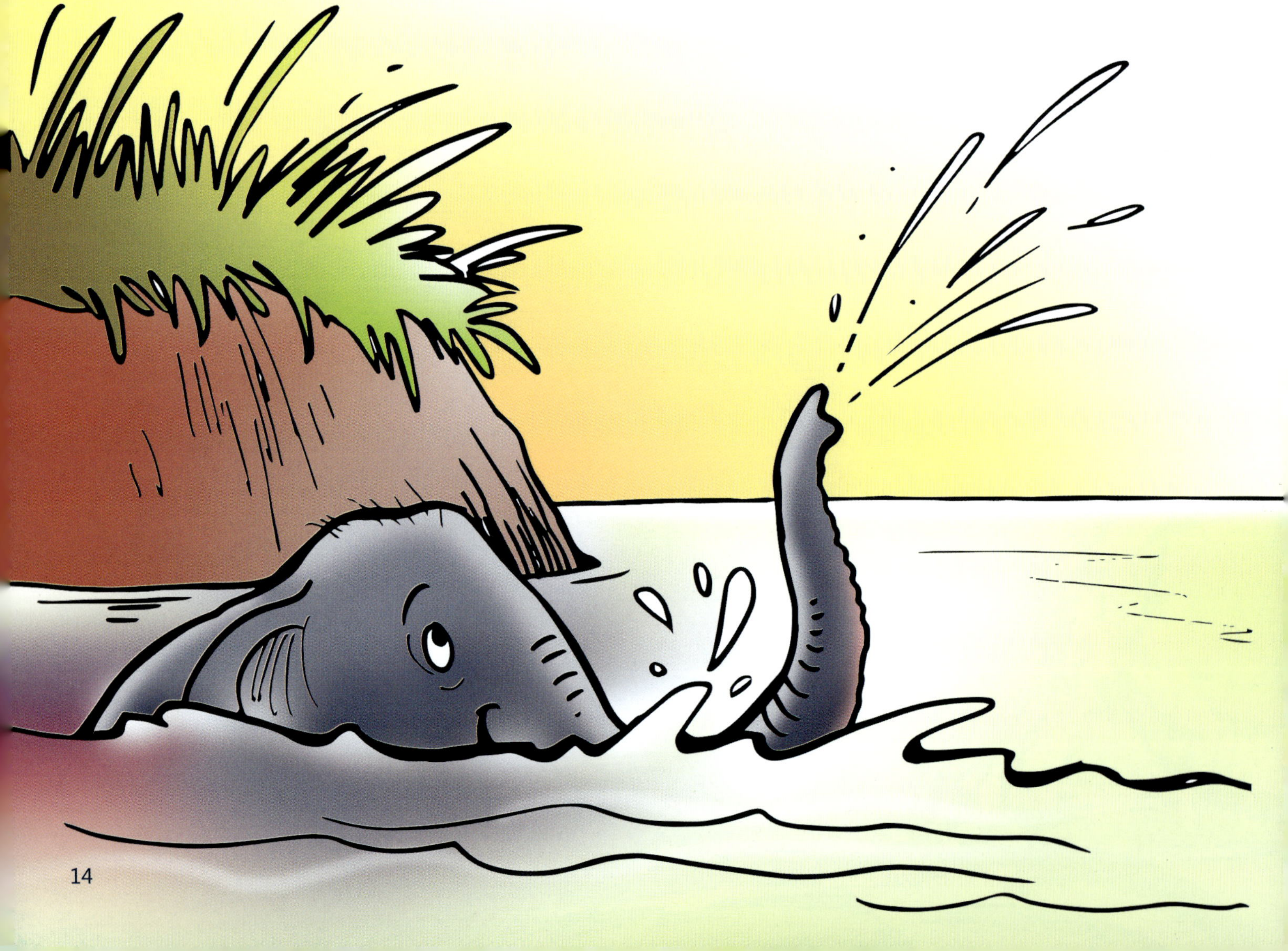

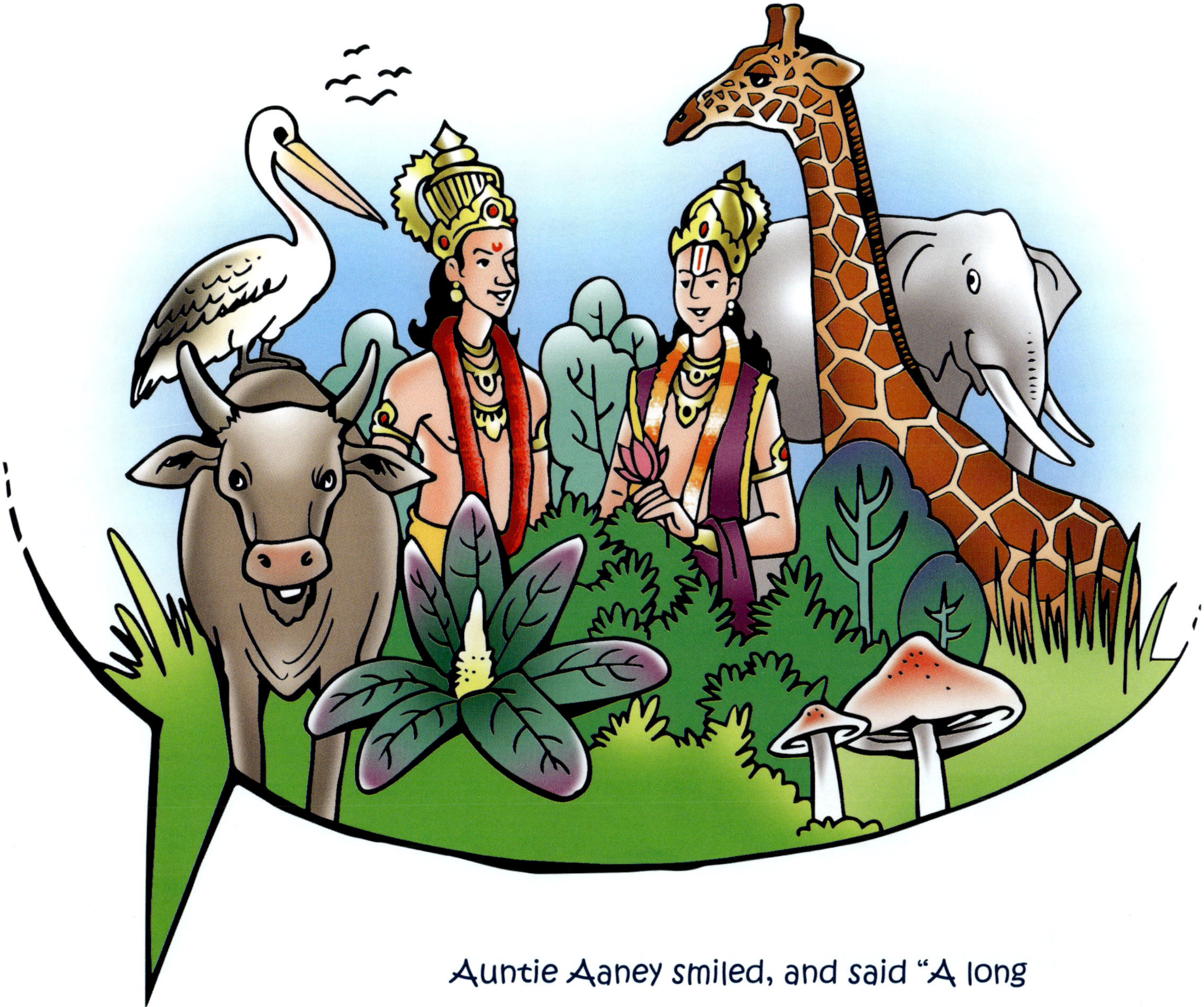

Auntie Aaney smiled, and said "A long time ago, longer than even we elephants can remember, gods roamed the earth, just like us. We were all very happy. We already lived in heaven..."

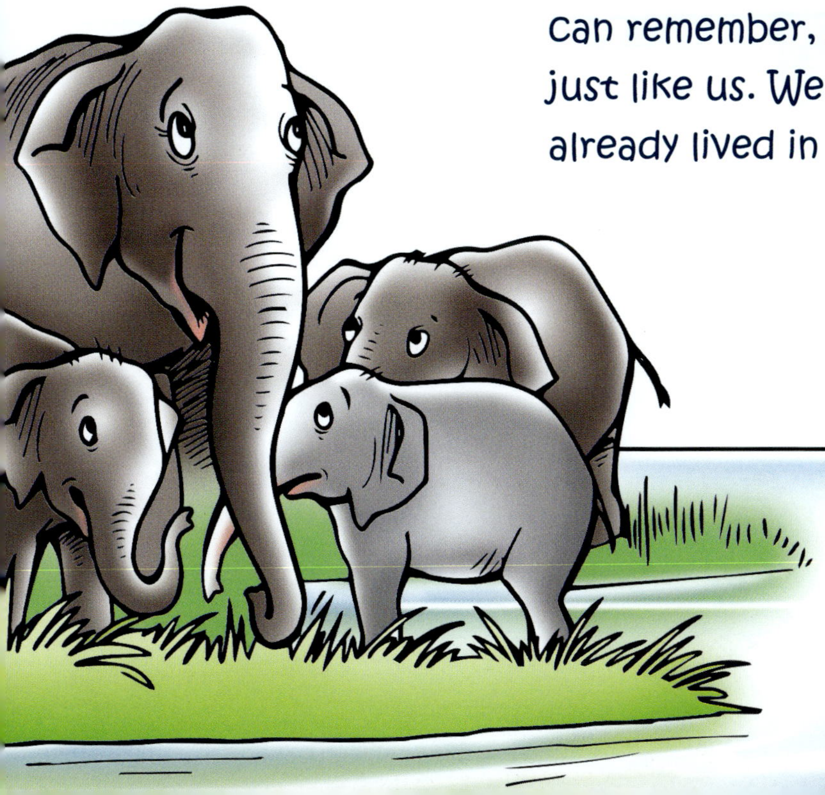

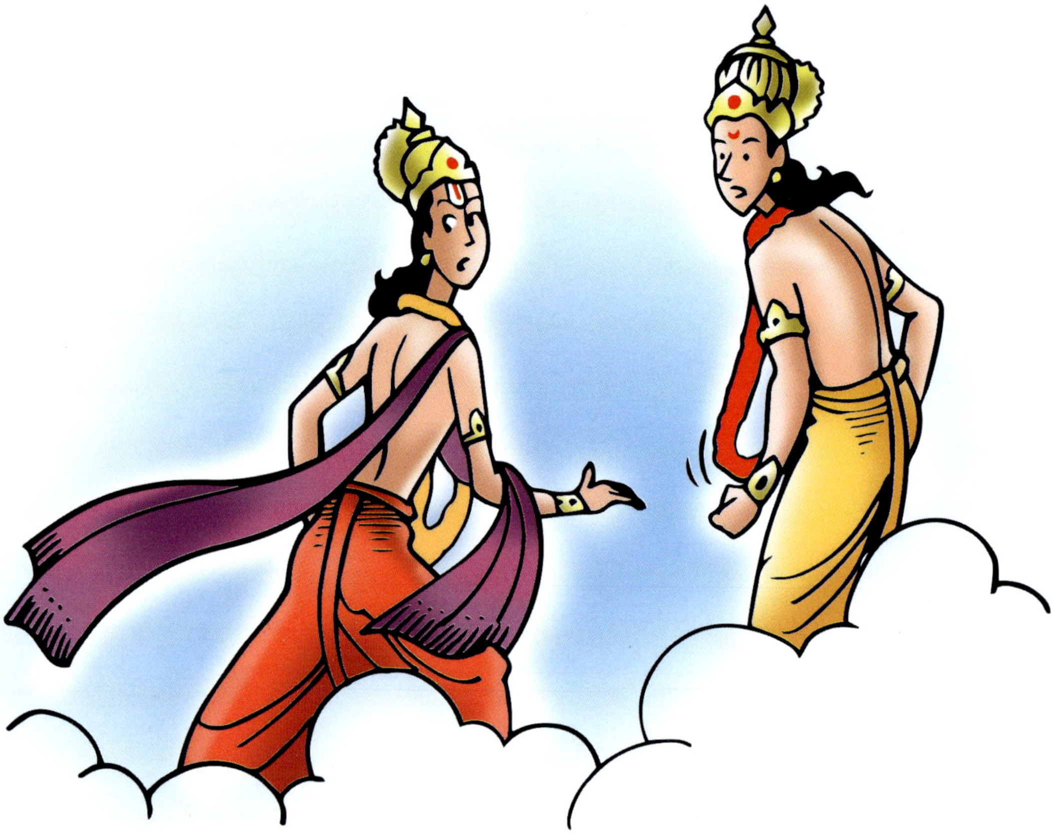

One day, human beings, men and women suddenly arrived, Auntie went on... and everything went wrong. The gods said, "We are going to another world, a new heaven. These humans are dangerous. Why don't you come too?"

The elephants said "Oh no! You go on ahead. We are big, We are mighty, and powerful. What can these tiny humans do?

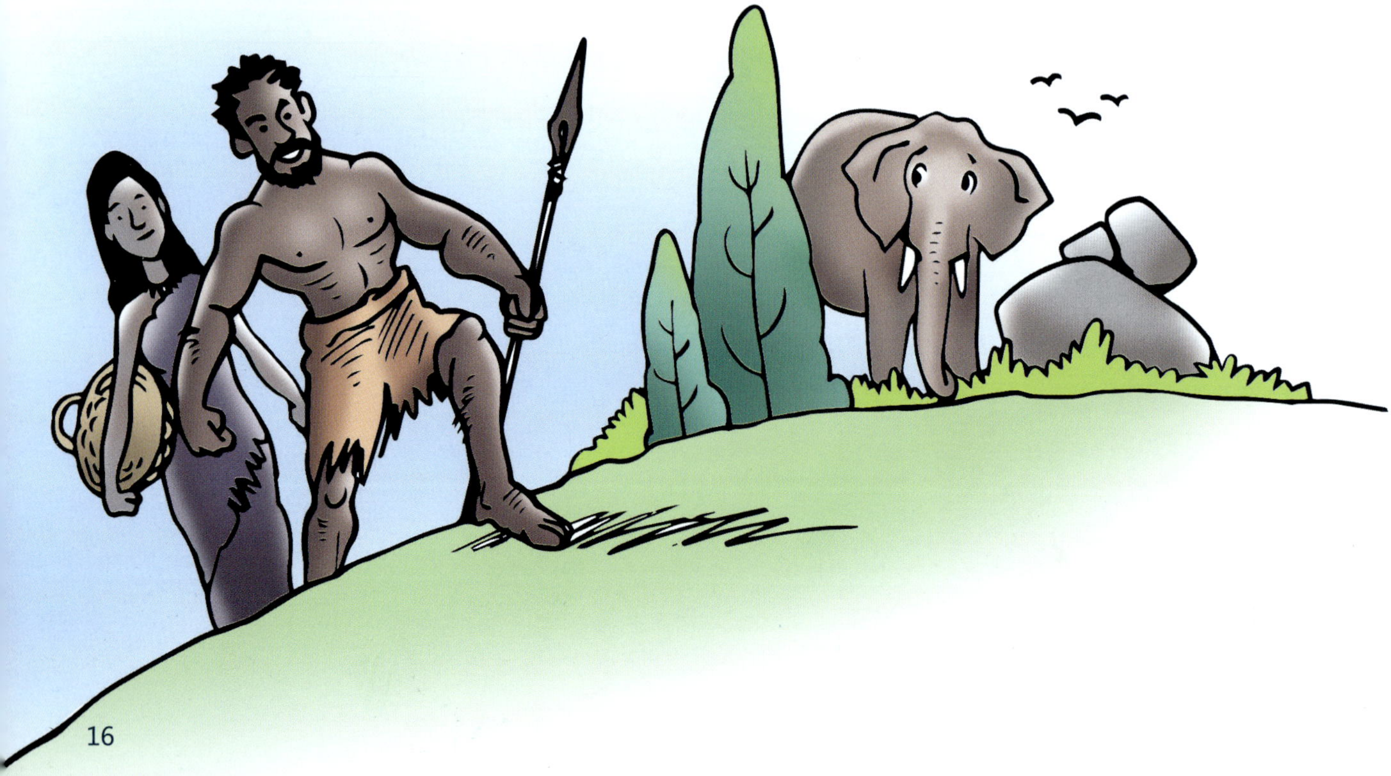

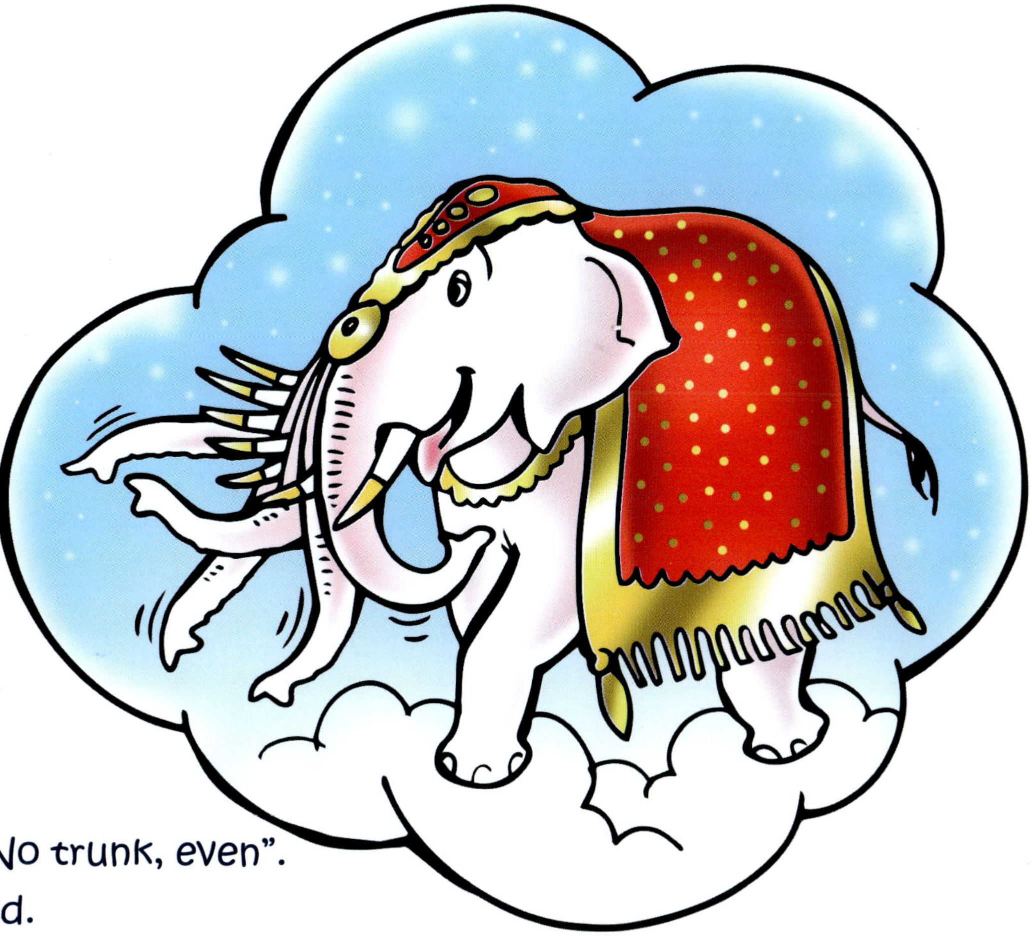

They have no tusks, No trunk, even".
The elephants laughed.

The earth was beautiful and big. The sky, the jungle, the river, the grassland and the mountain... we could share it with the humans, the elephants thought, and waved the gods off on their journey to their new heaven.

All the elephants stayed back. Except one, The Airavata! A very odd looking elephant he was with five trunks and ten tusks. He decided to go with the gods, Auntie was saying, but Balarama, who tried to imagine the Airavata, began to laugh. He forgot all about the wicked humans who were tiny but very, very scary.

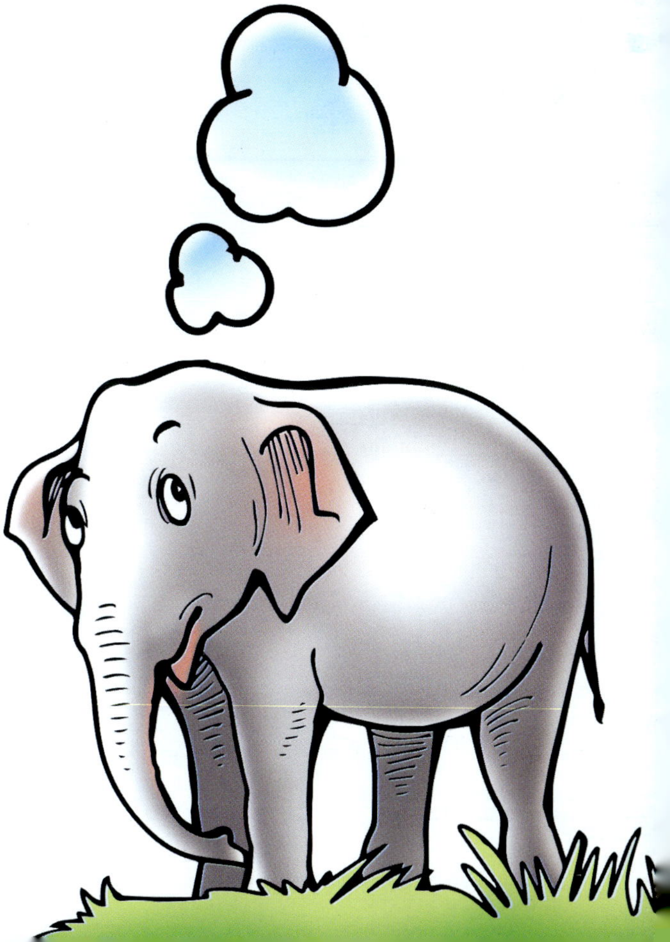

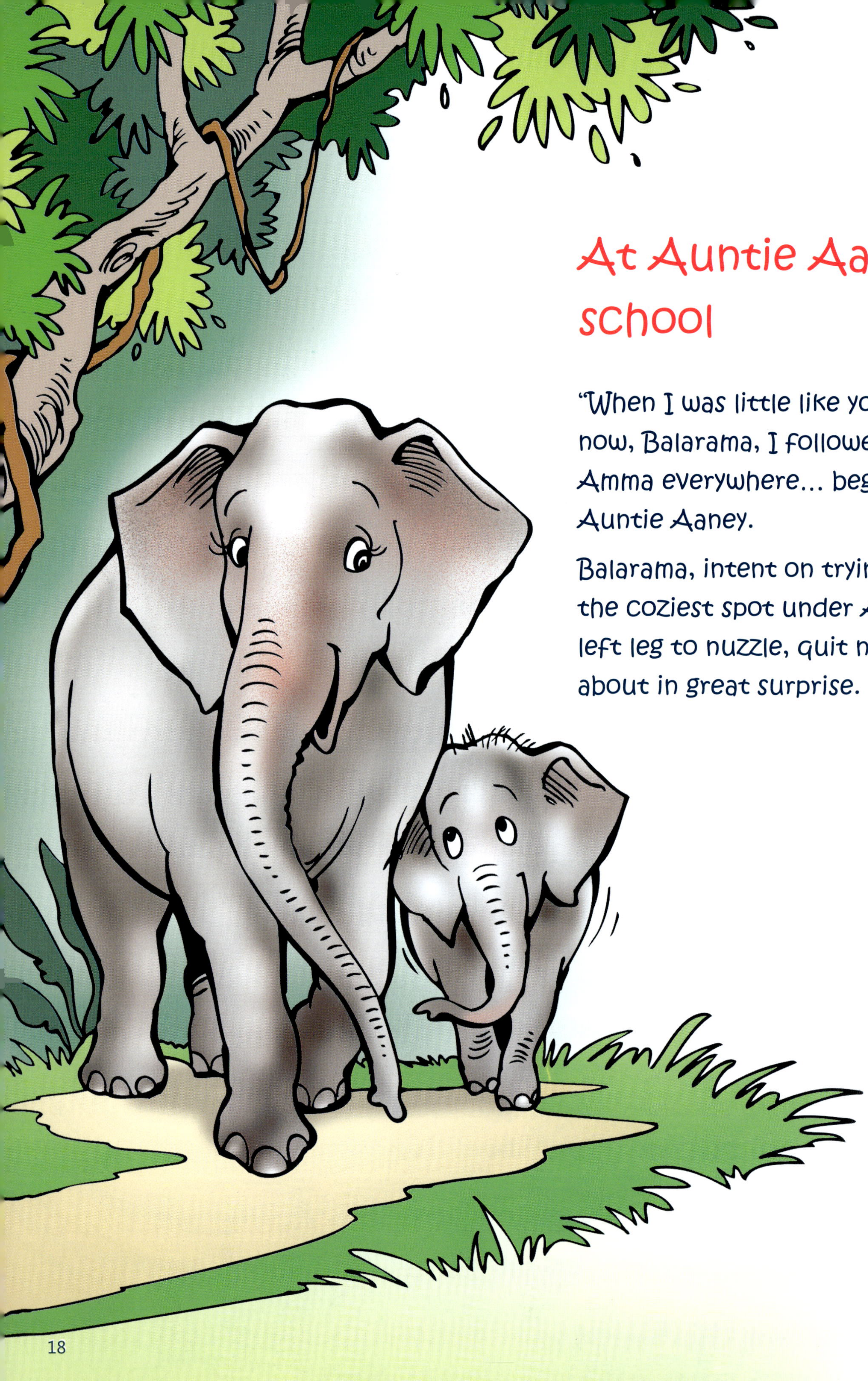

At Auntie Aaney's school

"When I was little like you are now, Balarama, I followed my Amma everywhere… began Auntie Aaney.

Balarama, intent on trying to find the coziest spot under Auntie's left leg to nuzzle, quit nudging about in great surprise.

"You are Auntie!" he cried. "You had an Amma!!!? And you were once little? Like me!!!?

Auntie Aaney laughed. "Yes, Balarama! One day you will be big! Bigger than me, and you will have long tusks, and everyone will stop and stare when you go stomping by" she said.

"Like Appa!" Balarama squealed excitedly. "Oh I can't wait to be big and have fine tusks!'

He rushed into the water, and drawing deep with his trunk sprayed himself

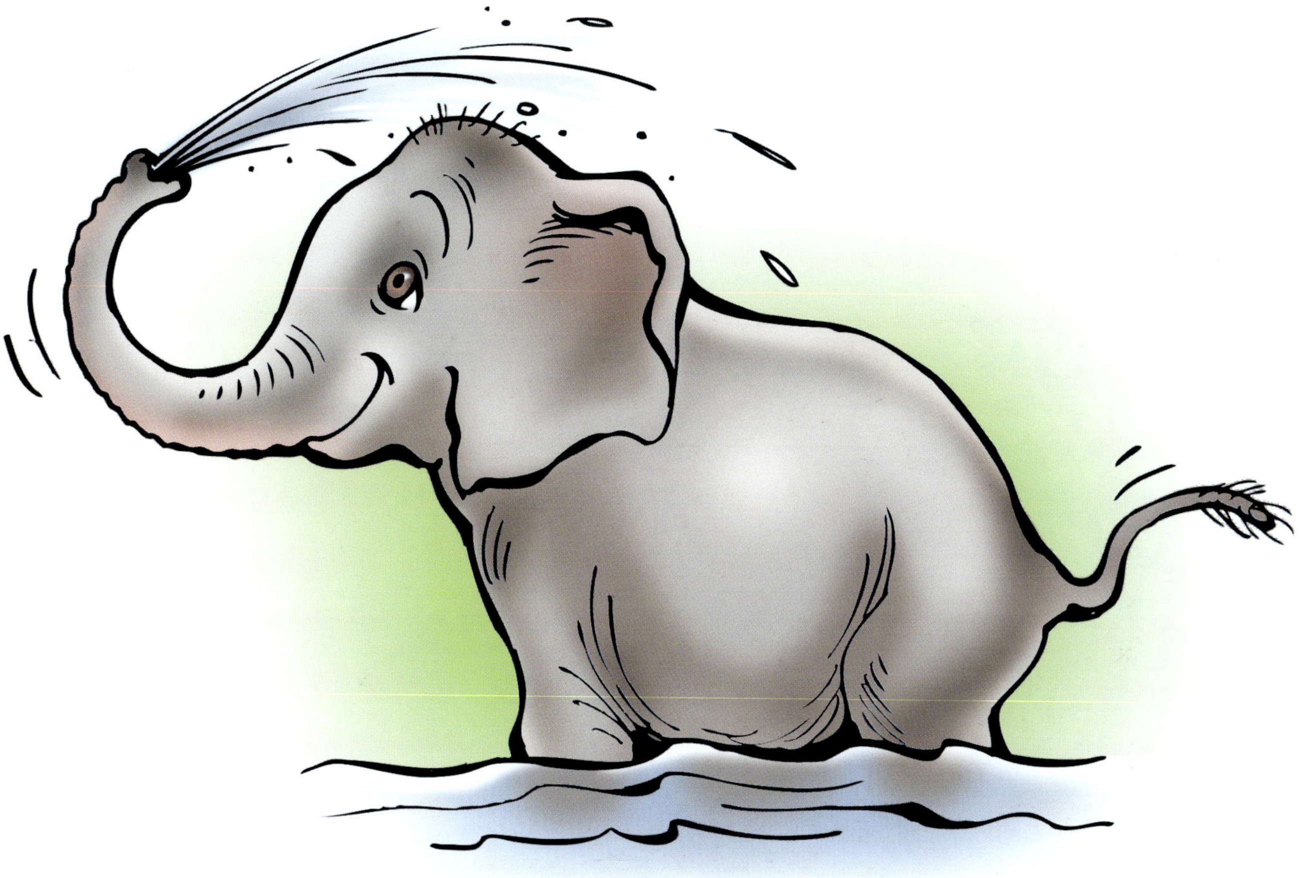

with a baby jumbo-sized shower. Then he found a muddy spot with a puddle, and he sat down and began to daydream...

He was strutting up to the stream where his friends waited, at their favorite hangout, Kakanakote, across the Kabini. Polka the leopard was sliding by, and stopped to stare... Hayday the cobra stopped slithering and raised his hood... but Balarama, the mighty jumbo, was only after one thing... to catch the eye of Mohini, who had strayed from her herd and was hiding behind the bamboo clump, pretending to ignore him.........

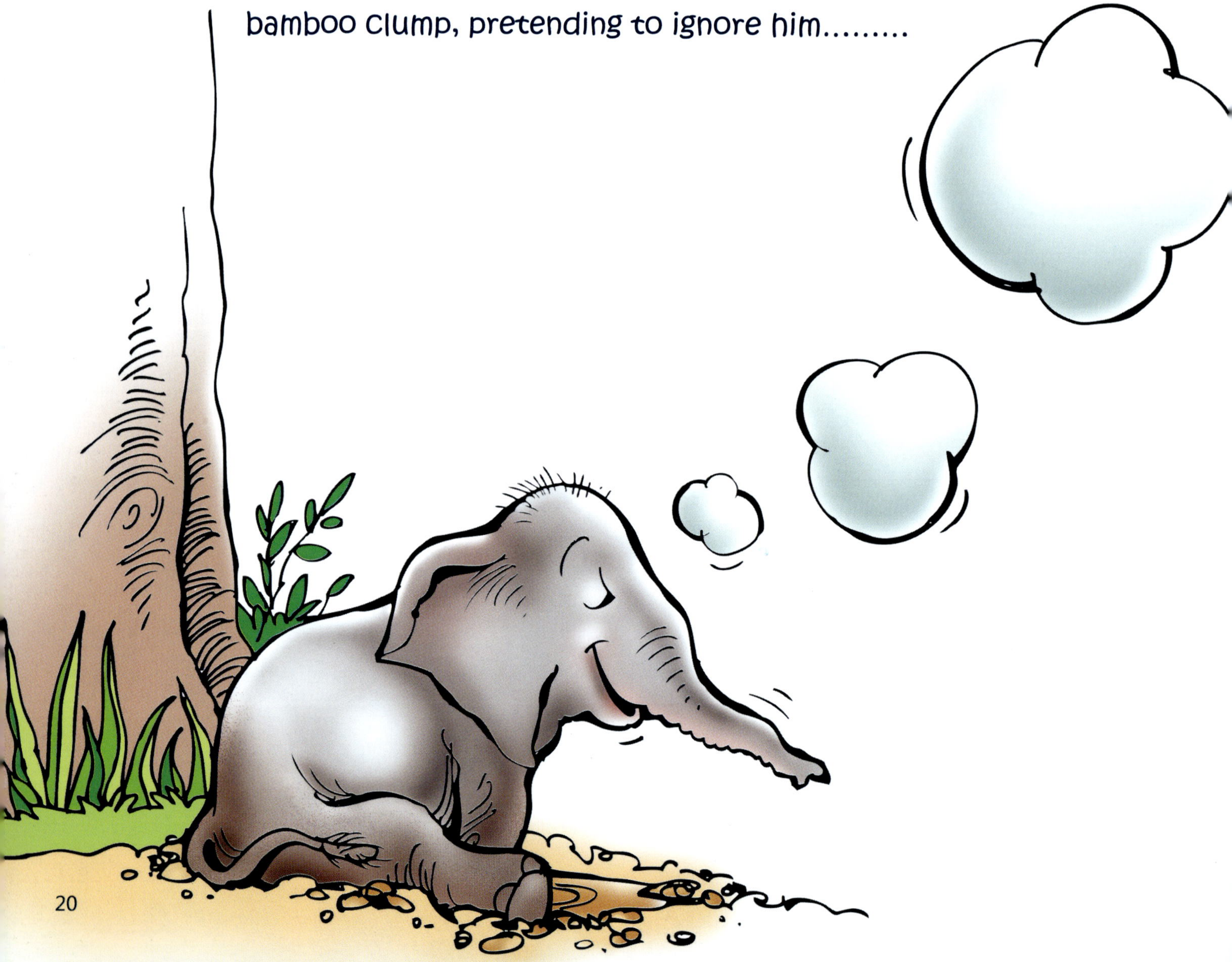

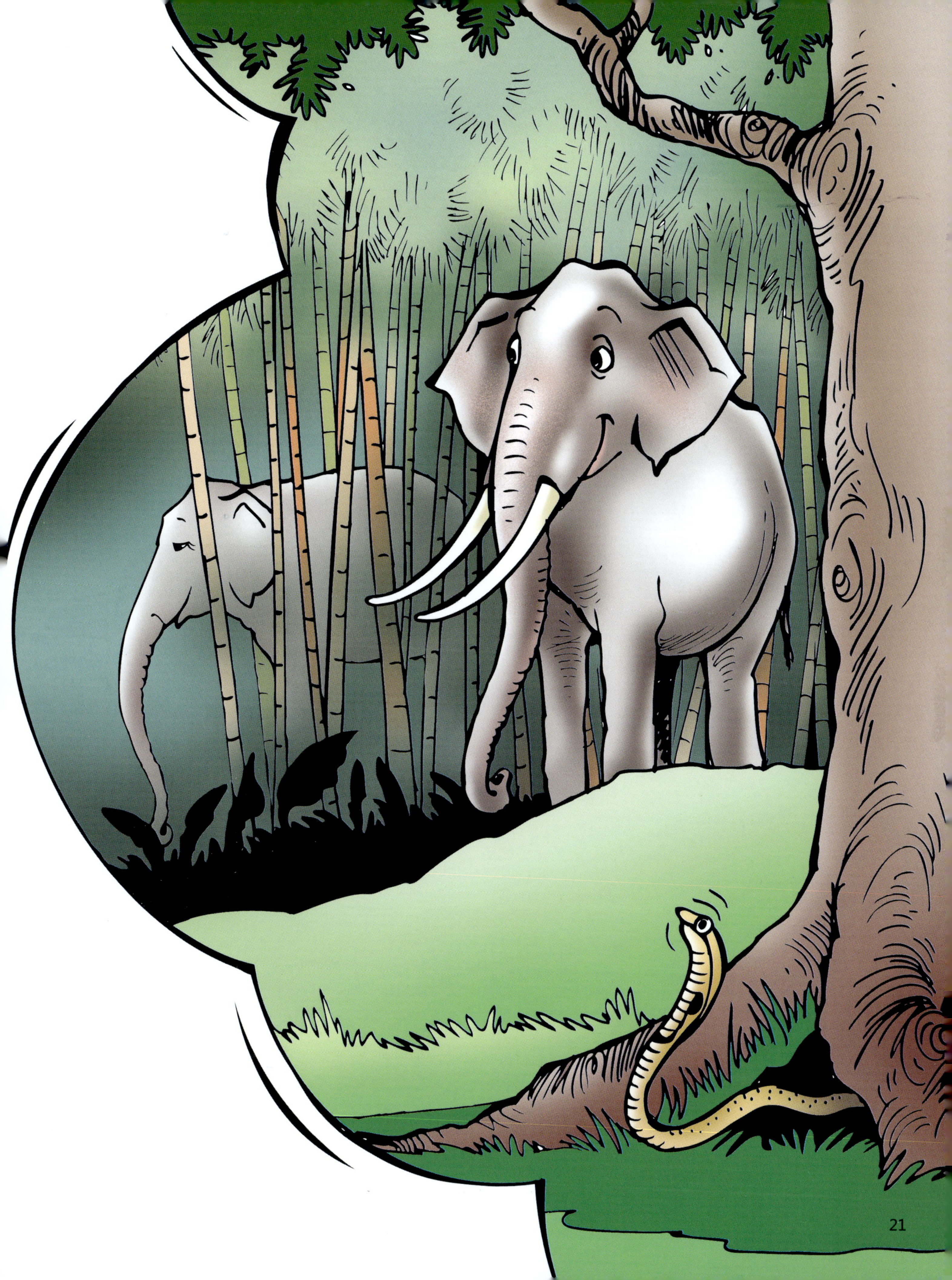

"Come Balarama", Auntie Aaney's voice boomed.

Splat!... went his dream as he tried to stand up and fell down on his tail.

He thought he heard someone crying out "Ouchie! Ouch! Ouch!" And then realized it was his own voice.

He ran to Auntie Aaney, as fast as his legs could carry him. He was only four, and just left his mother's side. He no longer tripped on his own trunk, and he had become very clever at using it to nibble at plants, and drink long and deep at the river.

Not like his cousin Arjuna, who was just six months old, and waddled more than he walked,

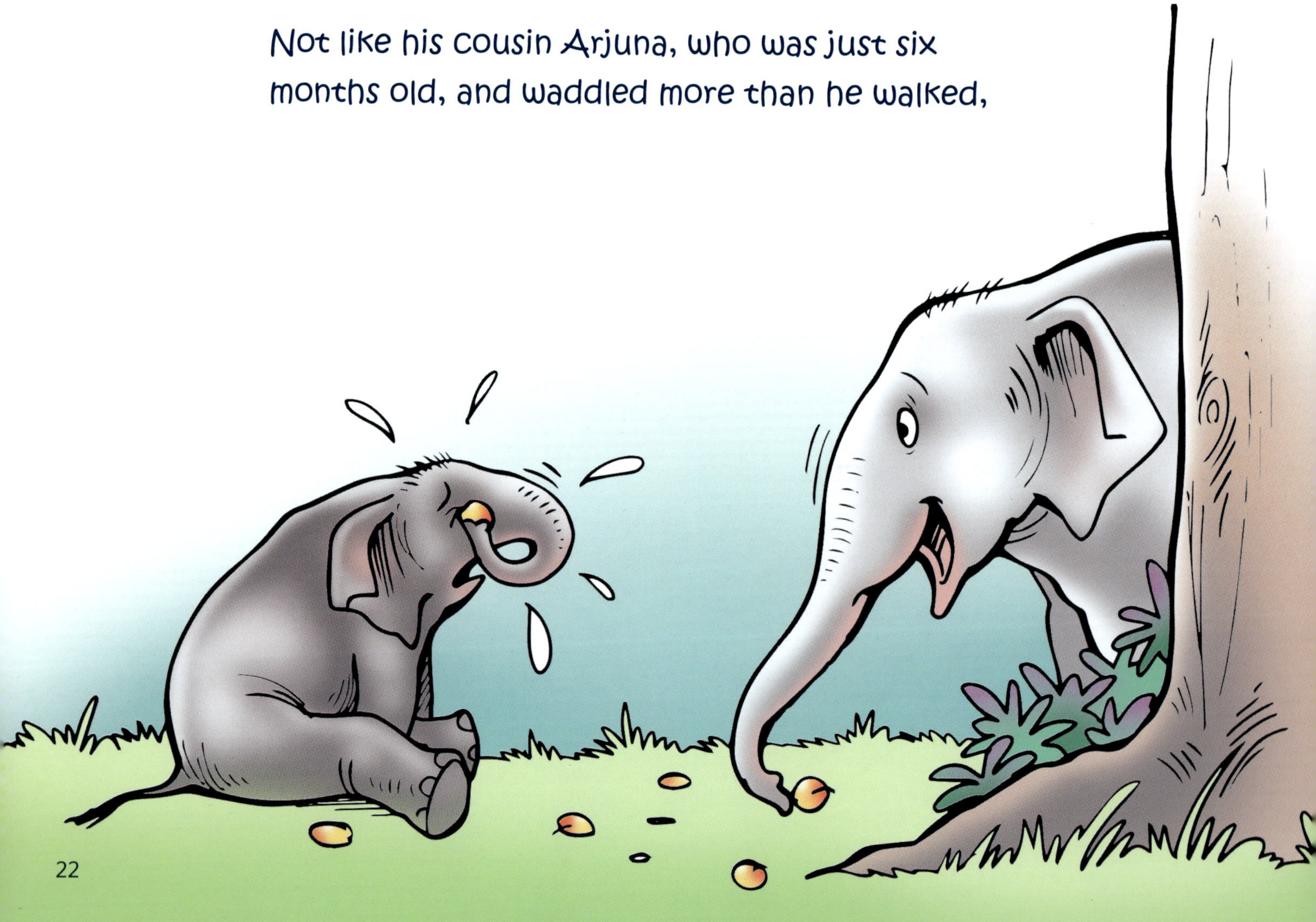

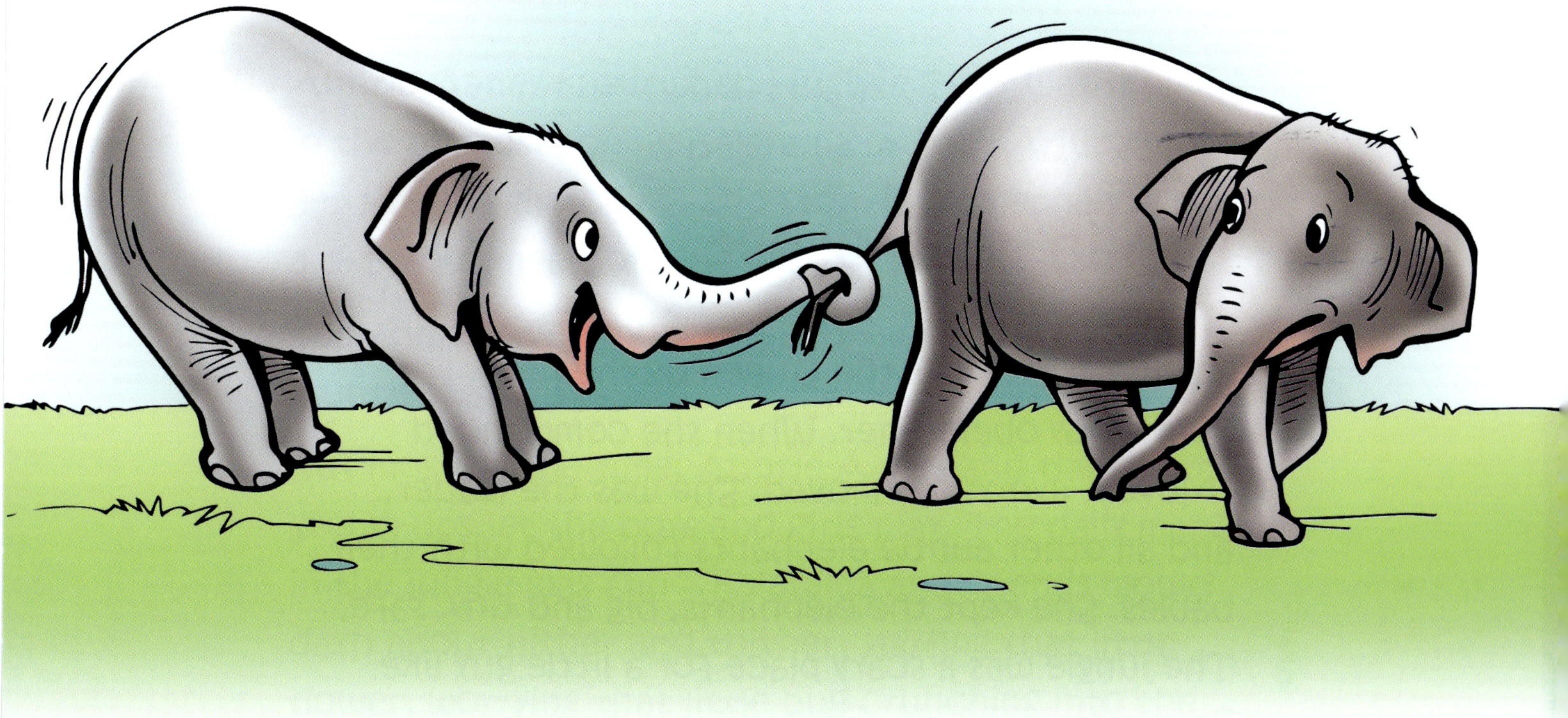

and often put his food into his eye, and squealed in pain. Balarama laughed at Arjuna's little accidents. He forgot his own tangles with the trunk when he had been like tiny Arjuna!

"Balarama"! His aunt sounded really angry now, and he went, remembering Auntie Aaney's enormous trunk landing on his rear the other day, when he had been caught pulling little Mohini's tail.

Really, Balarama was the naughtiest little elephant to be born in Nagarahole in a long, long time! Well, not since Auntie Aaney had been a little girl. But that's a story for another day.

Auntie Aaney let them play, always watchful, like she had eyes behind her ears. She never let them stray beyond the edge of an invisible circle. She knew the little ones got tired very quickly, and marching over 15 kilometres (9.5 Miles) of forest was hard enough for the grown-ups. She could rest a while as the children played, explored the nooks and crannies and then napped, as their tired little eyelids drooped shut, and they floated into Sleepy Land! It was a very hot day in May, and Auntie could use a nap, too!

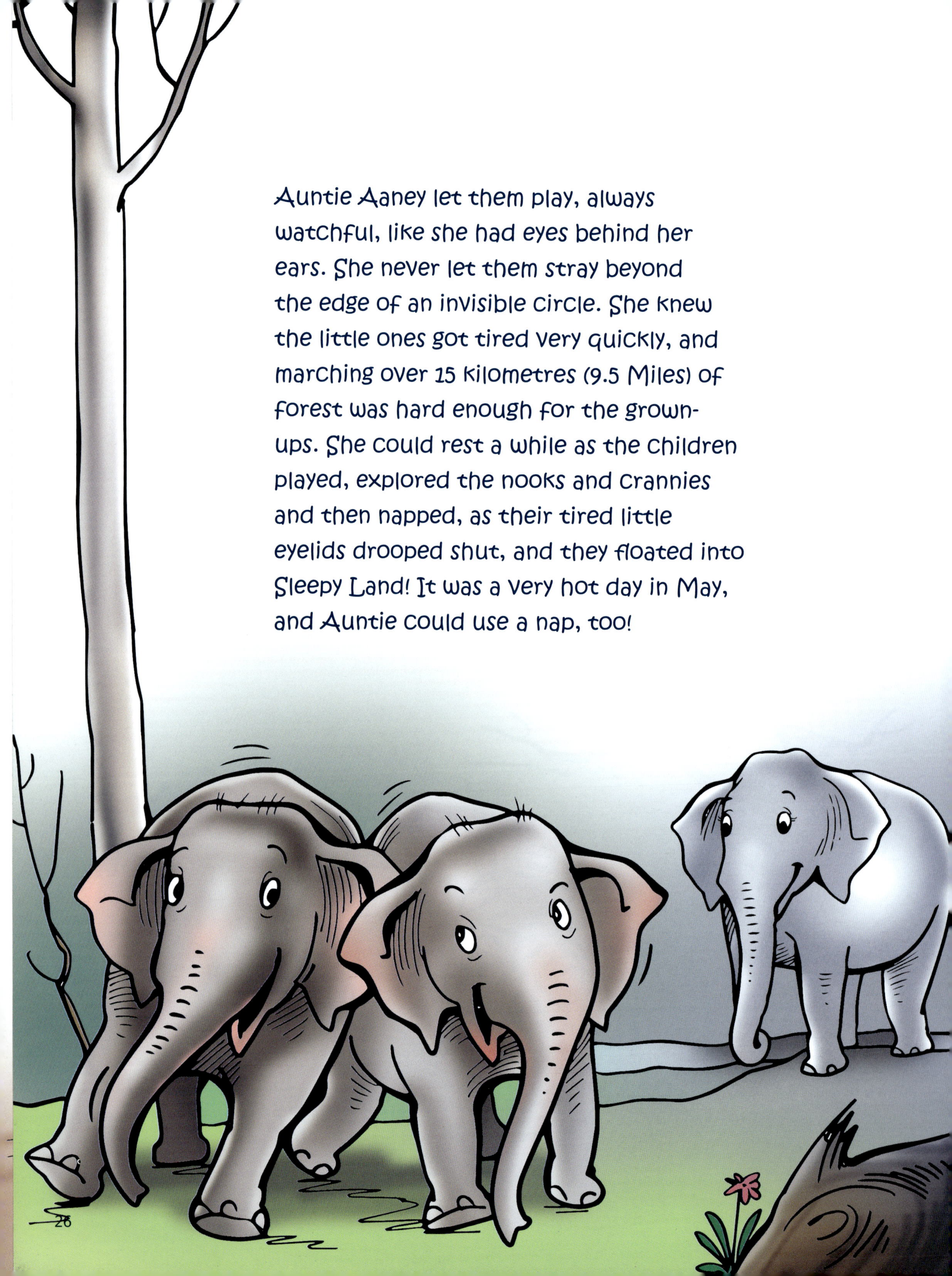

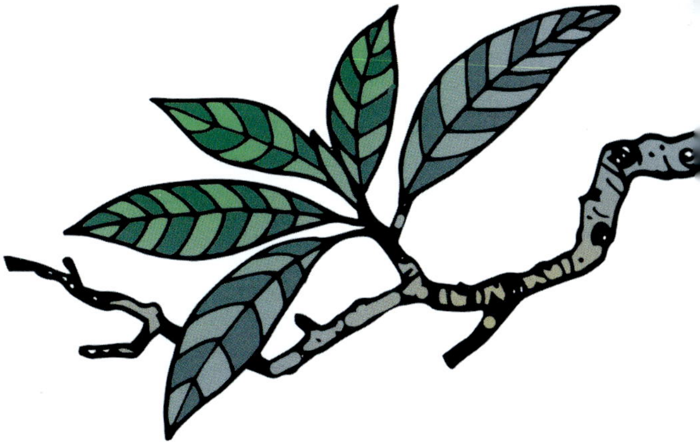

When they were older, Auntie said, Balarama and Arjuna would not be afraid of the tiger, or the leopard, for they left the big elephants alone. "But why are they here?" Balarama asked, He disliked being afraid of anything. Or anyone.

"Why, Balarama, the jungle is their home too. We must share it with everyone. The tigers, the deer, the sambar. See, that monitor lizard basking in the sun on that rock" Auntie said.

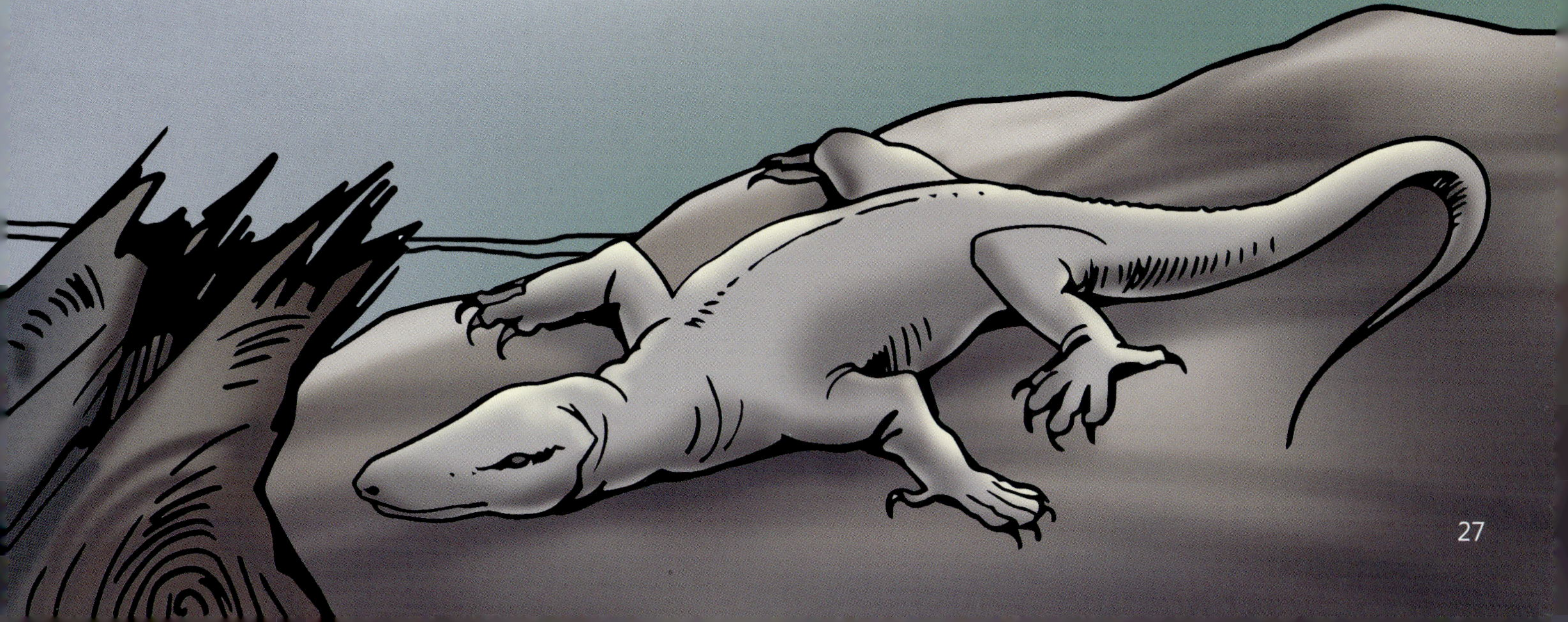

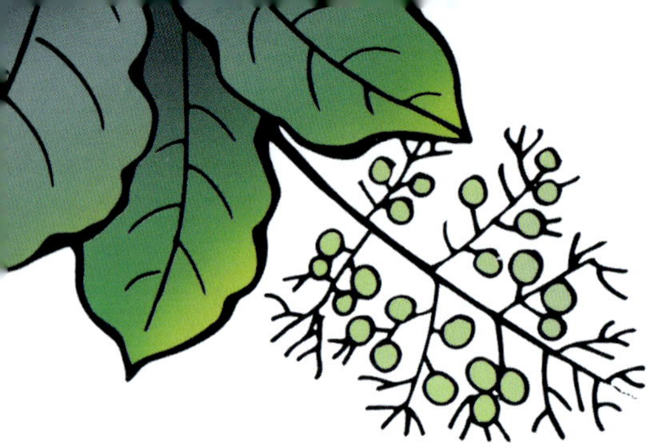

"Zzzz nqwmph!" said Balarama, and Auntie turned to look at him, and she laughed softly, for he was fast asleep, his little trunk curled up on his knees.

A while later, Balarama felt a gentle nudge on his neck, and mumbled, sleepily, "stop Mohini... you're tickling me..." and then, a little louder, "hey lemme sleep... I'll tell Auntie!"

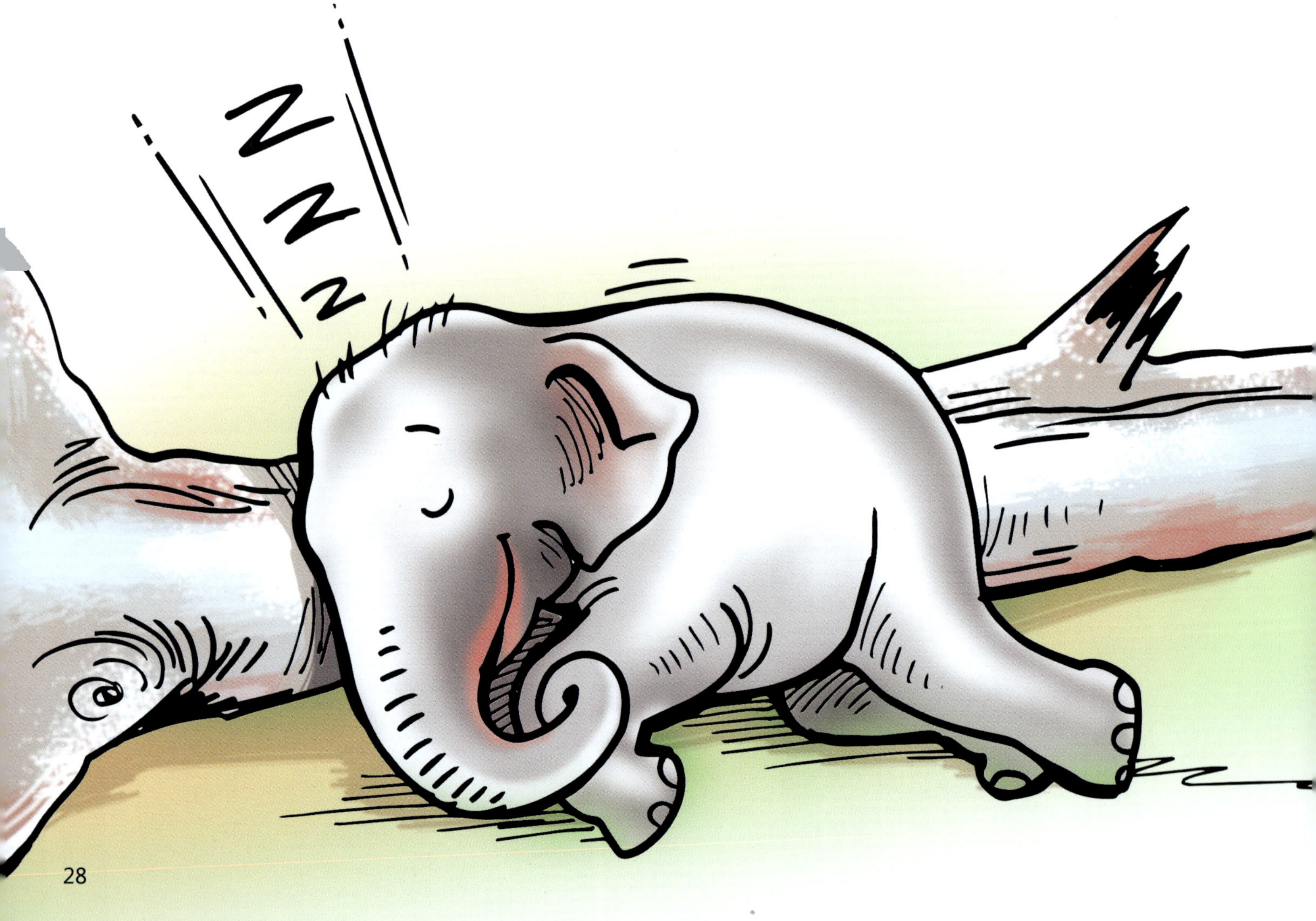

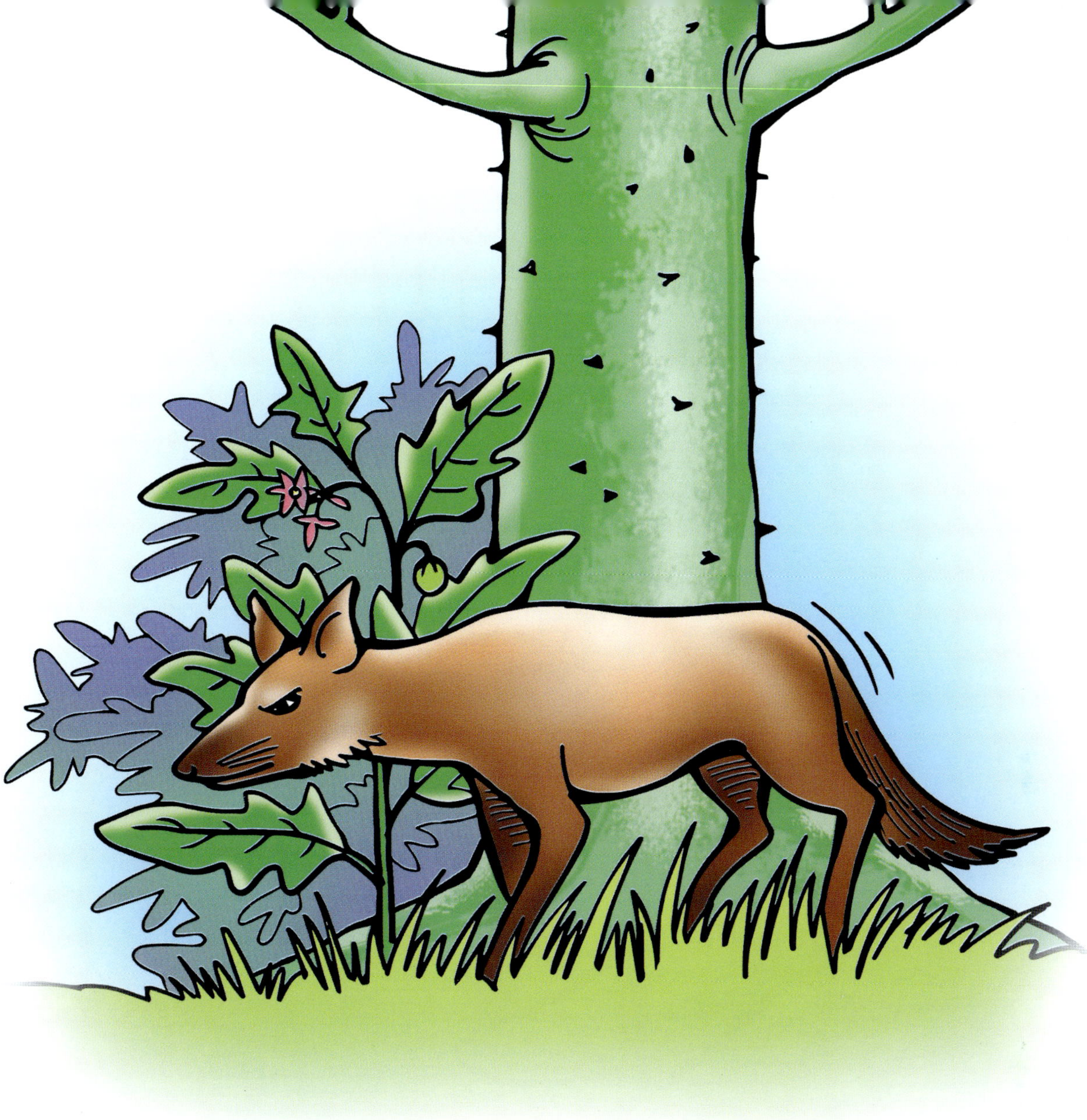

His eyes popped open suddenly when he heard Auntie's voice, "wake up Balarama, we have to leave now. Come on, you don't want to be left behind... I saw that dhole hiding in the horse nettle shrub behind the cotton tree and beechwood. He's a nasty piece of work"

Balarama bounded up at great speed, and ran to join the other kids who were waiting with their moms and aunties.

Big boy Balarama

Four years later...

Balarama stood, on the banks of the Kabini, where the water was shallow. He could see the fish darting about without a care in the world. This meant the crocodiles were not lurking close by. Who would want to have a leg locked in the powerful jaws of a hungry crocodile?

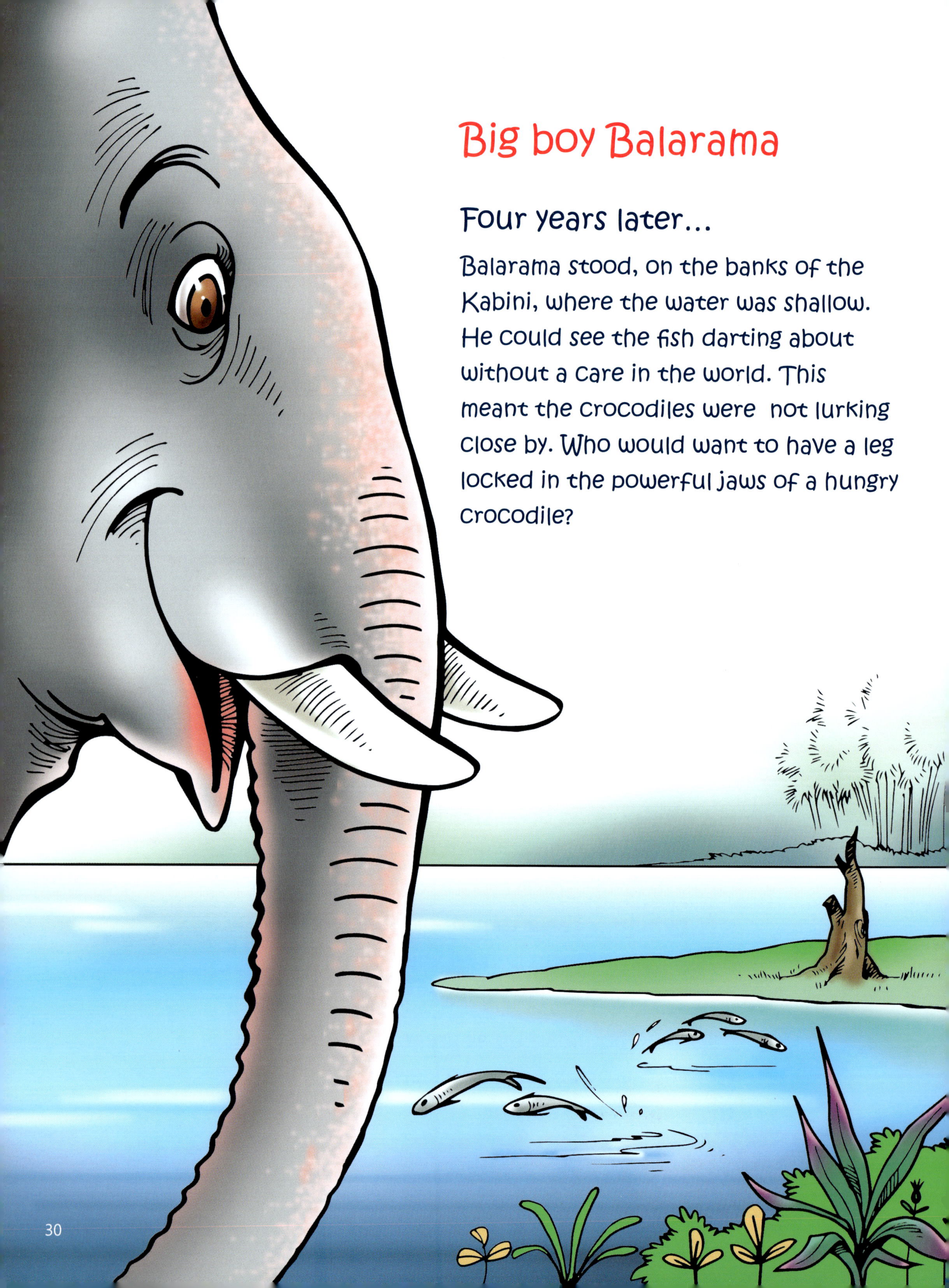

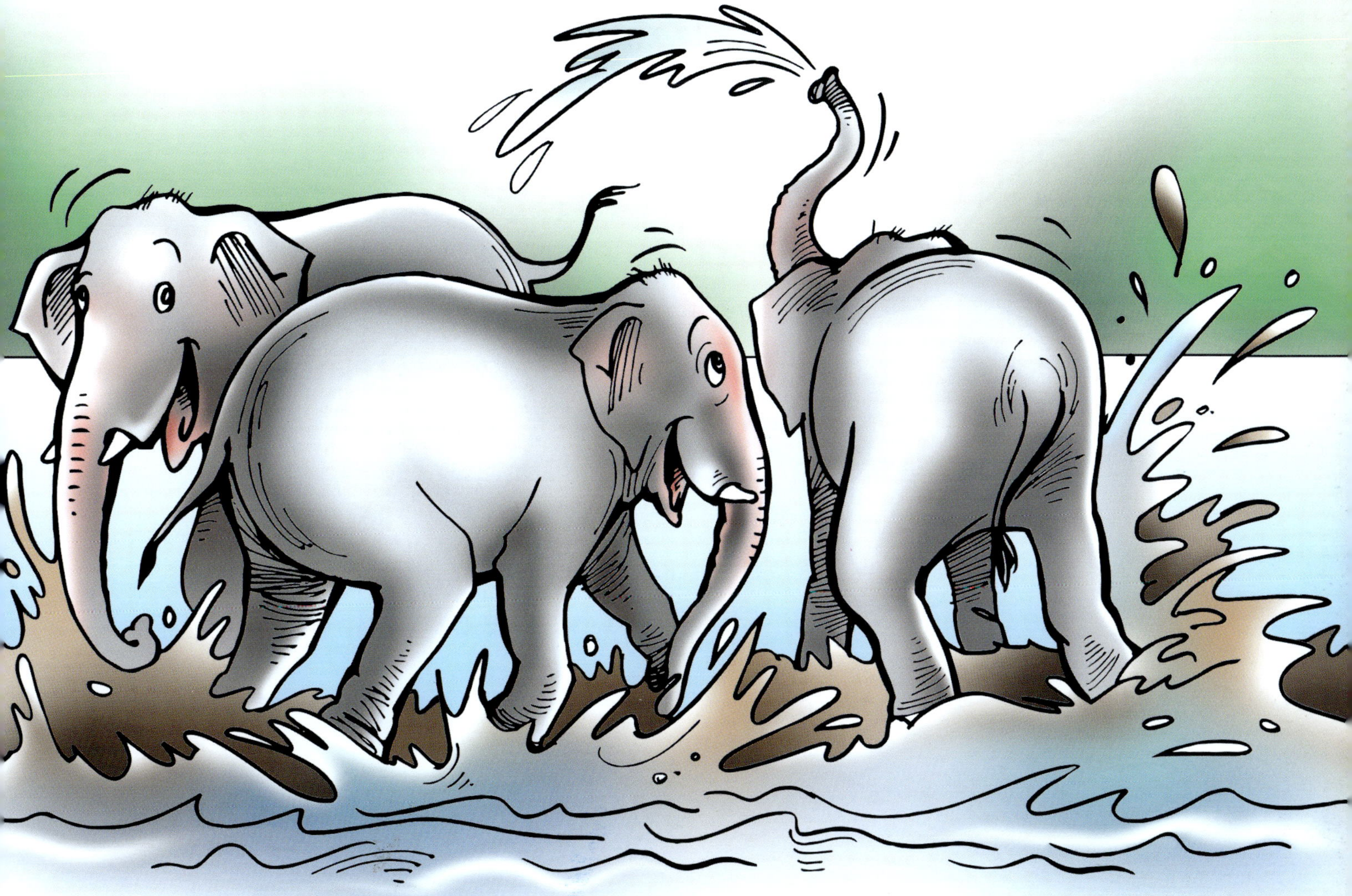

He meant to cross over to the Kakanakote side, and hang out with his friends- Bhima, Nakula and Rama who preferred to go stomping across the river from their home in Nagarahole. Now was a good time.

He watched Auntie Aaney and his mother herding the babies and toddlers to a safe spot in the river for them to bathe in and play. He laughed as the little ones tumbled about, and tripped on their trunks, and the really naughty fellow who pulled the tail of his buddy, who yelped in pain. That was him four years ago.

Mohini was there, too. One day she was going to be the matriarch, just like Auntie Aaney, who had taught him everything he knew about being a good elephant. He would be starting a herd of his own with Mohini, when the time came, and they would have many little elephant babies together.

That's what elephants had been doing forever. For 5.5 million years! Elephants had been here on beautiful earth since the beginning of Time!!

Balarama and other elephants living in Nagarahole were the Asian elephants, and their closest relatives were the African elephant. Another close relative was the Mammoth, which had become extinct 10,000 years ago! When Auntie Aaney told him that 50 million years ago, their kind were only about the size of pigs, Balarama wouldn't believe her. But of course it was true!

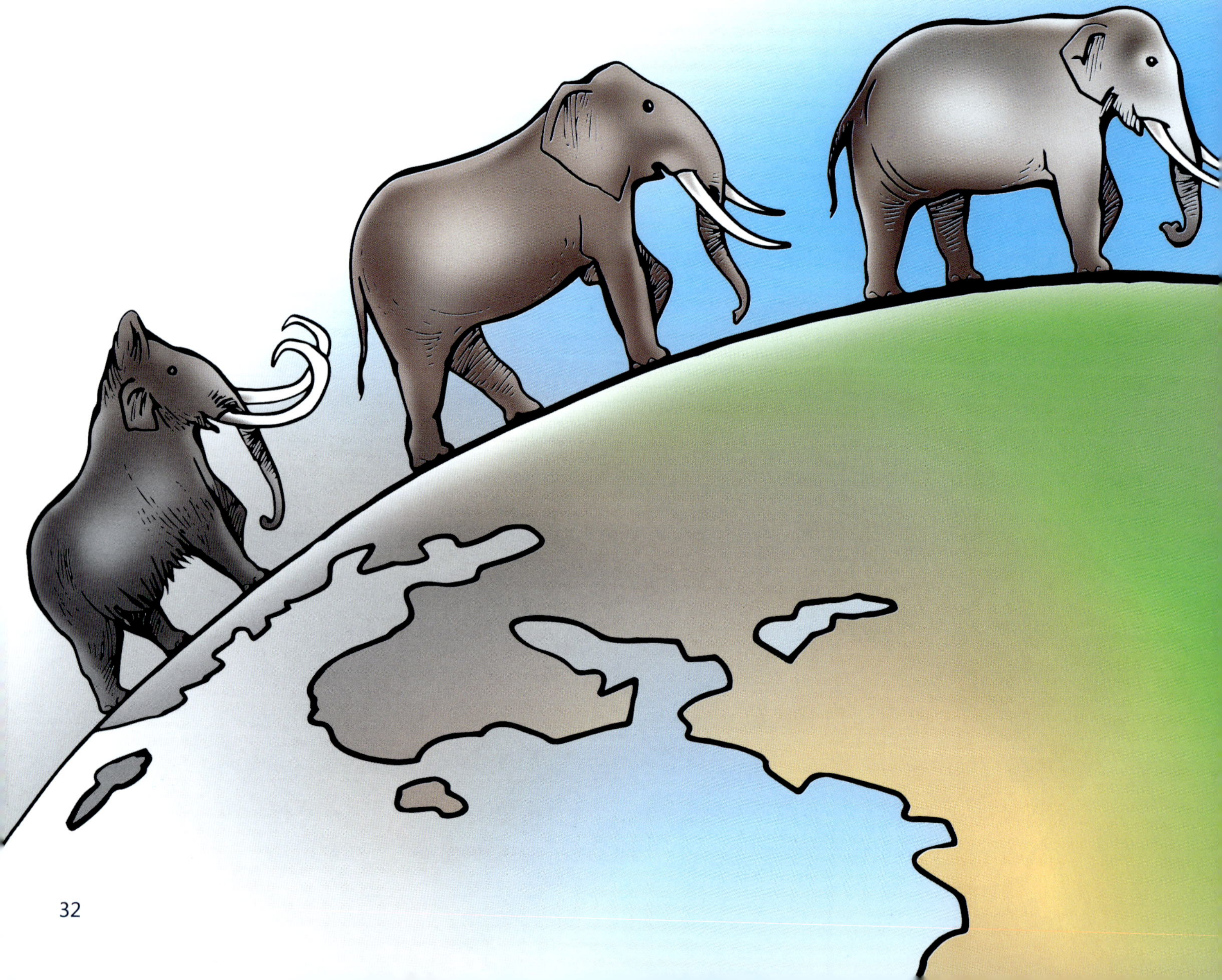

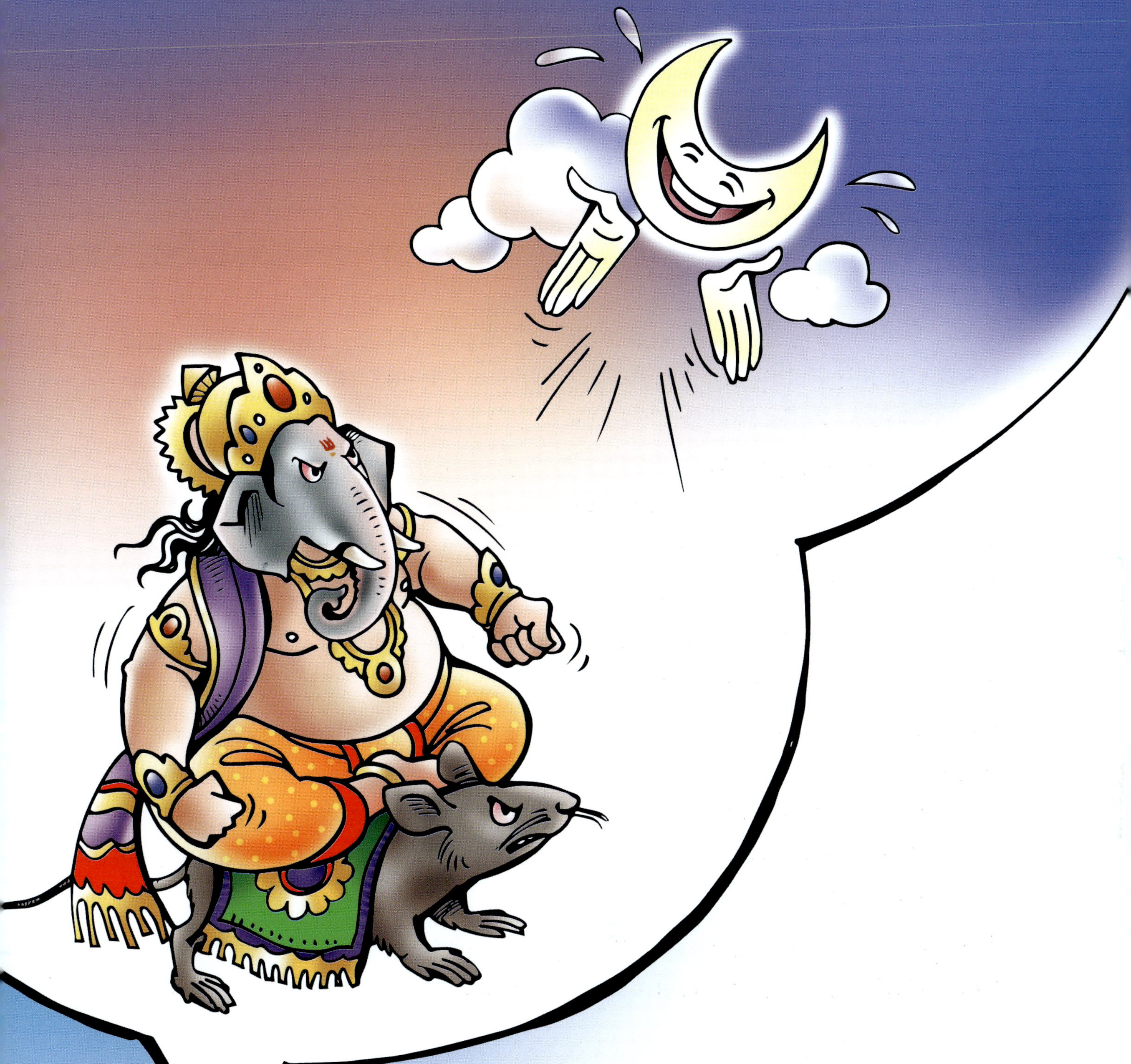

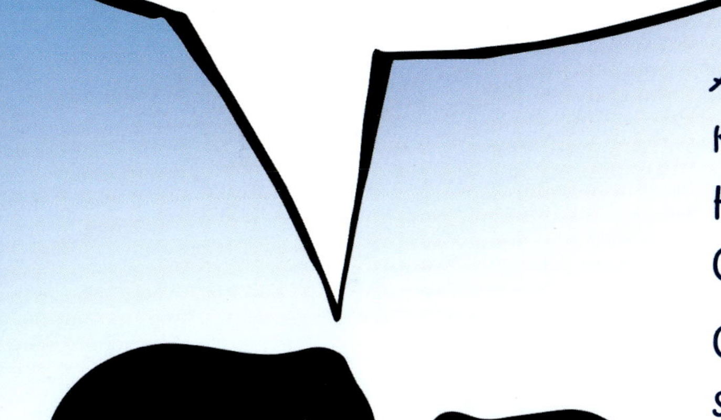

Auntie told him about Ganesha. You know, she said, "you know he's a god. He has a trunk, and tusks, just like us. Only, one of his tusks is broken"

Once, Moon was looking down from the sky and he saw Ganesha, fat, and round, pass by. He was riding a tiny mouse.

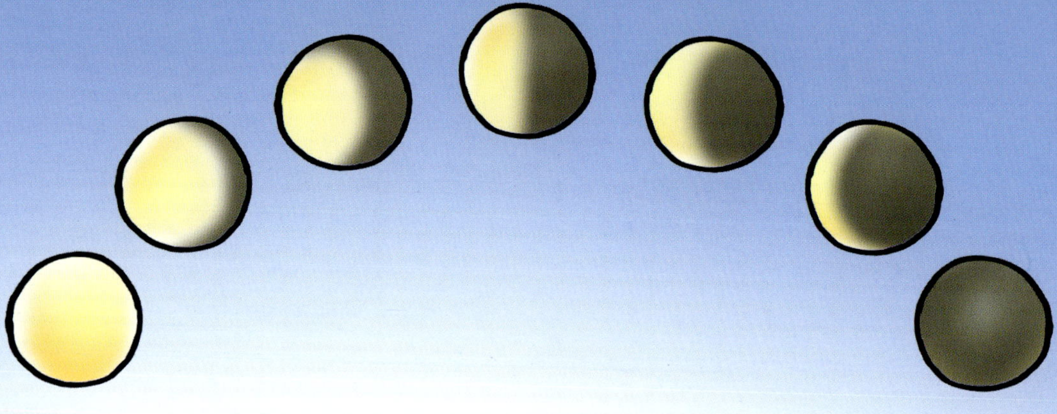

Moon began to laugh. He laughed till his tummy hurt, and when he finally stopped, he saw Ganesha was very angry.

Moon saw his angry face and he was frightened. Before he could begin to say sorry, Ganesha broke his tusk off and flung it at Moon, and said, "ho, you think I'm funny! Watch! You shall become dark, and you will stop glowing. And you will never be seen by anyone!"

Now everyone became worried. If the moon became invisible, there would be chaos everywhere!

Be merciful Ganesha, they pleaded. But Ganesha could not take back his curse. So he thought a bit, and said, "hmmm, from now on, you will wax and wane alternately every fifteen days. You will be seen as the new moon, half-moon and full moon, and there will be a moonless night".

Balarama loved this story very much, and often played Ganesha all by himself, when he thought no one was looking!

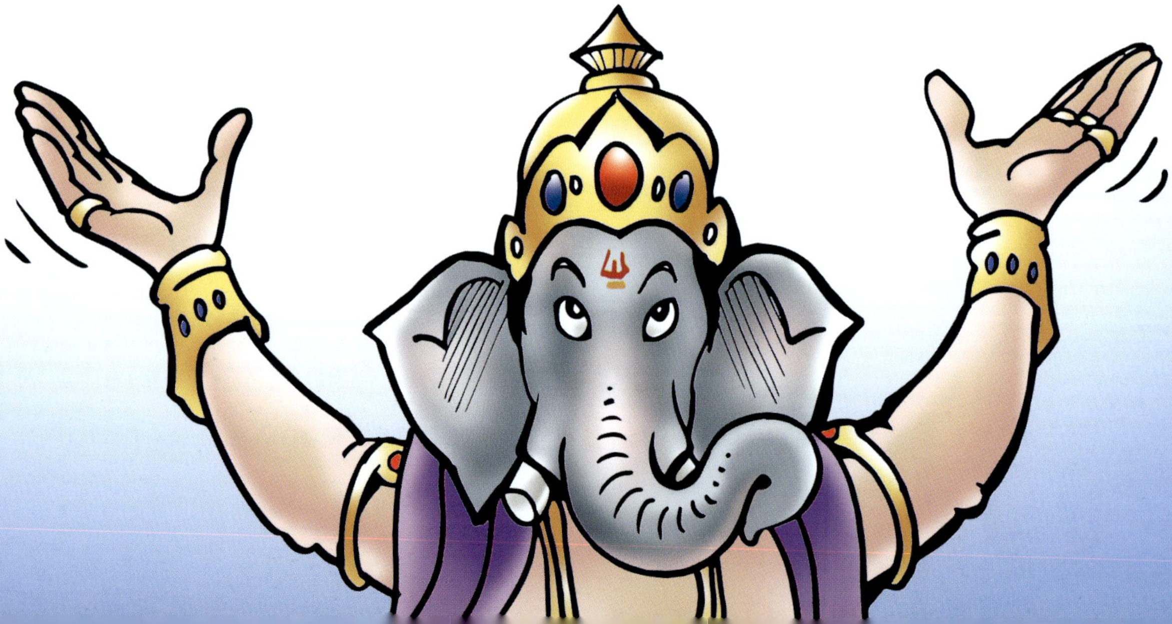

When he looked at the moon, which glowed softly on full-moon nights, and then began to grow smaller, he would laugh, and say, "hey Moon, I know all about you...."!

Balarama had heard that four mighty elephants hold the earth in place. They were given this task by the Gods Brahma, Vishnu and Shiva. Virupaksha stood at the east, bearing the weight of the earth on his back. Sometimes, when he grew tired, he would shake his head vigorously to ease the tense muscles in his neck. When he did that, the earth shook, rattled and rumbled, we called them earthquakes!

An elephant called Mahapadma is in the South, and the western side of the earth is supported by Somanasa. In the north is the elephant called Bhadra.

Elephants are very important, Balarama thought. If there were no elephants, the earth would fall down!

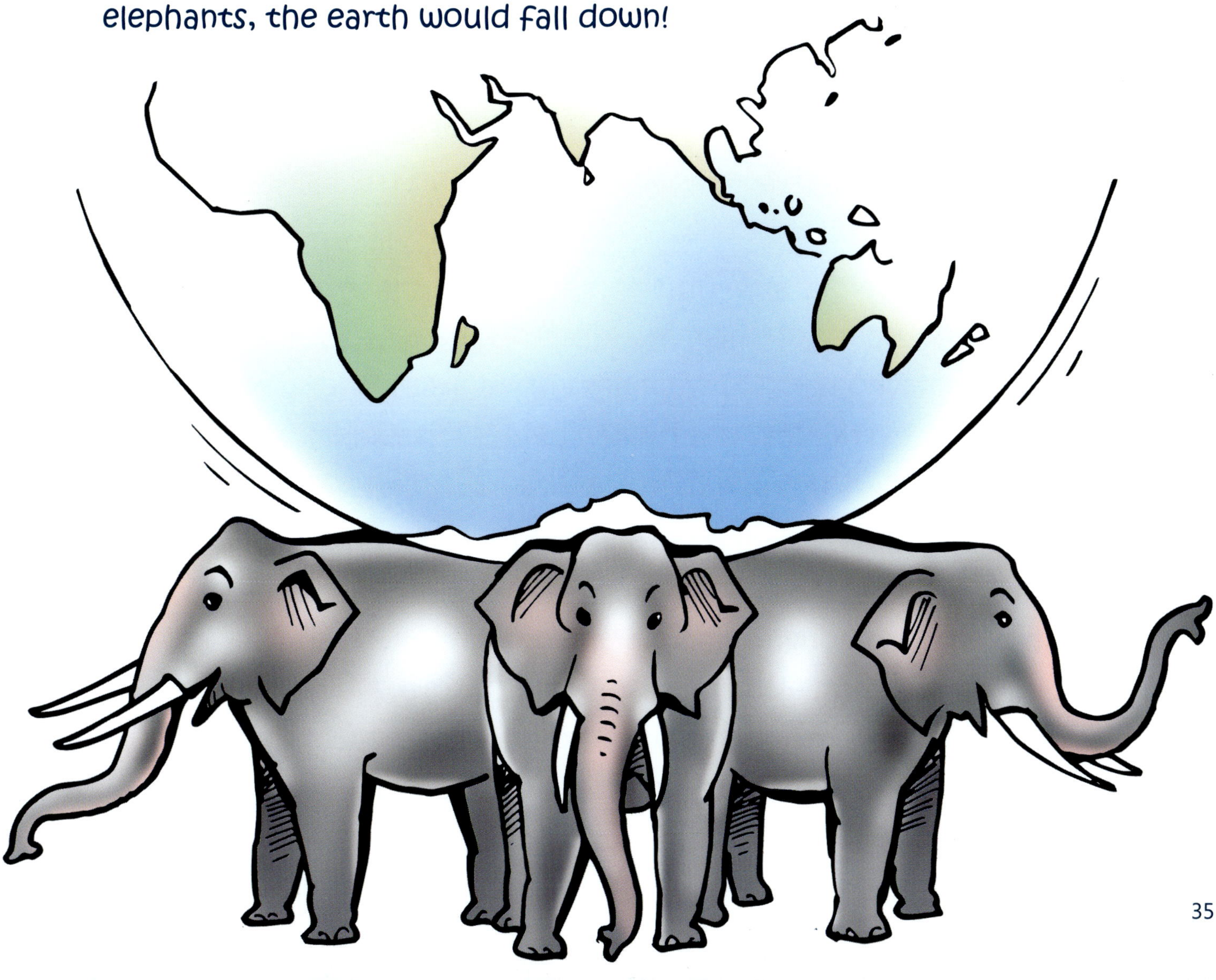

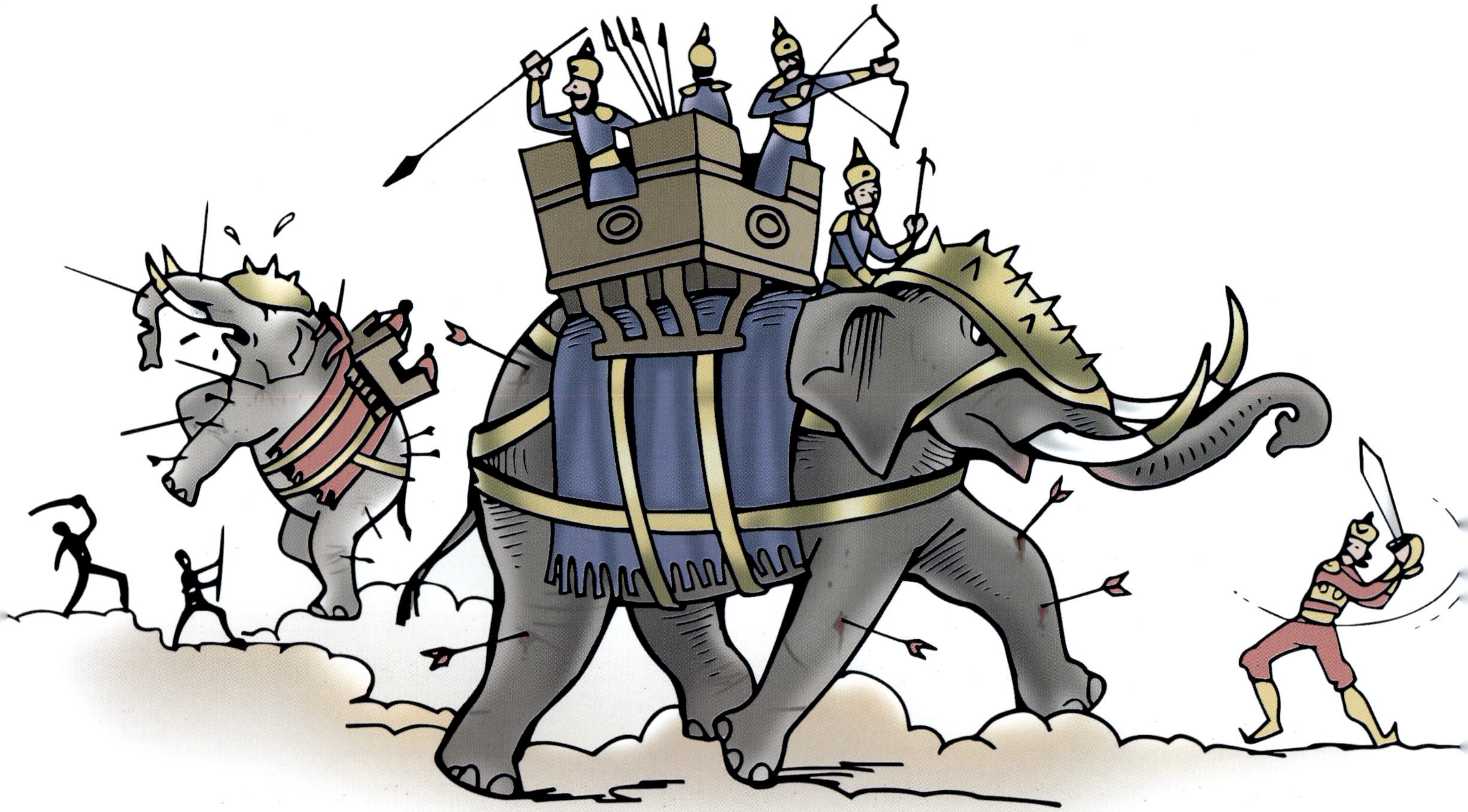

All about humans and khedda

One day. Auntie Aaney told Balarama and the other boys about war.

"War,"she said is a terrible thing. Man kills man, and in a war, thousands of them are killed. There was an Emperor, Ashoka, who had 700 elephants in his army. They went into the battlefield, and human beings rode them, and killed each other. Elephants, and horses died too."

Balarama didn't understand. How did elephants land up on the battlefield? And what were these creatures, horses? He thought elephants lived here in the forest. As for humans, well, he was not quite sure. He hadn't even seen one, though Auntie told him there were kind humans, and there were mean, cruel humans.

“Child,” said Auntie Aaney, “its time I told you about khedda... “. She sounded extremely sad, and he could barely hear her.

Balarama grew alarmed. He had never seen Auntie like this.... eyes drooping, her face long , her whole body stooped sadly.

Sniffling loudly, Auntie gathered Balarama, Rama, Nakula and Bhima close, and when they were all huddled together close to her, began...

“Boys, listen carefully. Now you are all old enough to know. You must all promise not go stray far from home, or go anywhere alone. And never, ever go to the edge of the forest, where the big gates are. On the other side of those gates live the humans.”

These humans, they want us. They want you, boys, because you have tusks. They take away

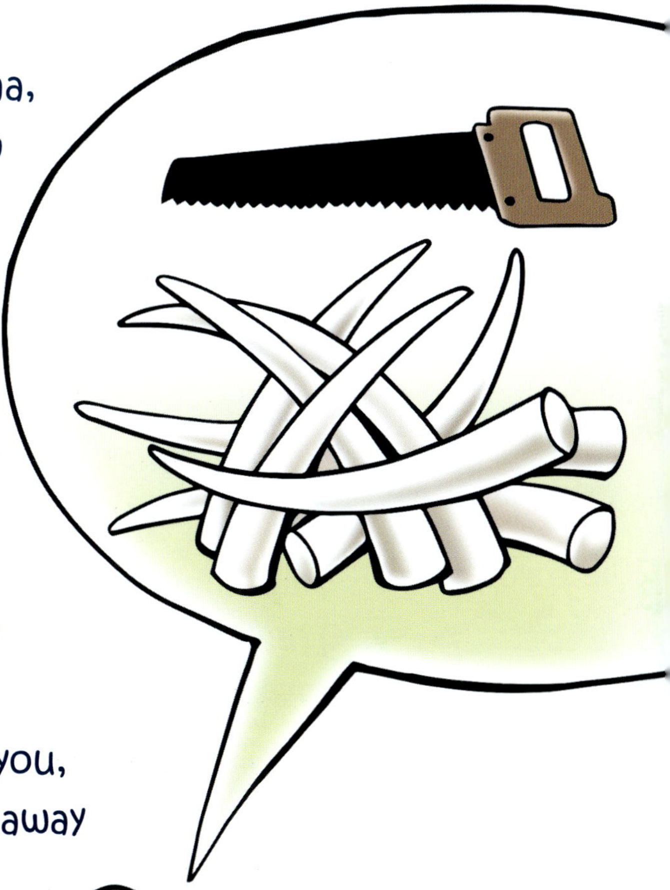

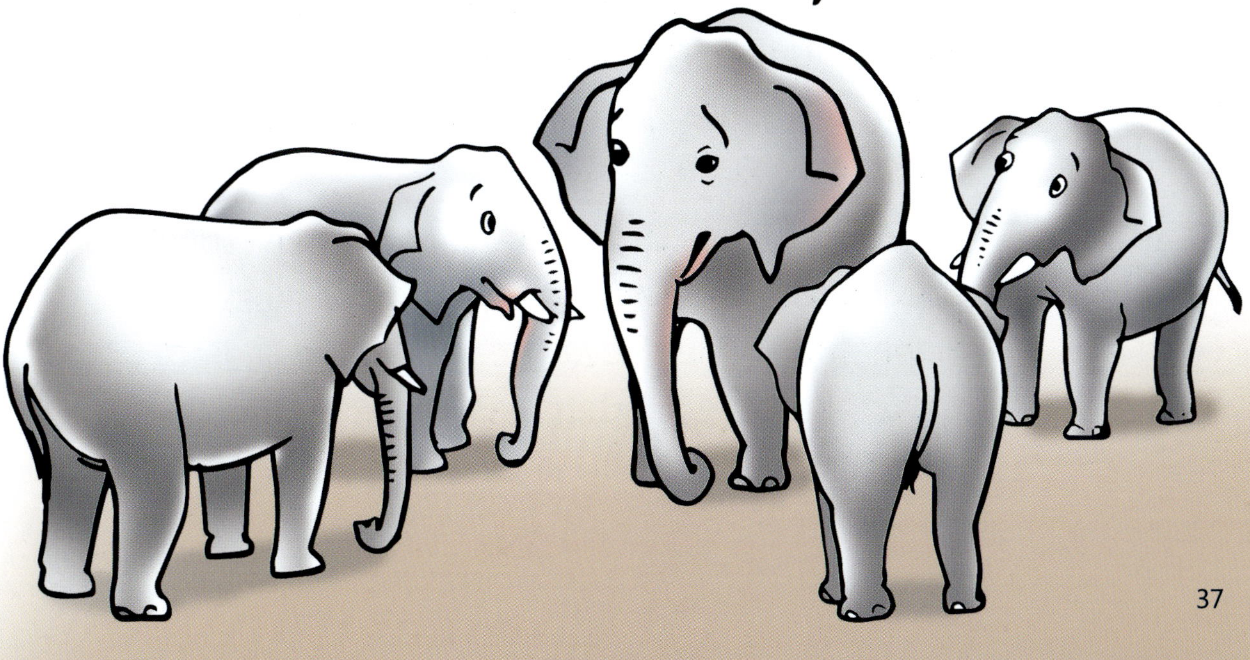

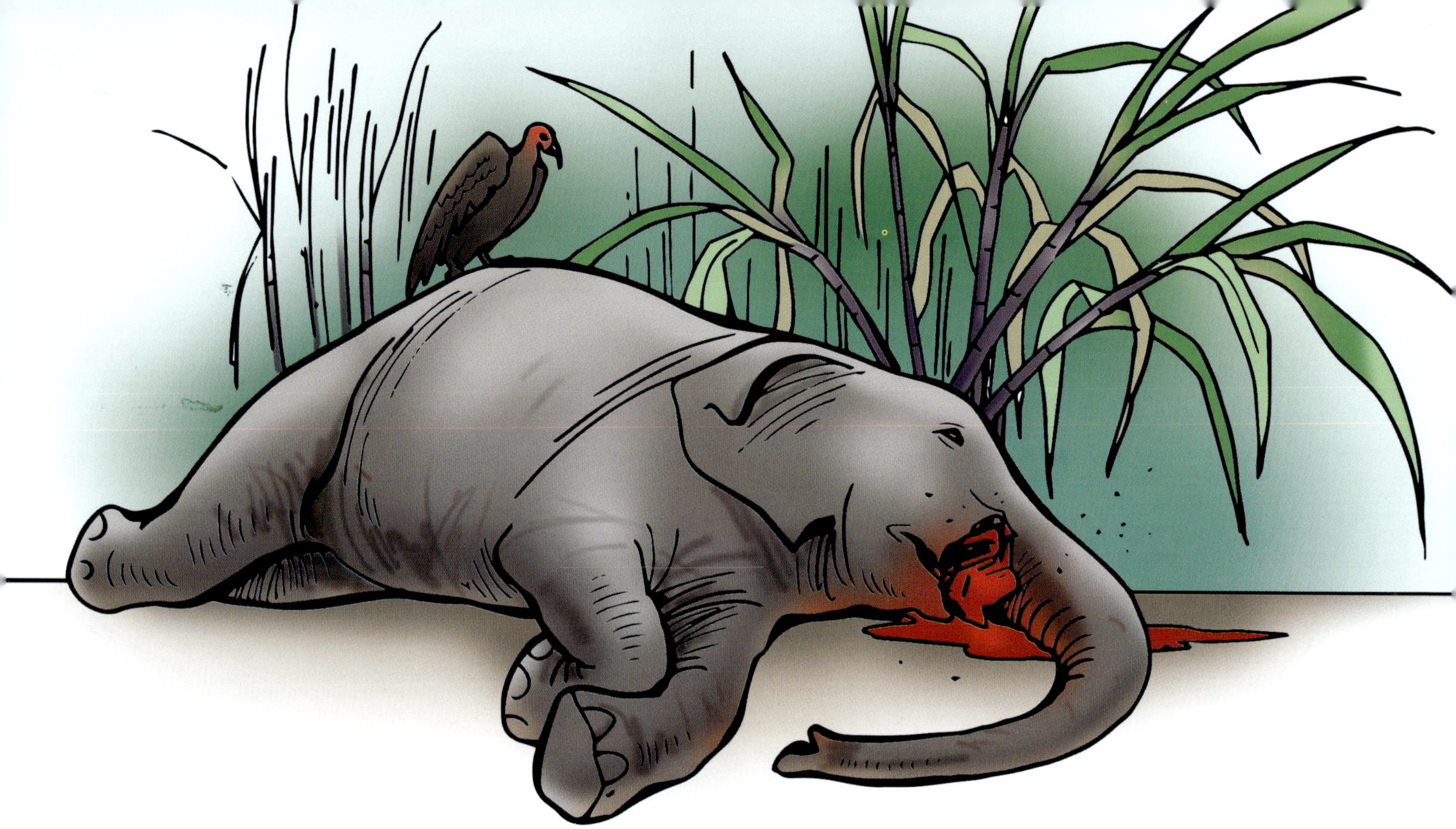

young elephants and they're never heard of again, Auntie was saying...

Balarama was terrified now. So were his friends. They huddled closer together, and stayed close to Auntie.

"Why would humans want our tusks?" Balarama thought, and jumped out of his skin when Nakula said, "My big brother Ramesha says he saw our uncle, Govinda lying on the grass by the sugarcane fields. I think he was dead... and his tusks were gone...!

Bhima, his voice quivering, said, "When Gunda told me that humans come and take away elephants and we never hear of them again, I thought my big brother was joking, and trying to scare me....

And now Auntie tells us this!"

The gang fell silent, and nobody wanted to go out across the Kabini to go stomping in Kakanakote. They would just stay home, close to Auntie, and their mommies.

After a while, the four young ones got tired of not doing anything. They were too nervous to play hide-and-seek, and splashing about in the water didn't seem fun at all today! They badly needed cheering up!! Suddenly, Balarama perked up, remembering something.

"Auntie," said Balarama, "what is khedda? You said you would tell us about khedda?"

"Come, darlings, "Auntie said, I will tell you about khedda. Once you know, you will learn to be very, very careful, and help each other, won't you?"

Balarama and friends nodded vigorously, their trunks touching the ground, and ears flapping noisily. They sat down around Auntie, nuzzling her and feeling safe.

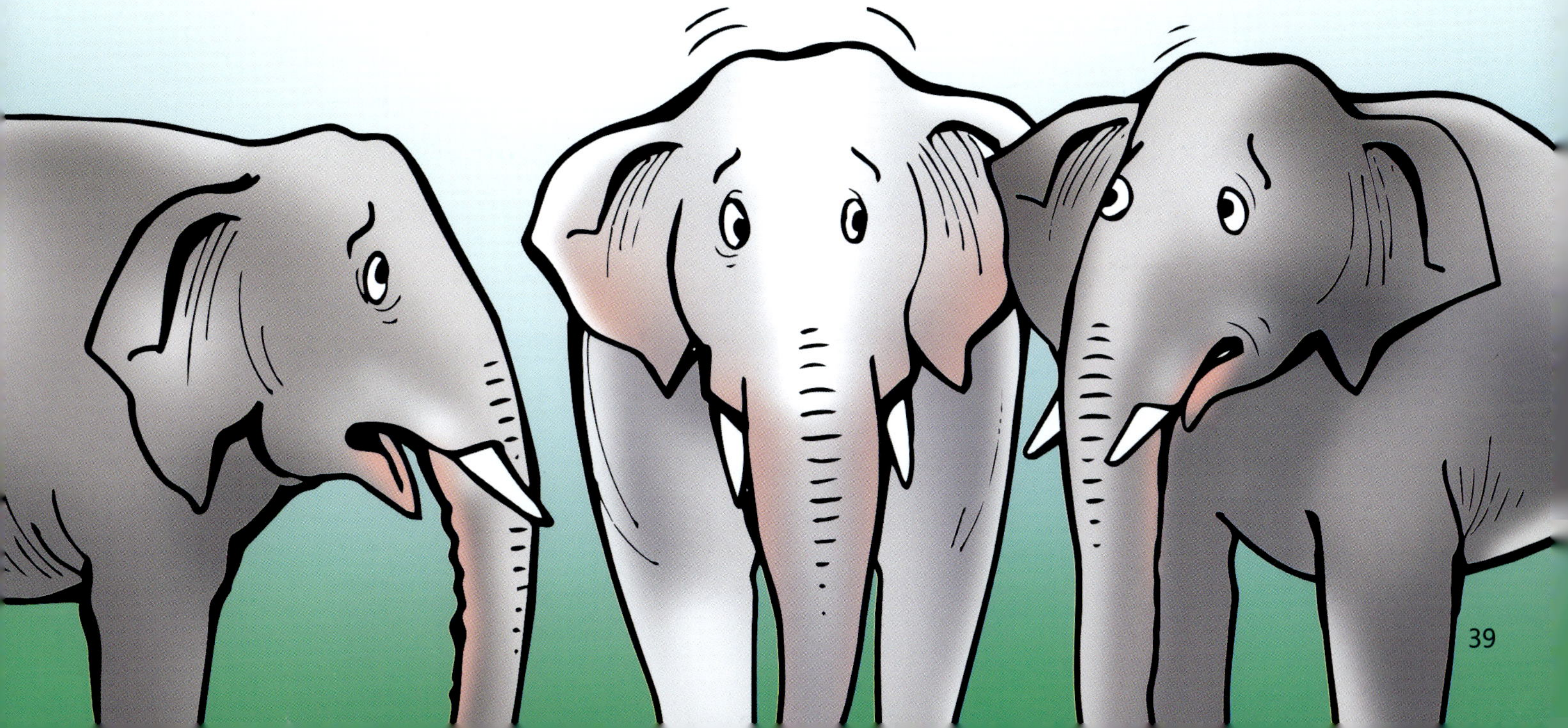

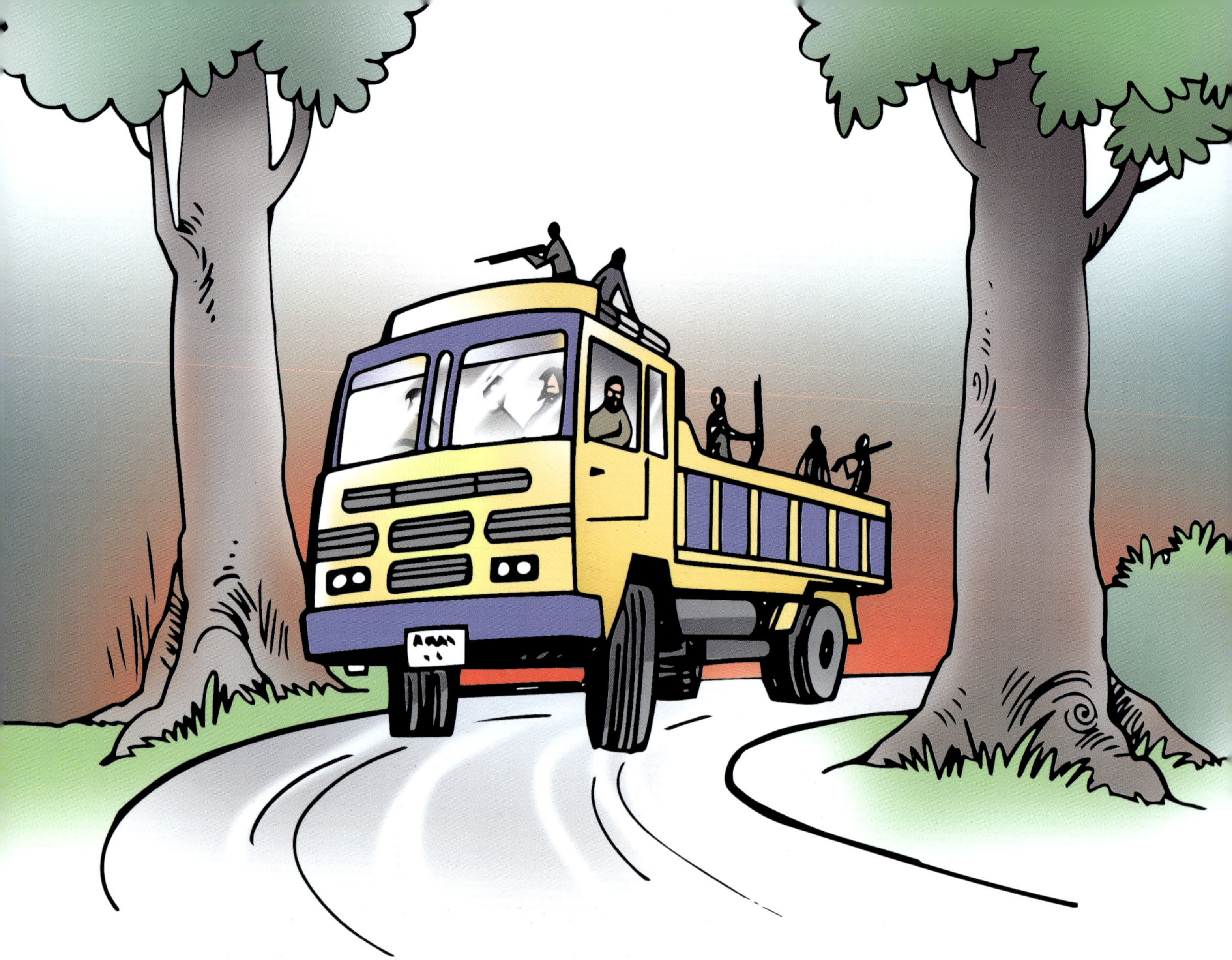

"Children, when you go near the edge of the forest, where humans often come, with guns, and big trucks, hide. Turn round, and very, very quietly, walk back home. Never let them see you" Auntie was saying.

"I know you've never seen a human, and you think he is too small to do anything to us. But they are clever, and cunning, and there are too many of them. "Auntie went on.

"They will lay traps for you. If you see sugarcane and grass in the forest, and not standing in the fields beyond, don't get greedy and run to it. The wily humans dig a big hole in the ground, and cover it with grass and cane.

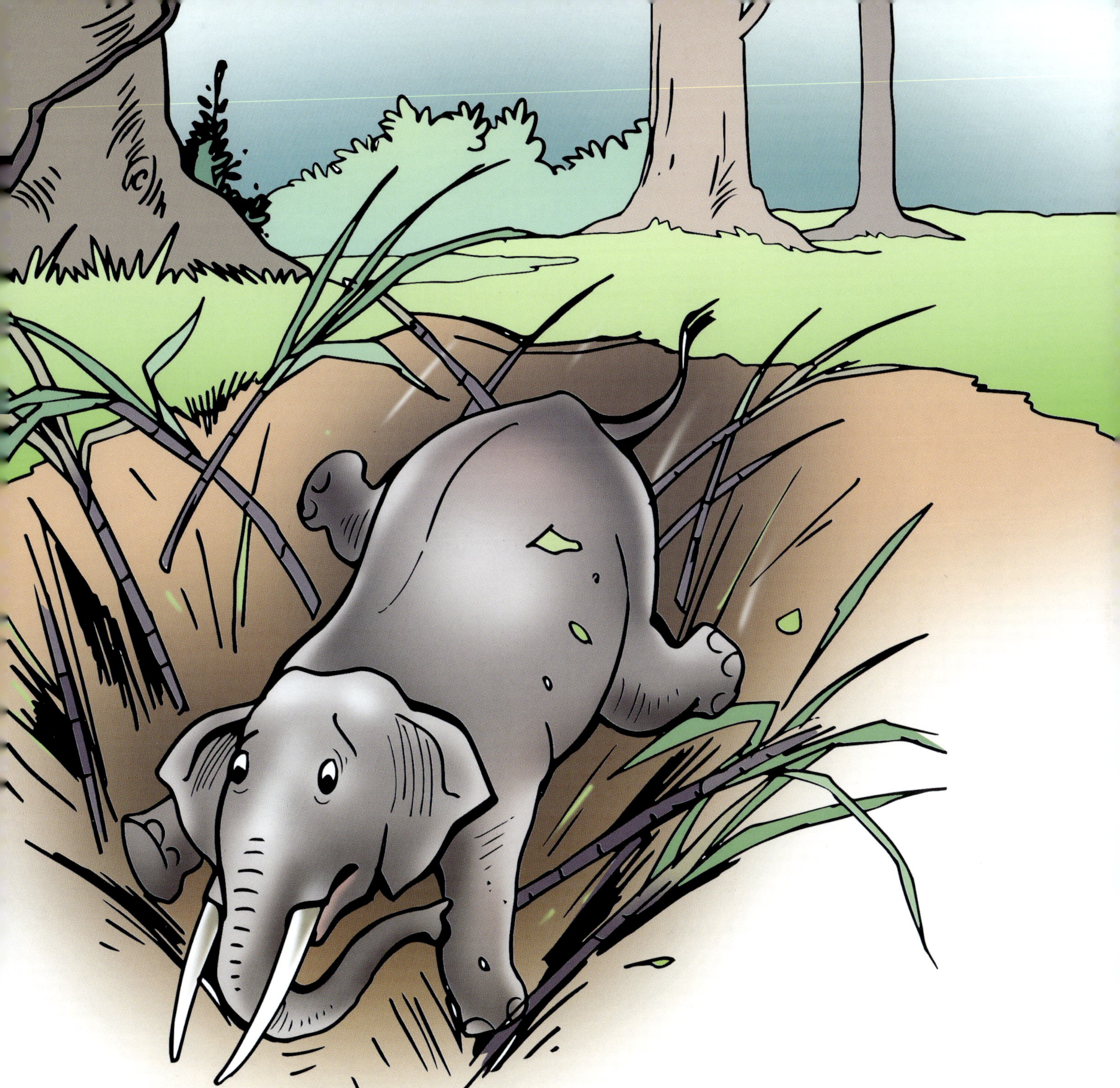

"Oooh! And when we go there, the grass will give way, and we will fall into the pit... that's scary, auntie..." said Balarama, shivering so much that he thought everyone could hear his bones rattling.

Of course, no one noticed. They could only hear their own bones rattling, as scary thoughts raced through their little minds. How horrible to be taken out of the forest! Never see Auntie again, or their friends...

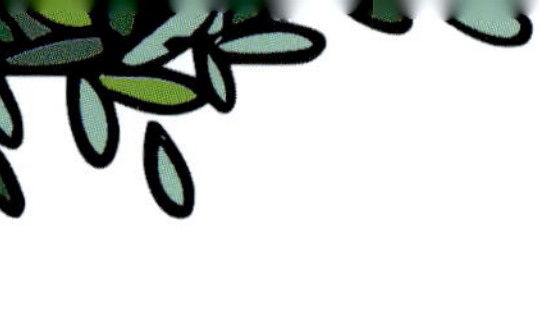

They come for Balarama

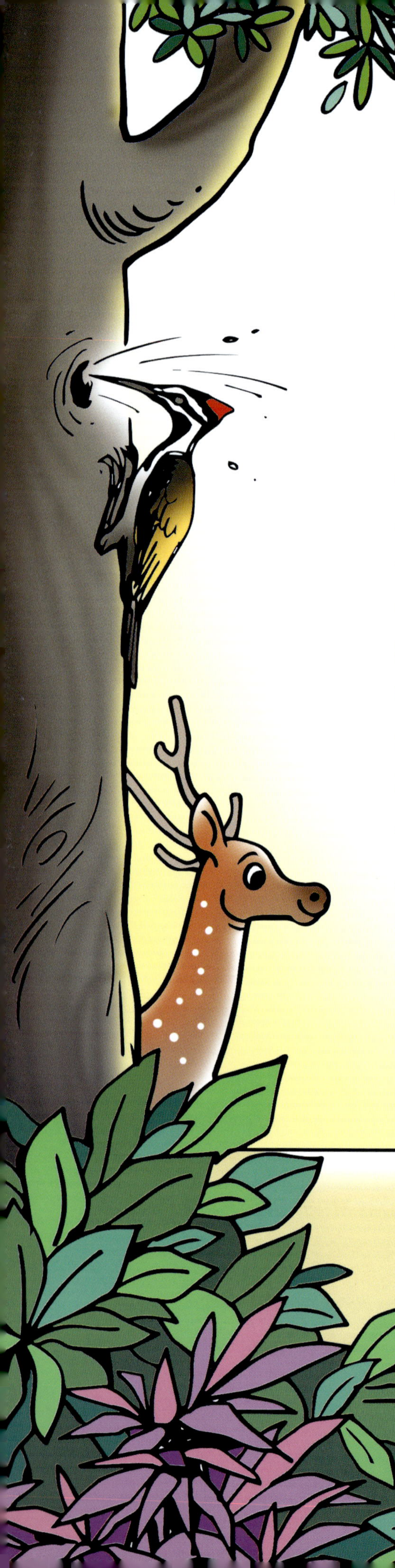

It was a fine day in Nagarahole forest. The Kabini flowed with a merry gurgle and caught the sun's rays in twinkling flecks of gold and silver. The cormorants, and storks stood in the water, occasionally dipping their beaks in the river to grab a fish. Kingfishers swooped in out of nowhere and flew off with a bite. Woodpeckers kept up their knocking on the teak trees, and deer flitted about behind the bushes. Burray, son of old Hughlie who had been killed by hunters many moons ago, skulked about, wondering if he ought to go for the kill, or wait another day to lunch on deer.

The baby elephants, under the care of Chikki Aaney, were learning to stand in the water without falling down on their tail. One of them had his trunk caught under another baby, and there was

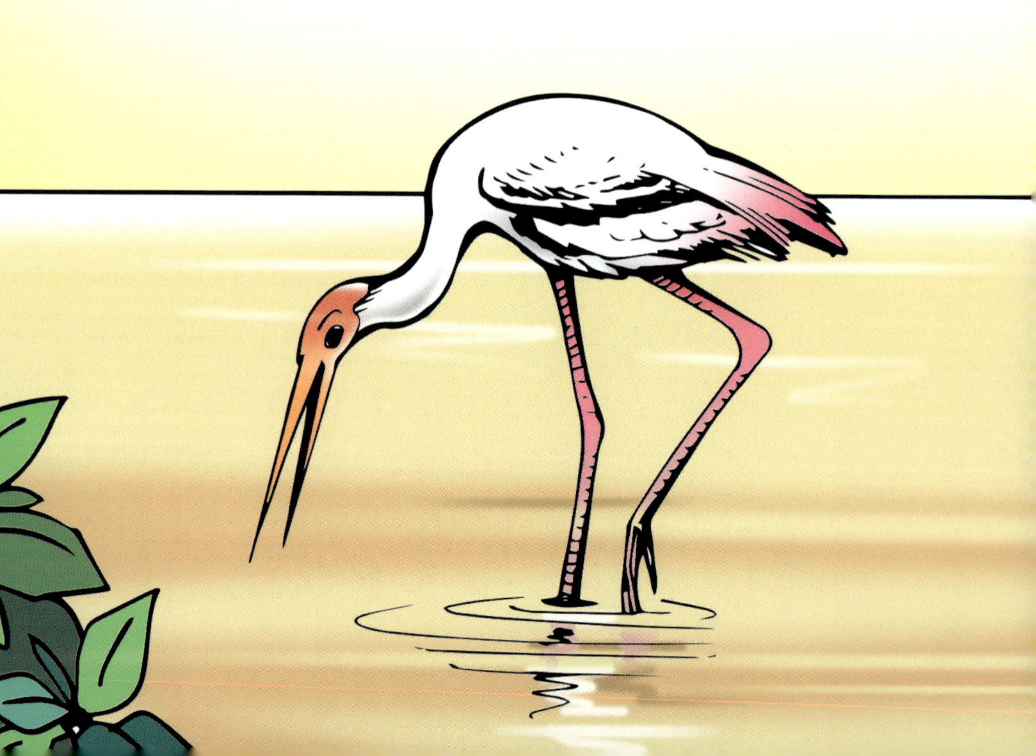

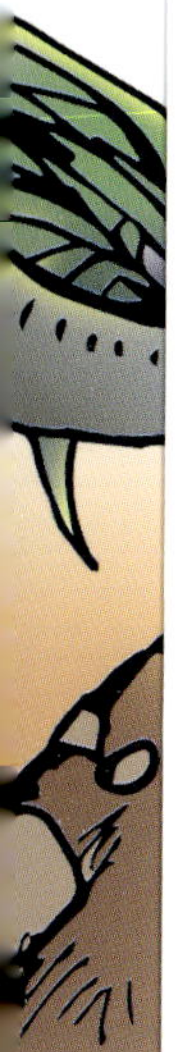

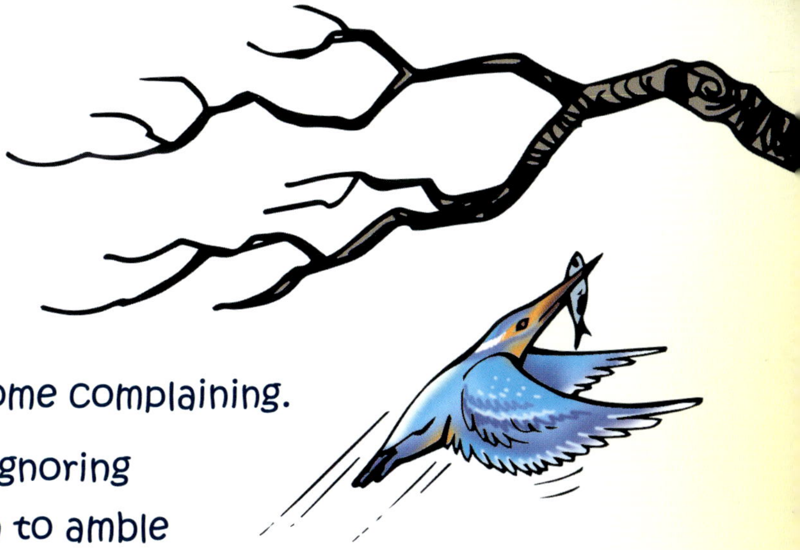

laughter, and wailing. And some complaining.

Balarama strode past them, ignoring the admiring looks. He began to amble with an extra swagger, shamelessly showing off long trunk, and the smart pair of tusks that grew long and awesome. Chikki Aaney came up behind him, and he felt a sharp nudge on his huge, imposing (in his opinion) behind.

"Ouch!" he cried, in sudden pain, wondering which young elephant had dared to do this.

"Get moving, young man," Chikki Aaney growled, and Balarama obeyed hastily. He liked Chikki Aaney a lot. She was only a few years older than him. When Auntie Aaney, who had raised him, and taught him everything he knew, died, she had taken over the herd.

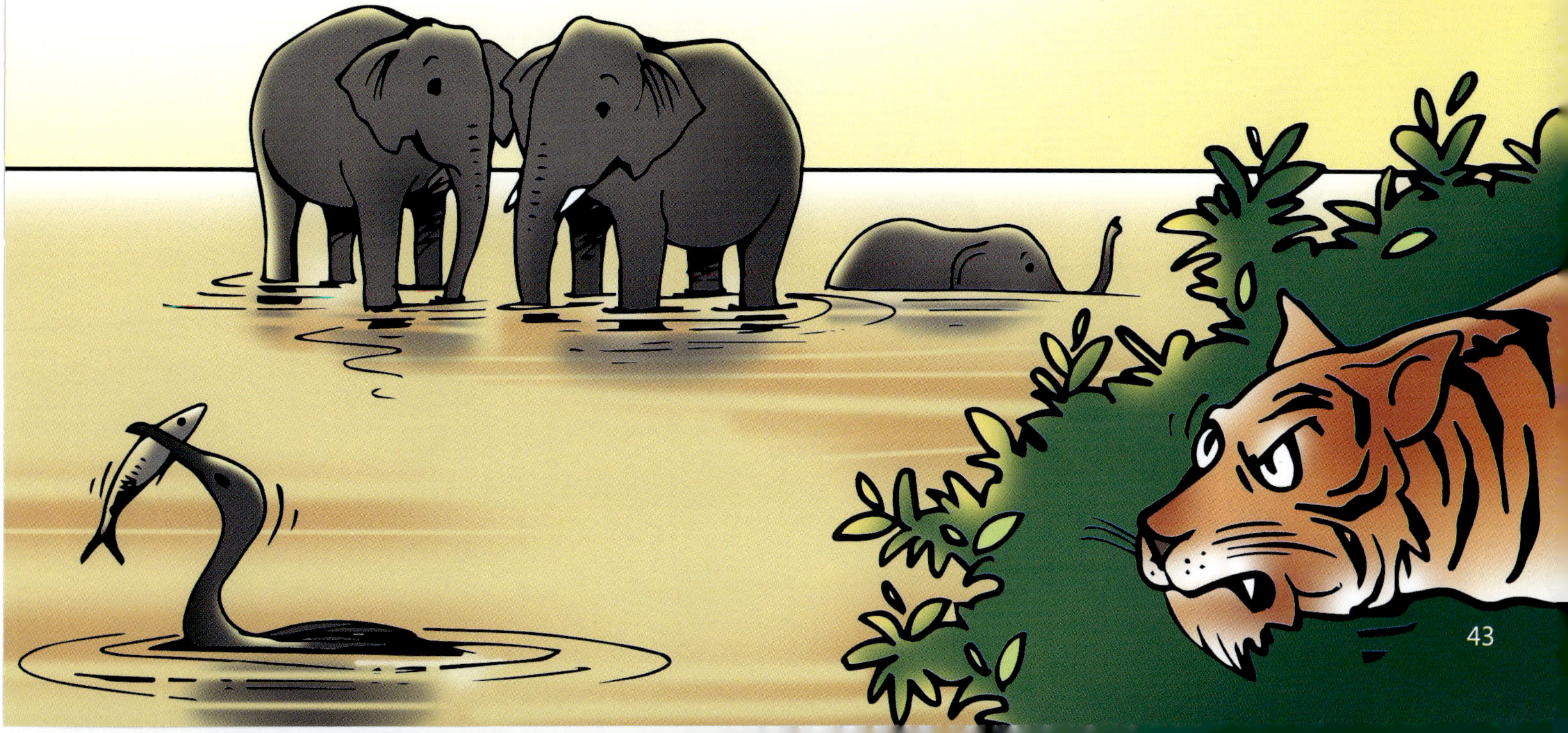

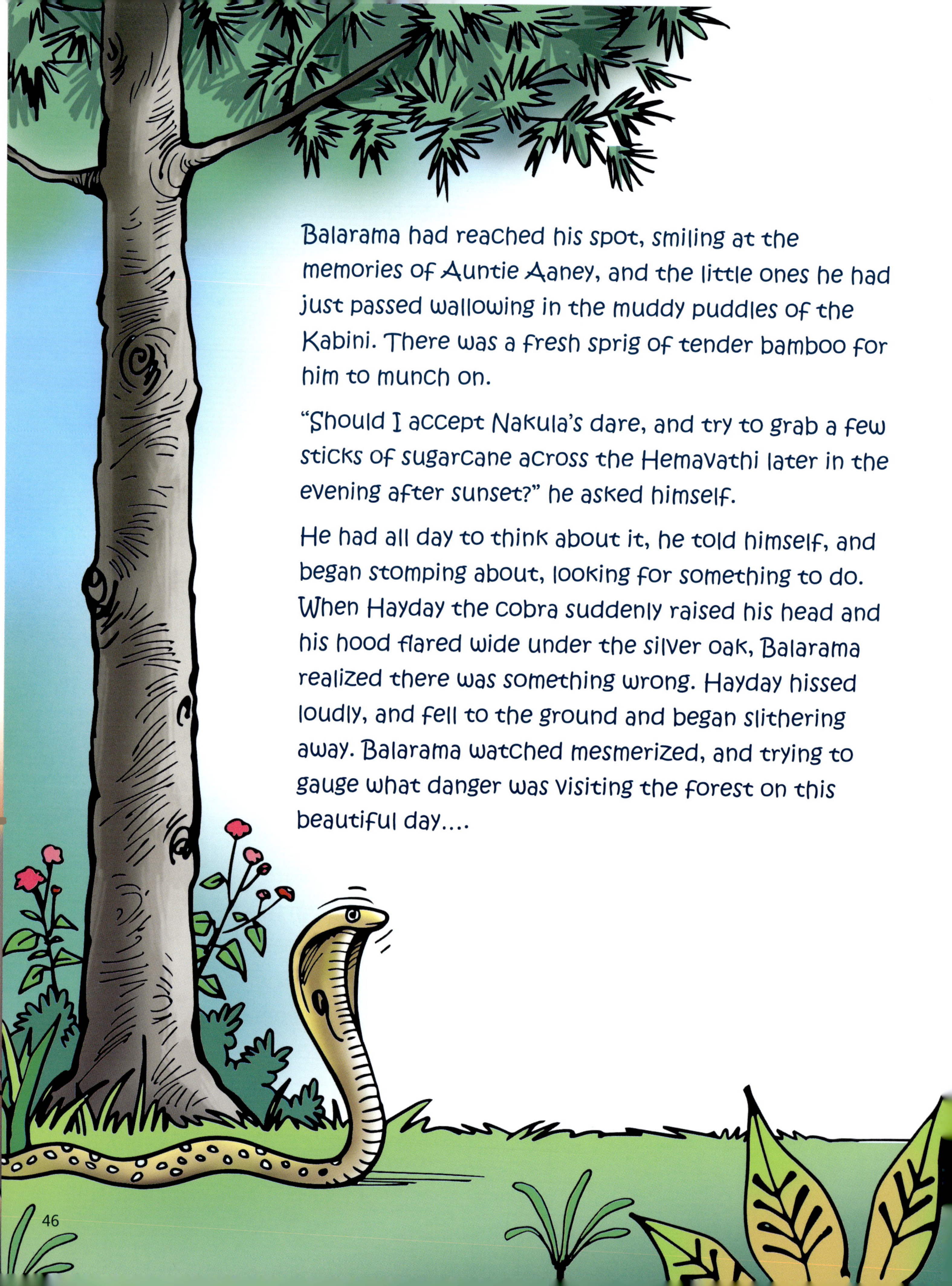

Balarama had reached his spot, smiling at the memories of Auntie Aaney, and the little ones he had just passed wallowing in the muddy puddles of the Kabini. There was a fresh sprig of tender bamboo for him to munch on.

"Should I accept Nakula's dare, and try to grab a few sticks of sugarcane across the Hemavathi later in the evening after sunset?" he asked himself.

He had all day to think about it, he told himself, and began stomping about, looking for something to do. When Hayday the cobra suddenly raised his head and his hood flared wide under the silver oak, Balarama realized there was something wrong. Hayday hissed loudly, and fell to the ground and began slithering away. Balarama watched mesmerized, and trying to gauge what danger was visiting the forest on this beautiful day....

He ought to make for the gooseberry and horse nettle shrubs behind the bamboo clumps, he was thinking...and turned, trunk raised, ears fanning slowly. When he felt a sharp pain shoot up his left hip, he knew he was not going to make it...

"A thorn... oh Ganesha.... What is happening.... "Balarama mumbled, before his legs folded up under him, and he fell on the grass with a great thud that could be heard a mile away...

"There's a handsome one... "He heard a voice. Humans. The dreaded humans were here in his spot... and he was down, slipping into a strange new kind of sleep...

"A worthy successor to Drona...." the human was saying...

Drona... sounds familiar... who? Where had he heard that word? It was the last question on Balarama's mind as he slipped into a dreamless sleep...

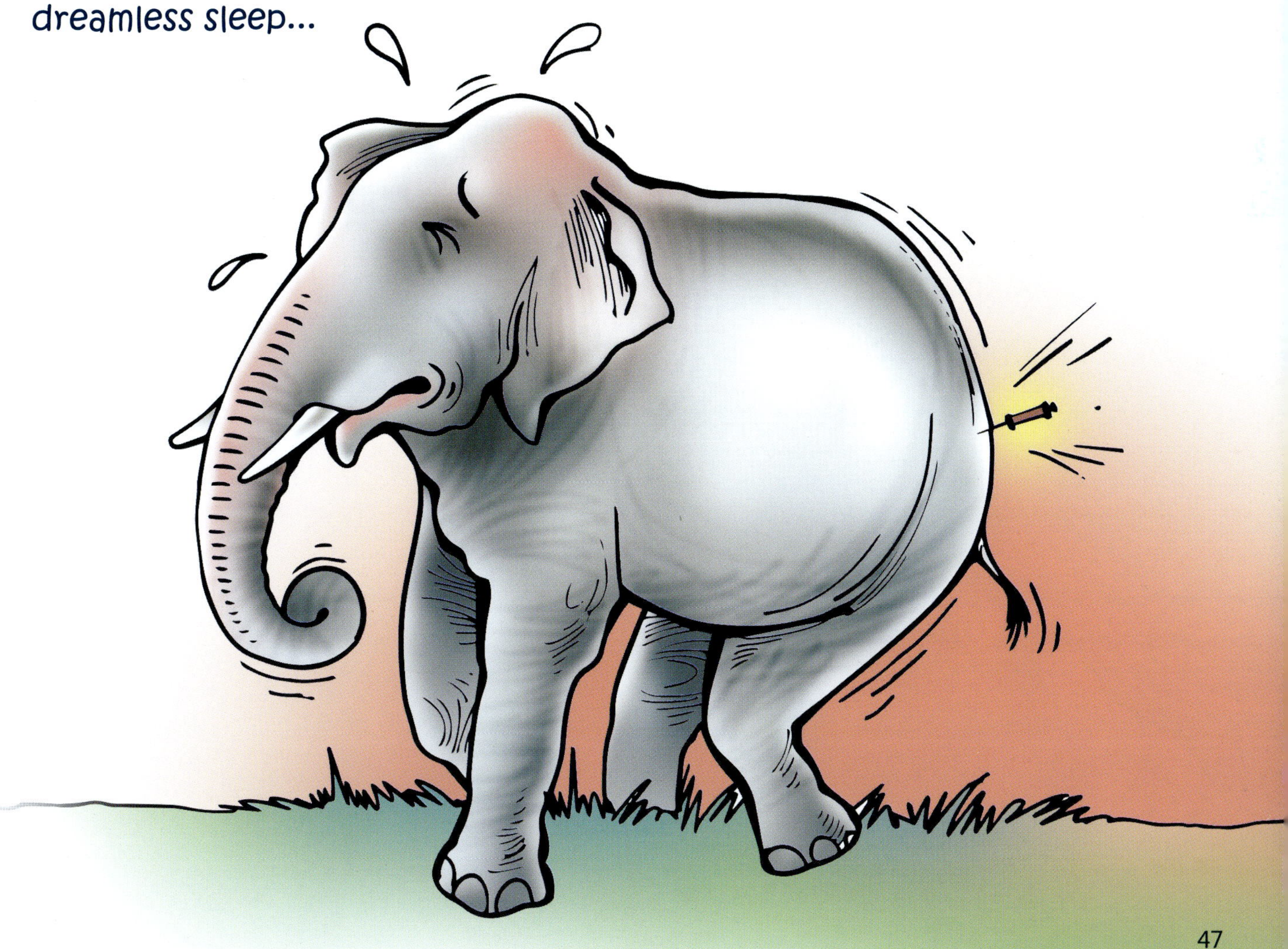

Balarama is taken

Balarama opened his eyes slowly. He felt groggy. "A drink of water.... And a splash in the Hemavathi..." he mumbled. His words came out sounding like a low grunt.

He got up. No really, he tried to get up, wondering why he was lying down like he was sick. But he could not move his legs at all! In great panic, he raised his trunk and let out a loud, agonised trumpet.

Balarama's "turraaaaauntmph!' rang out so loud that he was sure it could be heard in the watering hole at Kabini. Alas! He would never know!

As the echo of his trumpeting subsided, he heard voices again. "He's waking up, "someone was saying. Balarama tried to turn his head to see where the voice was coming from.

Of course, he could not turn his head... there was a rope cutting into the folds of his neck, and the pain was unbearable. He whimpered, and flapped his ears. He could only move his right ear!

There were humans-he knew they

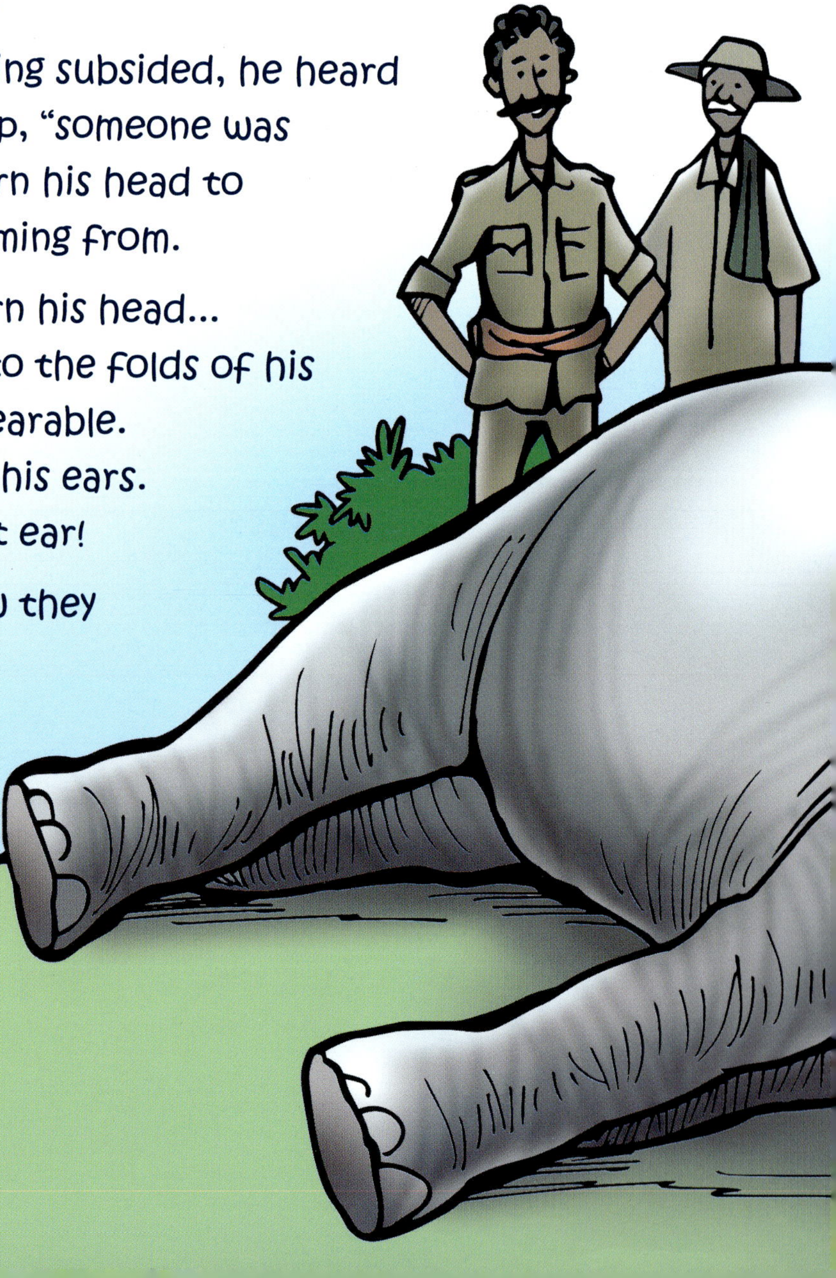

were humans, though he'd never really set eyes on all around him... prodding him, touching him and talking loudly as if he wasn't there!

As Balarama felt the ground firmly under his four feet, and found that he was not falling, he turned his head from left to right. He found he could!

He also saw these strange creatures a dozen of them, at least, standing on two legs. With their forelegs they were tugging at the ropes that bound him. They had no trunks! And no ears, apparently! Definitely no tail!!

He was hearing strange new sounds, words, and strangely, he knew he was going to hear more of them from now Balarama felt himself move. He was being lifted... His feet no longer touched the ground. "So this is how Chiroo, that annoying leopard cub must have felt", Balarama thought. He had seen Uncle Ramesh wrap his gigantic trunk around him and fling him into the bamboo clump 300 meters away!

He looked down, and gulped, as he had never had this view of his home. He was on level with the top of the jackfruit tree,

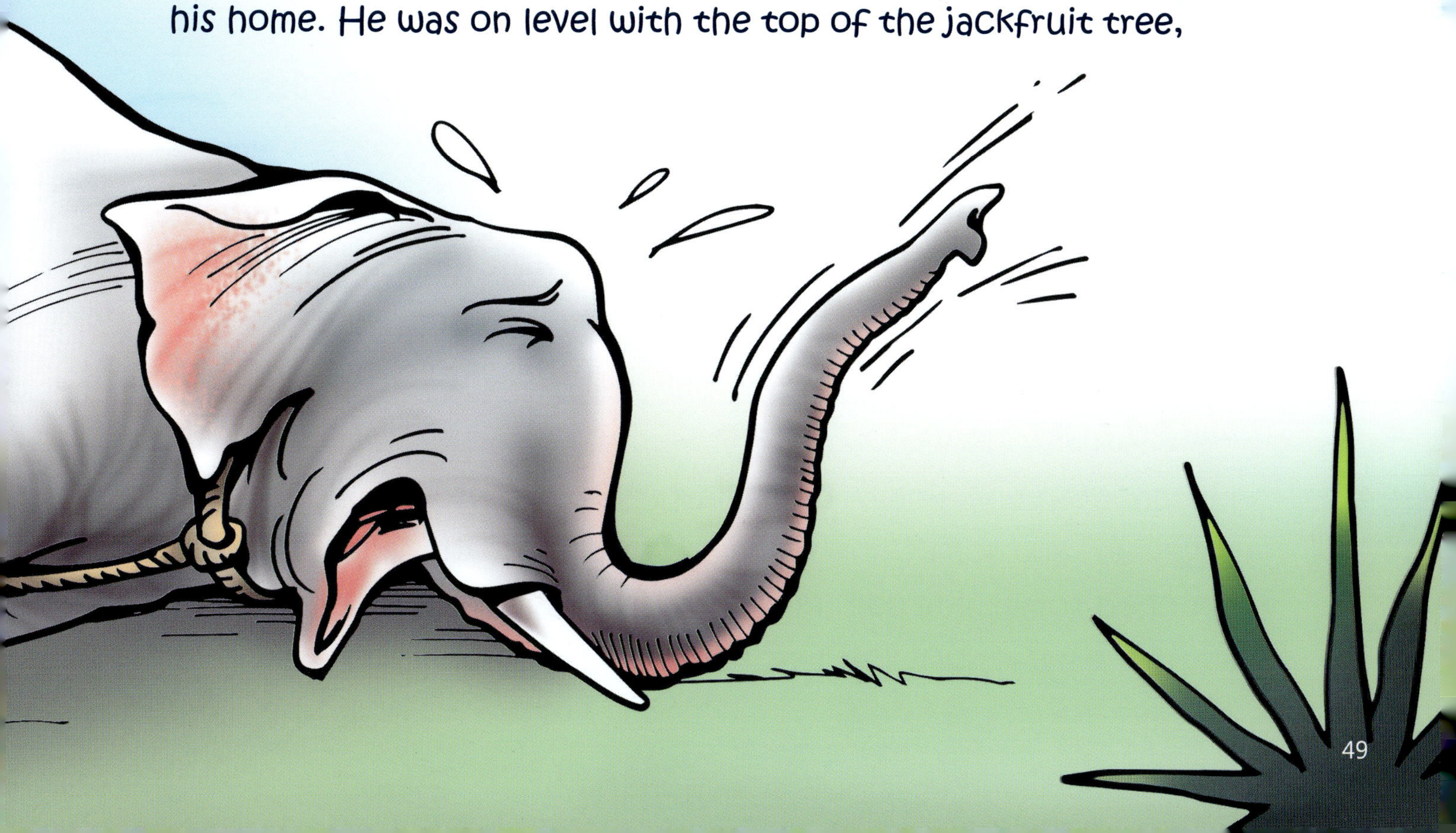

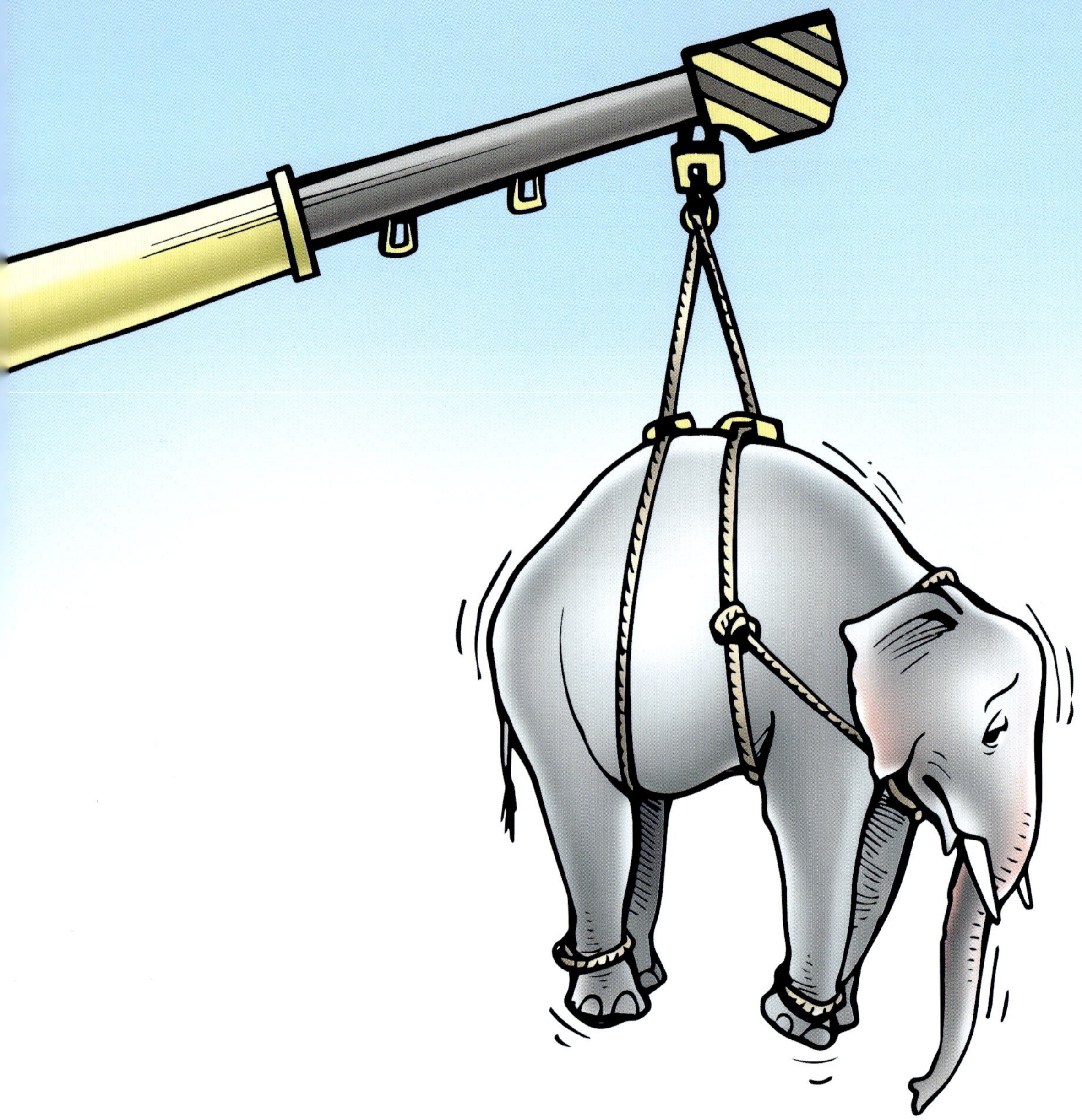

and he could feel the foliage brush against his ear. He was suspended mid-air, flying like the sharp-eyed Giduga the eagle.

His head was spinning and he thought it was the forest spiraling down. Before he could get used to it, he felt himself dropping down again. He hated what was happening to him. All trussed up, being pulled up, dragged down, and these noisy humans making him do all his!

He was standing, finally, on something. His feet were bound together, and something slammed shut. His trunk almost touched something cold and hard. He was in a cage, but he'd learn the names of what was happening to him, much later.

The cage was drawn by a truck, and soon it started moving. Balarama watched as the forest whizzed by. He began to whimper softly, and tears streamed down his eyes... The forest receded into the distance, and he could no longer hear the Hemavathi rippling merrily by. He thought he glimpsed Burray the tiger on one of the teak trees, watching him being taken away.

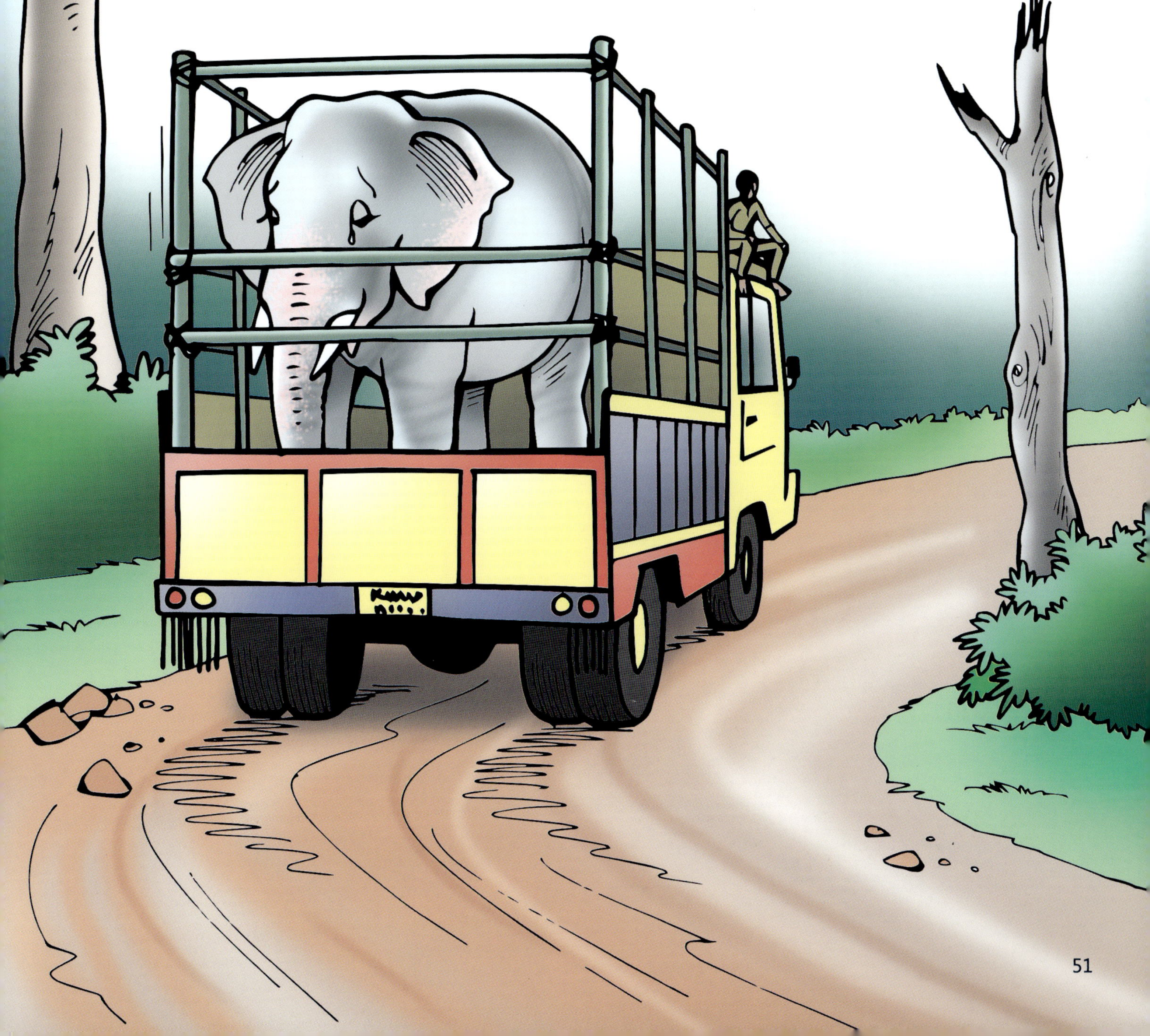

Balarama's despair and a new friendship

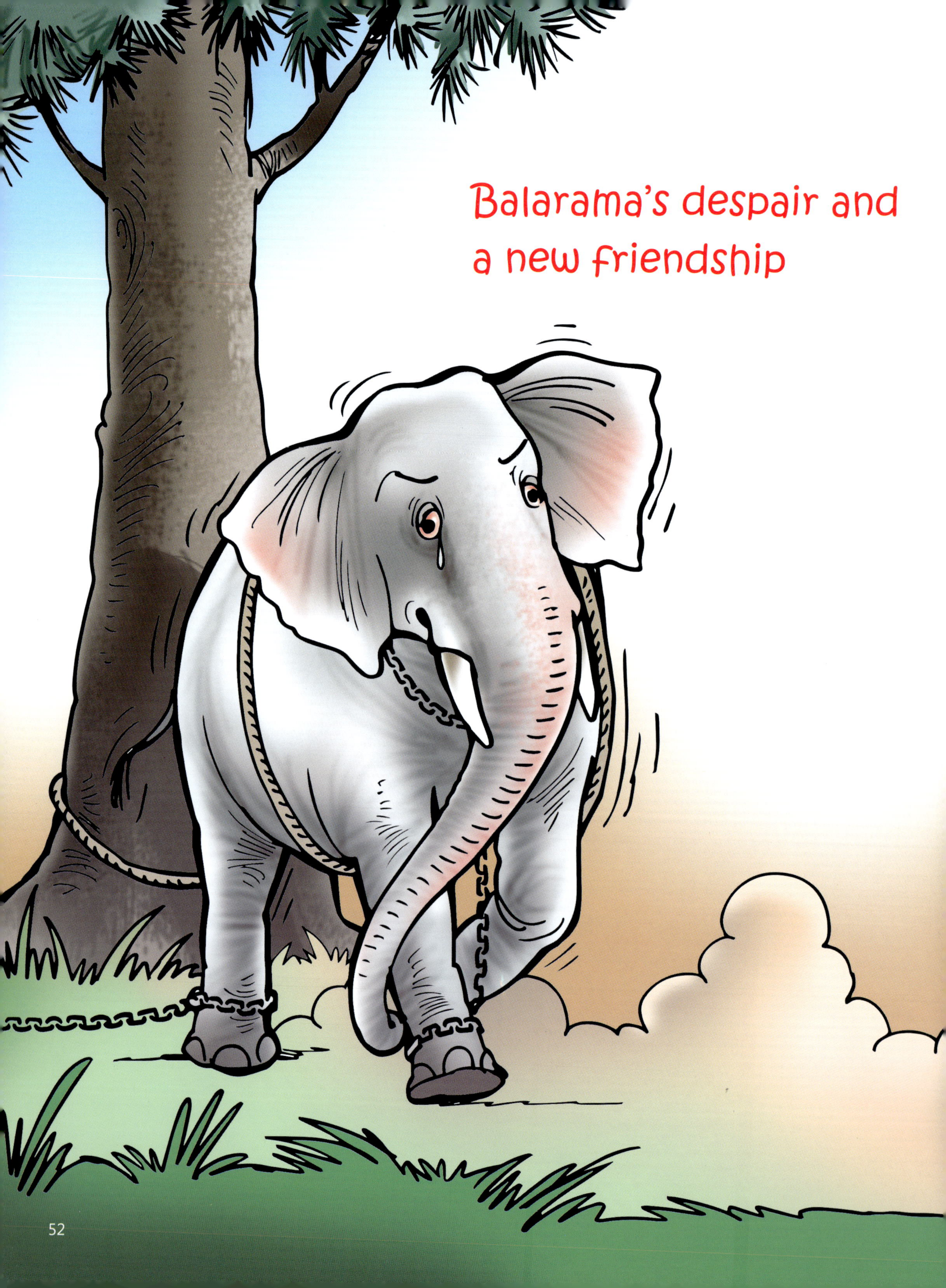

One week later...

Balarama stood under the giant silver oak, still as a rock. Aunty Aaney would have been pleased, he thought. Not that he could have moved even if he wanted to. His legs were bound in chains that snaked up from a stout iron post a few dozen feet away.

"I wish I were dead," Balarama thought, as tears welled up in his eyes and flowed down his drooping trunk. Was he being missed back home? Was Mohini looking for him desperately? Had Burray the tiger told the herd? What were Arjuna, Bheema, Nakula and Rama doing? Did they miss him?

In the seven days since he had been here at the elephant camp Balarama had cried a lot. More than he had all his life!

He was also very angry. On the first morning, Balarama slowly began to understand – he was never going to see his home, or his friends again!

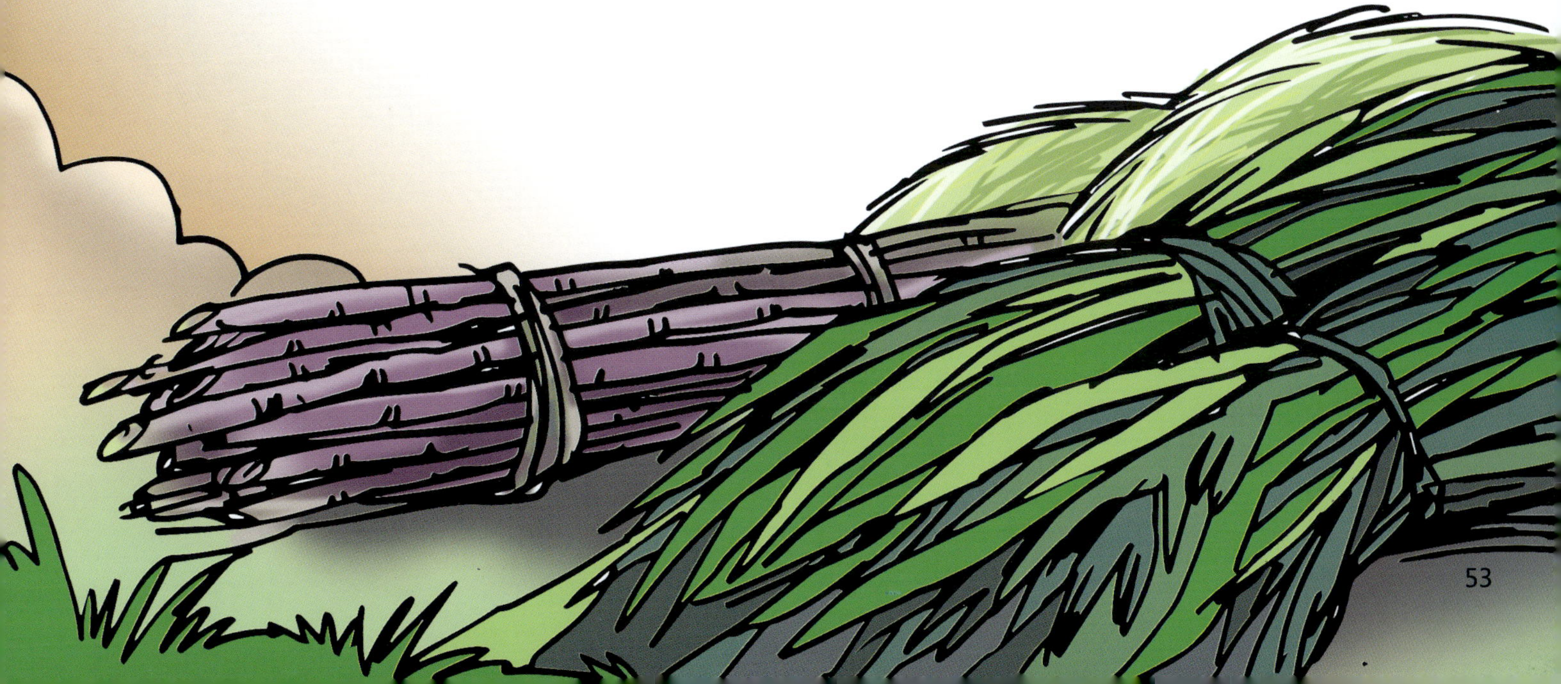

He strained at the chains and ropes binding him, and when he could not move as he wished, he trumpeted in great agony.

His "turrrrraannntph", was blood curdling, and every beast in Nagarhole and Kakanakote would have frozen its tracks. After which they would have run very fast, as far away as they could.

The humans here, were unimpressed. When he trumpeted, all he felt was a sudden sharp jab in his rear, or in the folds of his neck. His famed "turrrrrannnntph" would then end in a pathetic whimper.

A mound of grass and sugarcane was within grabbing distance of his trunk. But he had no appetite. The human, who was called Sannappa, came to him every morning, and coaxed him to eat.

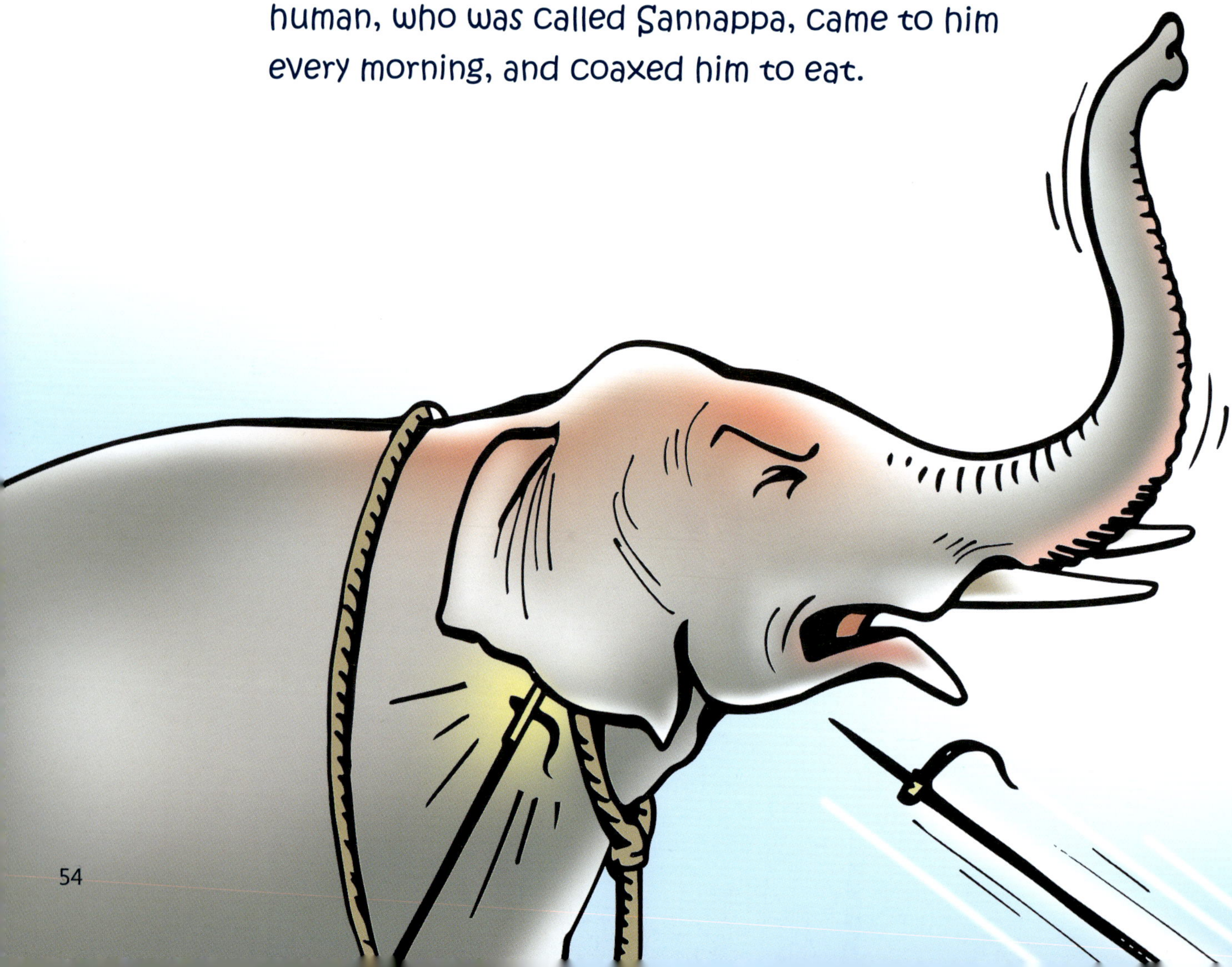

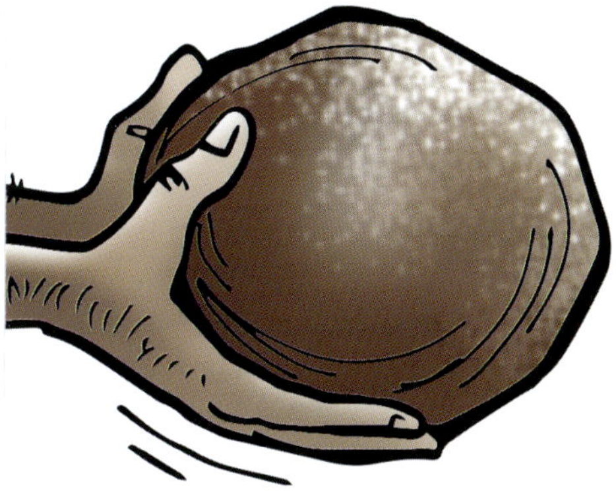
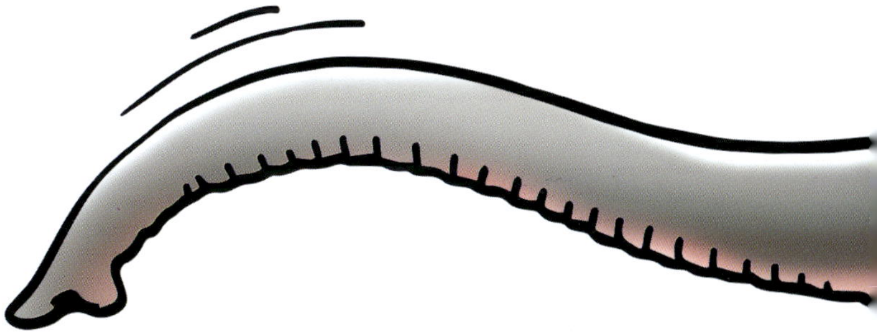

"Balaramoo, please eat. Here, I brought you ragi balls. They're good for you. ", Sannappa would say.

He would gently stroke his trunk, and fetching water in giant drums, which had stout pipes, he would spray Balarama with cool waters of the Kabini.

Balarama loved the feel of the water, and his tempers would cool a bit.

But he would remember how he would walk himself to the riverside when he felt like it, and become sad, kicking himself mentally for beginning to like Sannappa.

When he remembered to be mad, Balarama would go all stiff, and flicking his tail, raise his trunk, and pretend to nuzzle Sannappa, When Sannappa leaned close, he would dig sharply with his tusk.

But Sannappa was wily. "Don't, Balarama. I have tamed many elephants like you. You will soon meet Drona..." he would say kindly, while pulling the chains just a teensy bit tighter in an eight around his legs.

Every morning he woke up and saw his chains, the grass and Sannappa, and remembered where he was. What was he to do? Why had he been brought here? What about Drona?

hailed Sannappa, "hey, look who's here... so is he ready?" one of them asked.

"Yes, Annayya, "we are ready, replied Sannappa, "patting Balarama on his head.

Nudged by Sannappa, Balarama strode in through the wide gateway, whose logged gates were open.

He slowly raised his head, and looked around. His eyes widened in wonder at what he saw. There were seven elephants all with their right leg in chains, standing in a circle, staring at this newcomer. A human sat on three of them, while the other four were being nuzzled, stroked and gently spoken to.

Sannappa nudged Balarama, and guided him to a

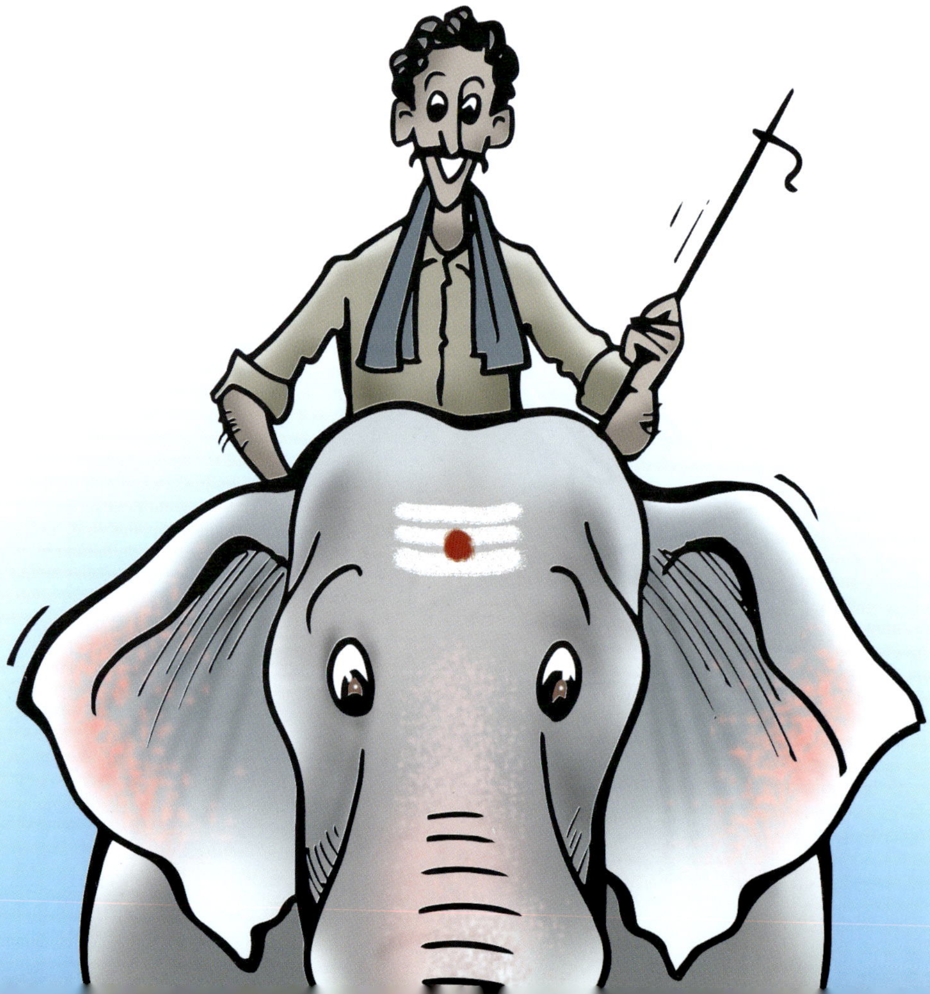

vacant spot in the circle of elephants. Balarama went, nervously, and stood in his spot, and turned to look at his neighbor on his left. He looked familiar, he knew those pink patch of freckles on the right ear!

"Arjuna!" he exclaimed,"how? What happened? You too?..." he was blubbering and soon Arjuna too was trumpeting excitedly, and making elephant noises of relief and comfort.

Arjuna had been taken from his own stomping ground on the same day, and he had been kept, not far from where Balarama had been chained. His human was Annayya.

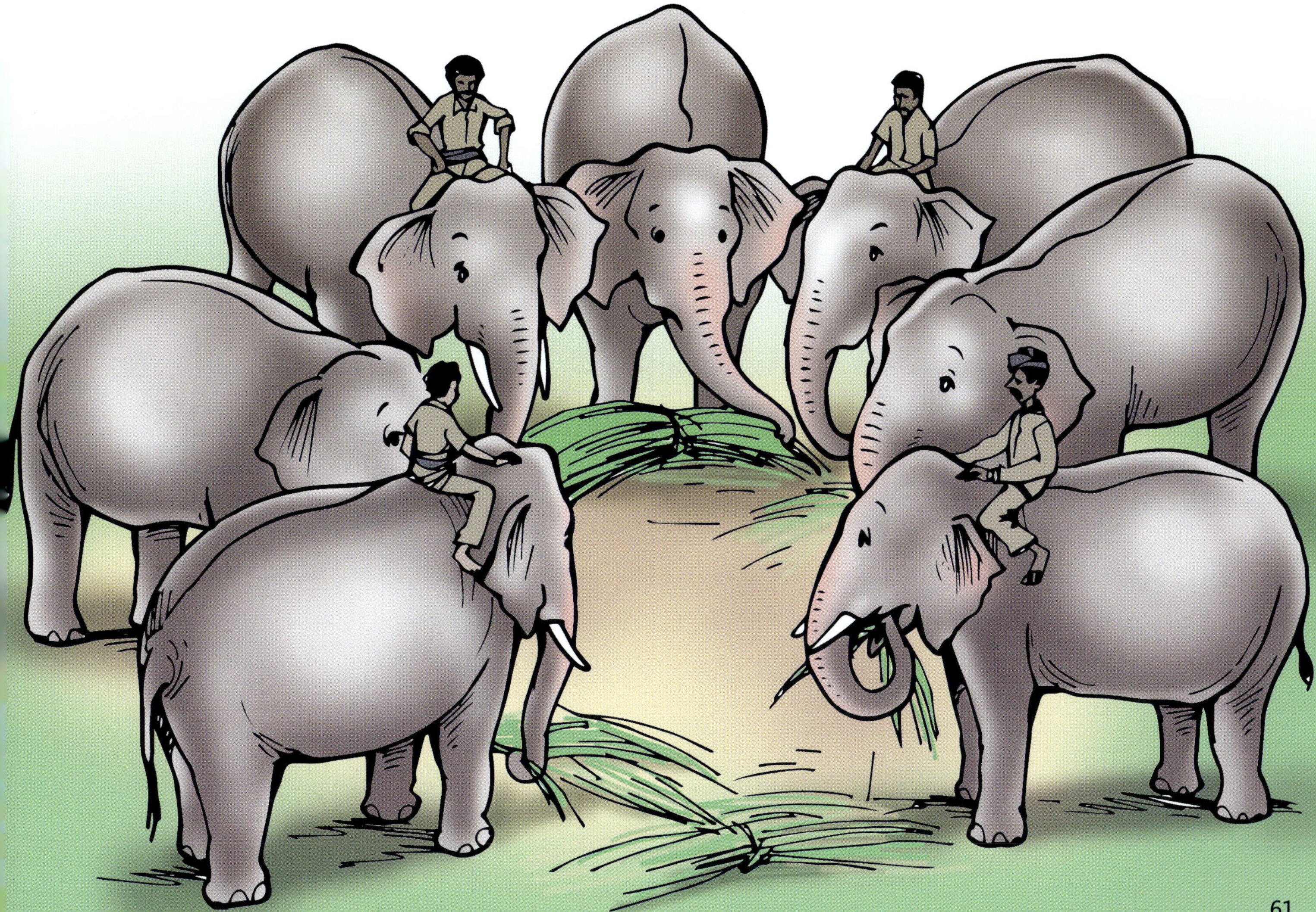

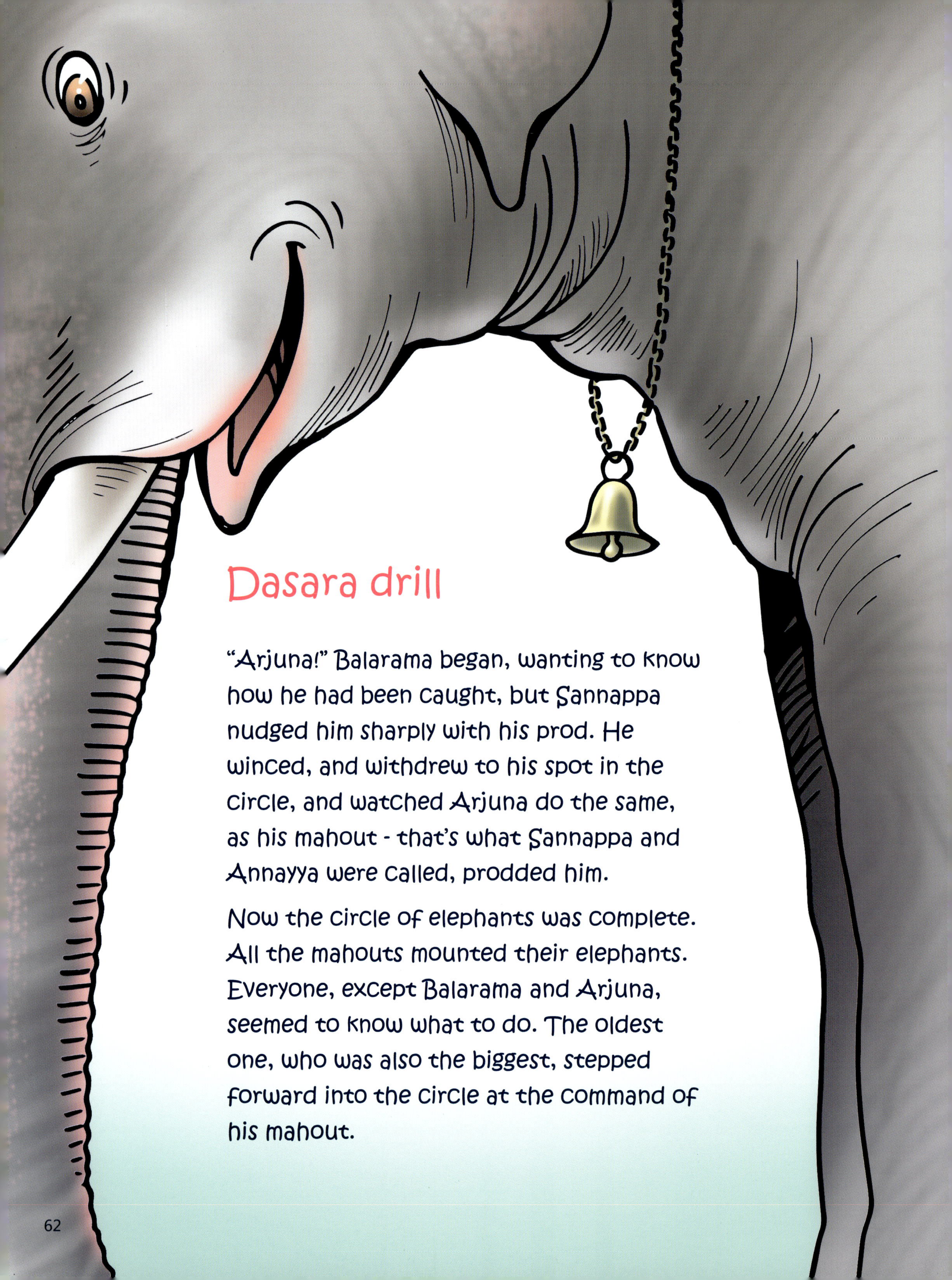

Dasara drill

"Arjuna!" Balarama began, wanting to know how he had been caught, but Sannappa nudged him sharply with his prod. He winced, and withdrew to his spot in the circle, and watched Arjuna do the same, as his mahout - that's what Sannappa and Annayya were called, prodded him.

Now the circle of elephants was complete. All the mahouts mounted their elephants. Everyone, except Balarama and Arjuna, seemed to know what to do. The oldest one, who was also the biggest, stepped forward into the circle at the command of his mahout.

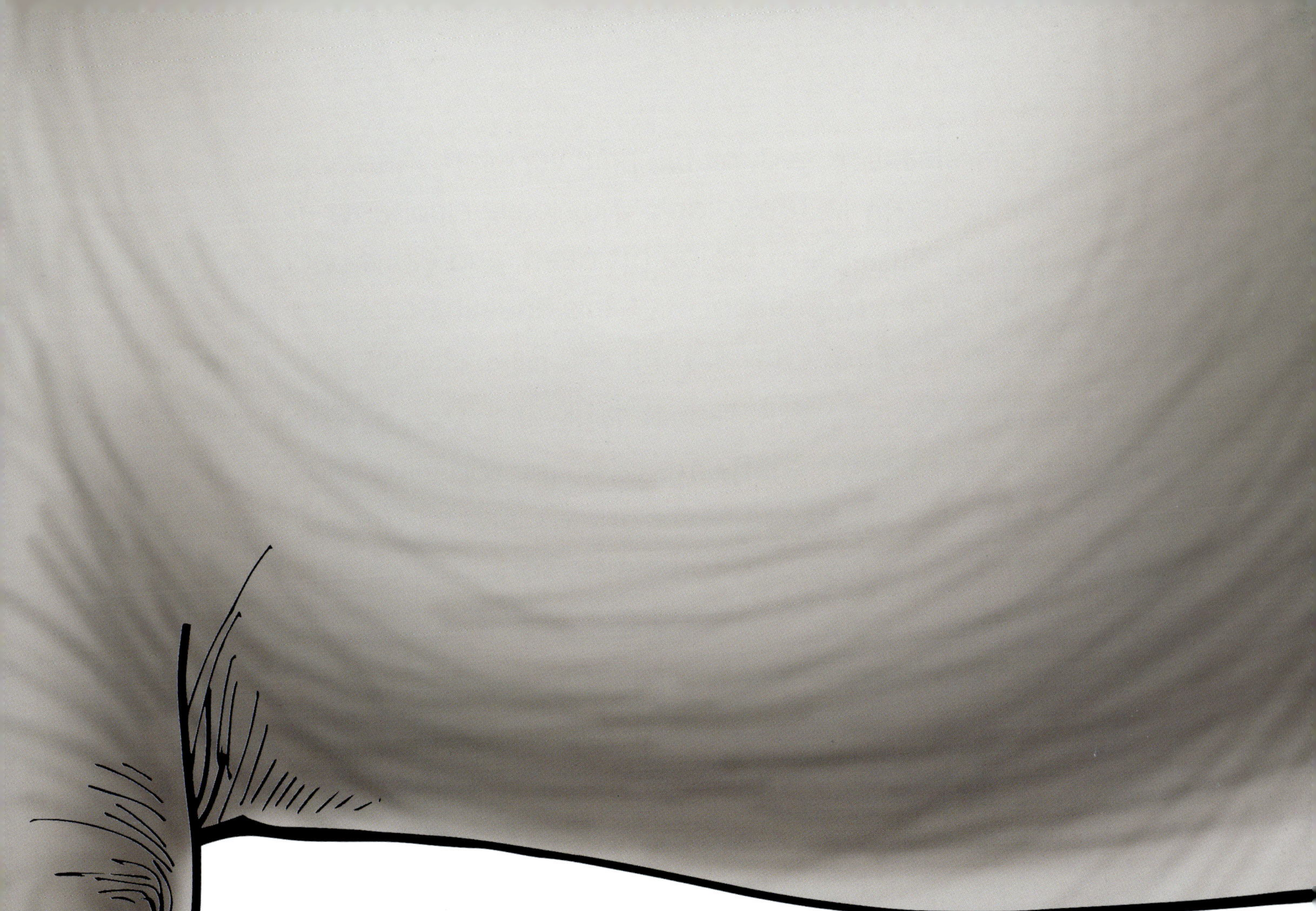

"Drona, kneel" said his mahout Basavaraju.

So this was Drona, whose legend was told to all young elephants by Aunty Aaney. His strength, his powerful trumpet that would send tremors across the forest. His majestic gait! His fearsome anger! The ease with which he had once wrapped his trunk around Hughlie and flung him 200 metres away into the Kabini.

Balarama stared at him, wide-eyed. He was awed.

Drona was kneeling. He raised his trunk and shook his head until the big bell tied around his neck tinkled merrily.

As Balarama watched, he became very sad. And angry. Humans were vile! Why didn't they leave elephants alone? Balarama felt a sharp tap on his head, and came back to the present. The other elephants were kneeling too, and their bells were ringing. Only Arjuna and Balarama were standing.

Sannappa spoke softly, "kneel, Balarama. You can do it..." With a deep, sad sigh, Balarama knelt, and watched Arjuna do the same. He would never understand all this - Was he taken from his home to be a performing elephant for humans?

Kneel. Stand. Sit.

Kneel. Stand. Sit.

At noon, their first lesson ended, and the elephants were taken away to rest and have a meal. He finally got a chance to speak with Arjuna.

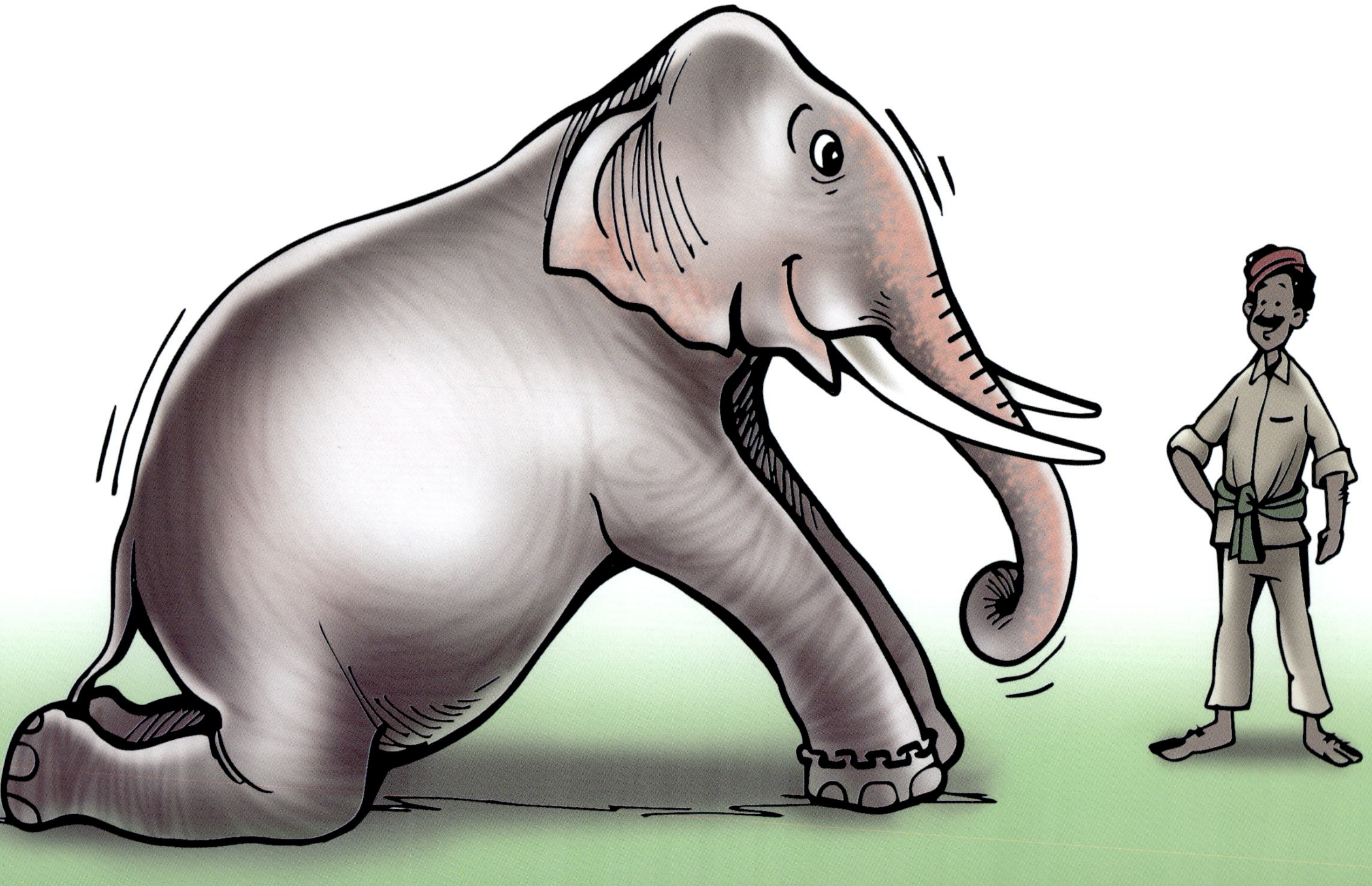

"I was going to see Lila, "Arjuna said, his eyes brimming with tears. Balarama was silent, thinking of his own Mohini.

"I was racing along, very excited, for Lila had made their secret sign touching her trunk to her right ear," Arjuna. That meant Lila would wait at their special place in the bamboo clump...

When Arjuna tripped over a pile of bamboo and sugarcane, he fell, it give way, and he found himself going down. He was frantic. He tried to break his fall, but only slipped further down into a hole. It was a trap, that Auntie Aaney had warned them about, when they had been little.

Balarama and Arjuna stood close, nuzzling each other. This was the only comforting link they had, with their past.

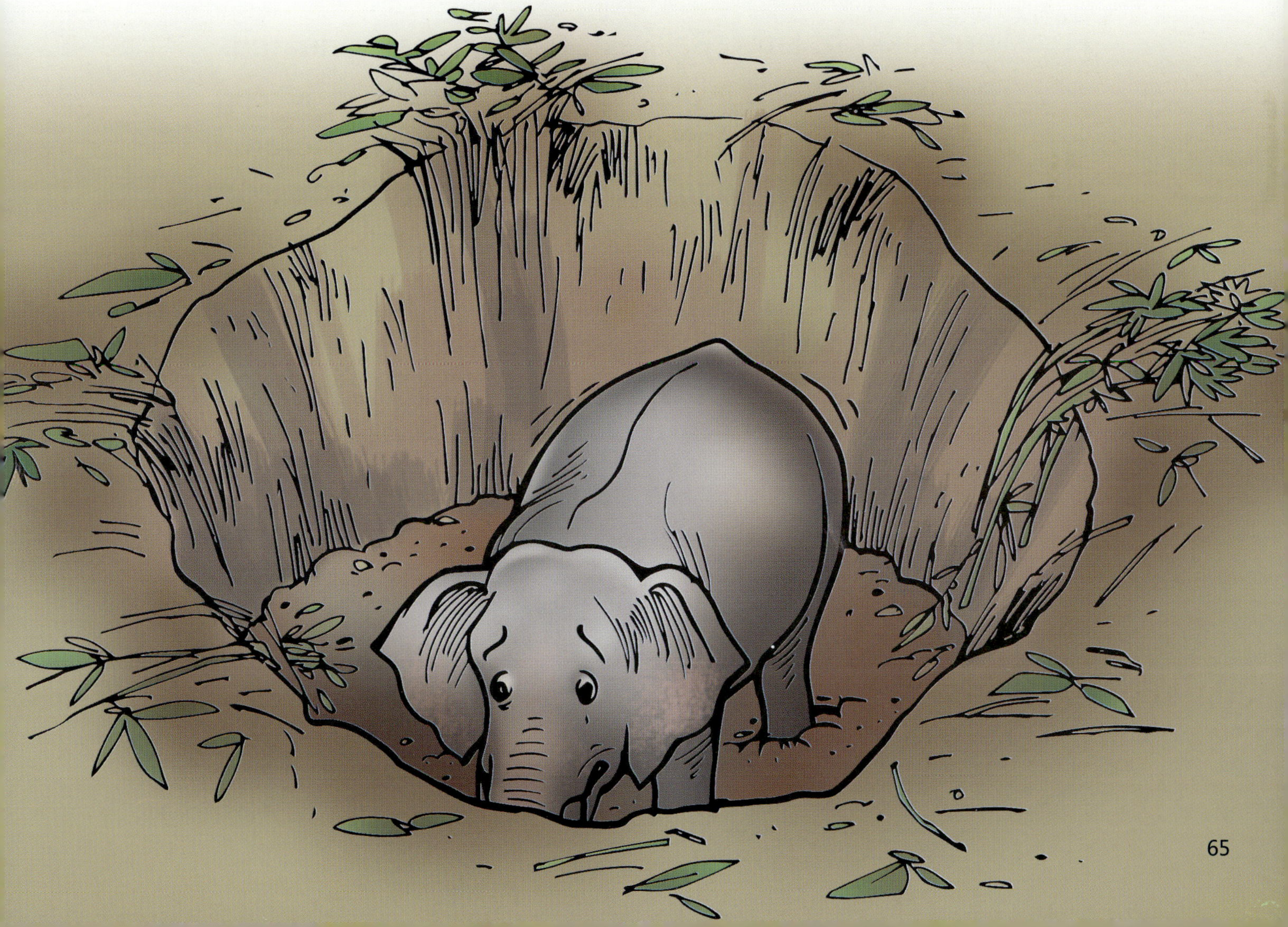

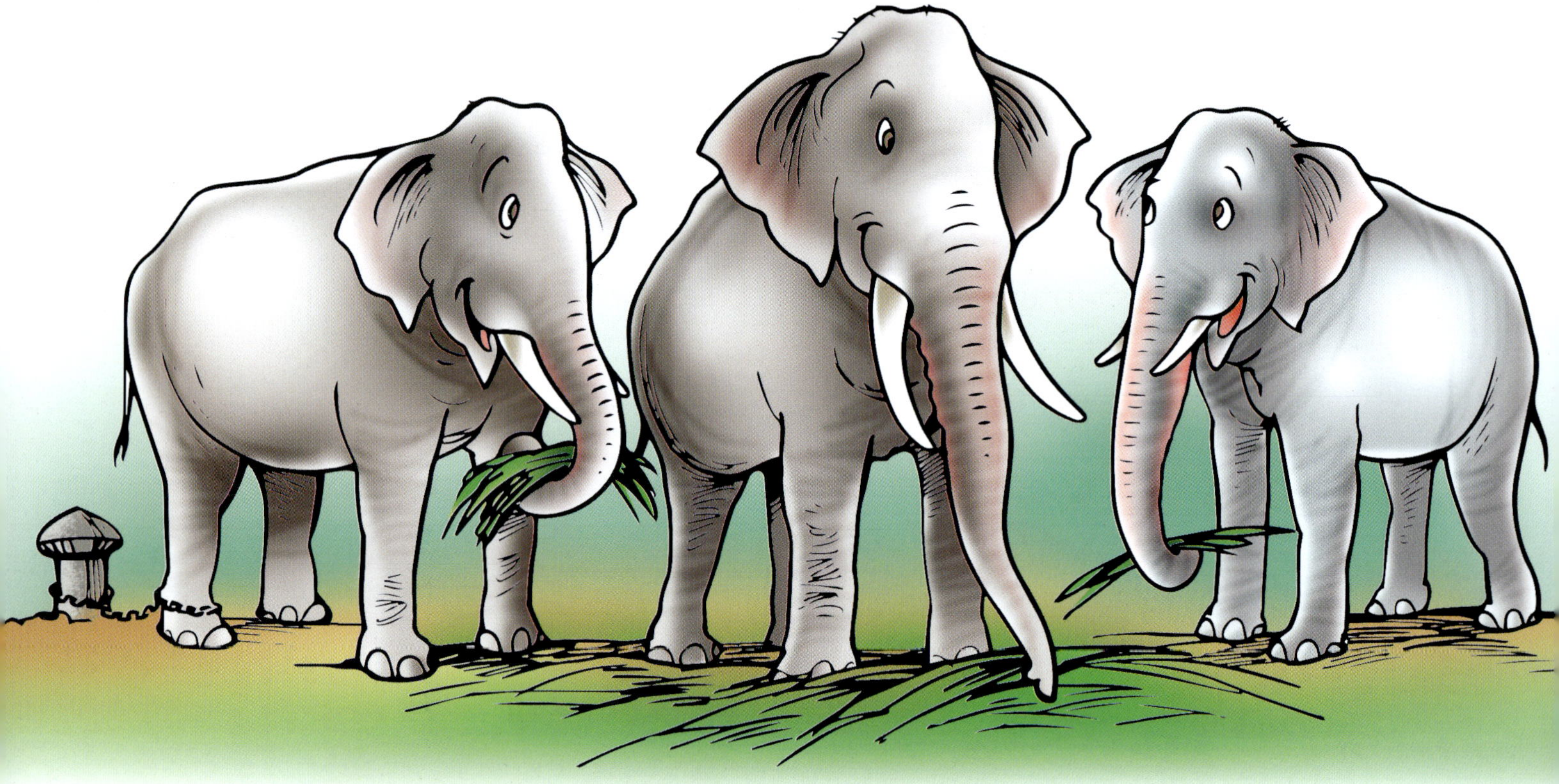

March to Mysore

Three months later, Balarama and Arjuna graduated. They were in great awe of Drona. He spoke little, and ignored all the humans around him. Except Basavaraju. They were very fond of each other, and Basavaraju often said only he could predict Drona's mood. Drona always obeyed Basavaraju without a fuss.

But Drona was kind to Balarama and Arjuna. He patiently repeated the drills so they could watch and learn. Soon it would be Dasara in the royal city of Mysore. And the final day, of the Jamboo Savaari-- the march from the palace to the Banni Mantap.

Balarama wasn't sure what Dasara was. He thought it must be a grand show, where he would have do all the kneeling, bending, and dancing a few steps in front of important humans.

When Dasara festival, which means ten-day festival, was three months away, the elephants in Dubare were taken to Mysore. They walked some way, through villages. People gathered on the wayside, and some gave them coconuts, bananas and cane.

They offered aarathi, and applied kumkum on their foreheads.

Balarama watched the senior elephants, and Drona. Like them, he accepted the offerings, and placed his trunk on the human's head. Sometimes, they held out baby humans and Balarama patted them affectionately, and walked on.

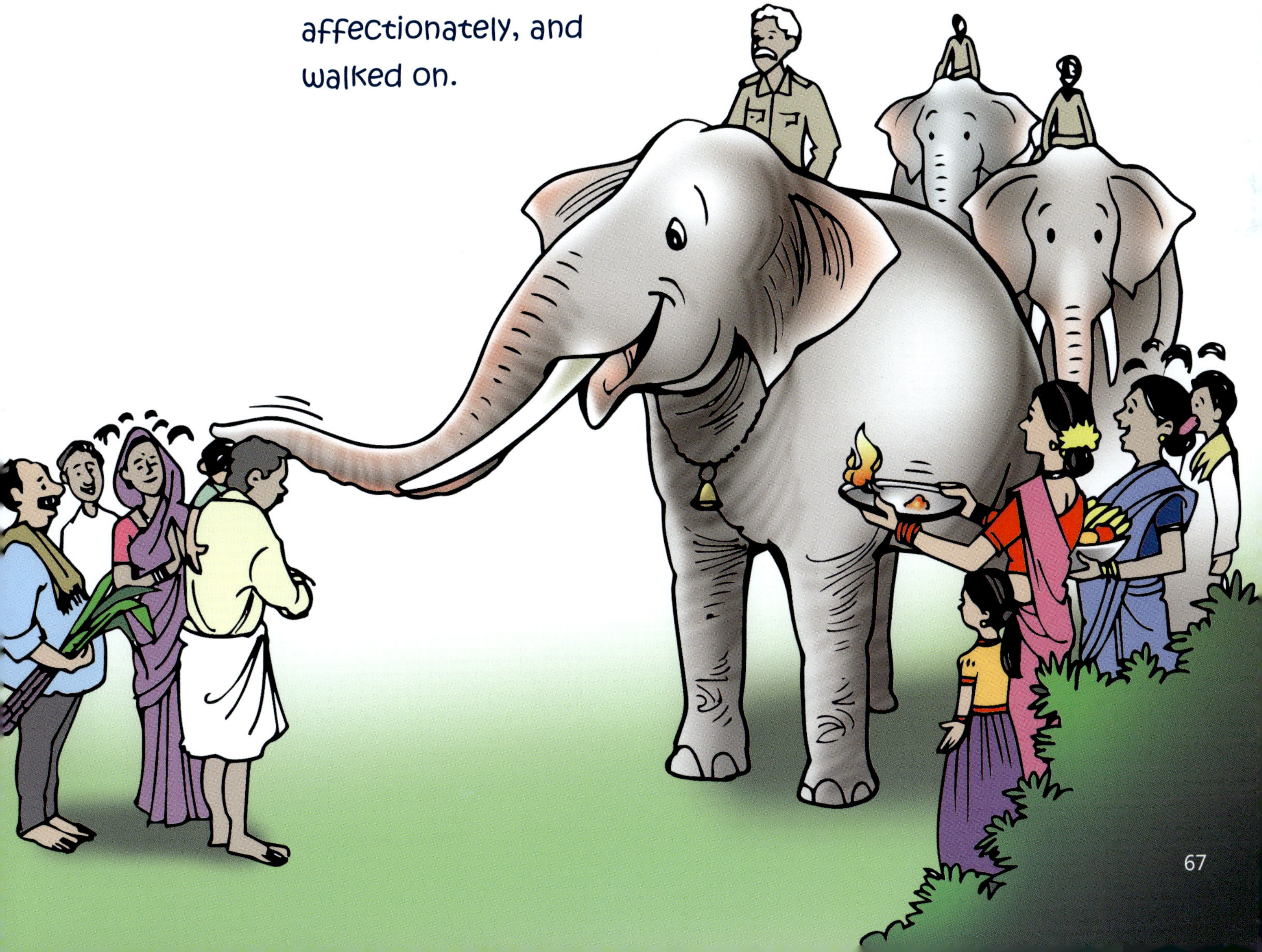

After walking for a day, they stopped in a wooded spot near Hunsur. It looked like the jungle, but there were strange noises through the night. It was, Balarama learnt later the hum of vehicles passing by on roads...

The following morning, the elephants were herded into trucks, like the one he had been brought in from the jungle the day he had been caught. They were driven through the roads, on which hundreds of trucks some small, some really tiny, with just two wheels were whizzing by in both directions.

They were honking, and humans were shouting at each other, and when the trucks reached the entrance to Mysore city, Balarama saw a policeman standing in the middle, waving his arms.

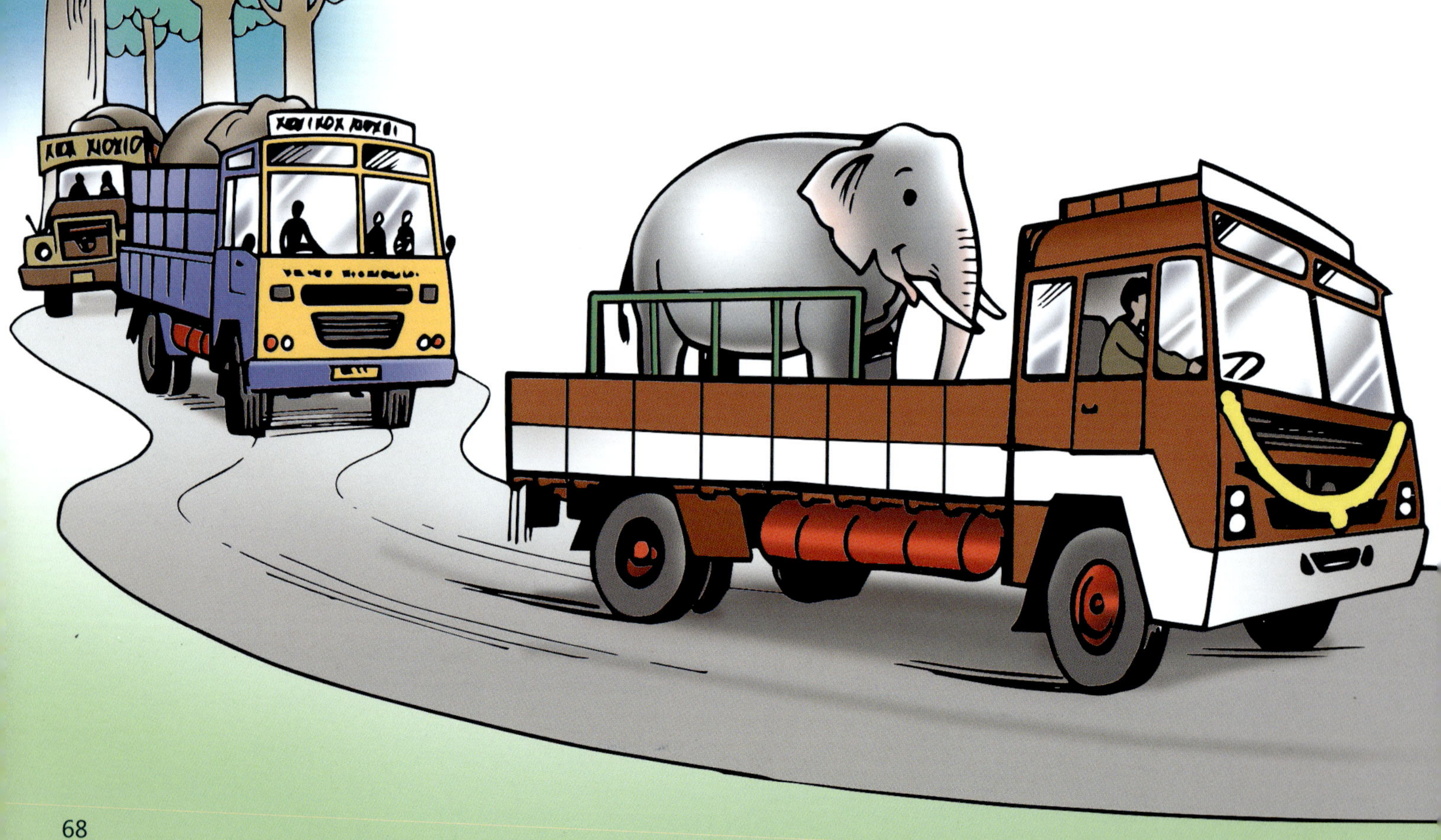

The elephants' caravan stopped behind a procession of other vehicles, and when the policeman waved them on, they moved.

Soon they were brought to the royal stables and the elephants trundled out of their trucks. This was going to be their home for the next three months.

Balarama was very nervous. He hated the noise and bustle in the city.

It was crawling with humans! They were a noisy lot. There were some who barked instructions, and others who ran to obey orders. Sannappa and the other mahouts were very respectful when "officers" came to inspect the elephants. Six new elephants from another camp had now joined the Dubare friends.

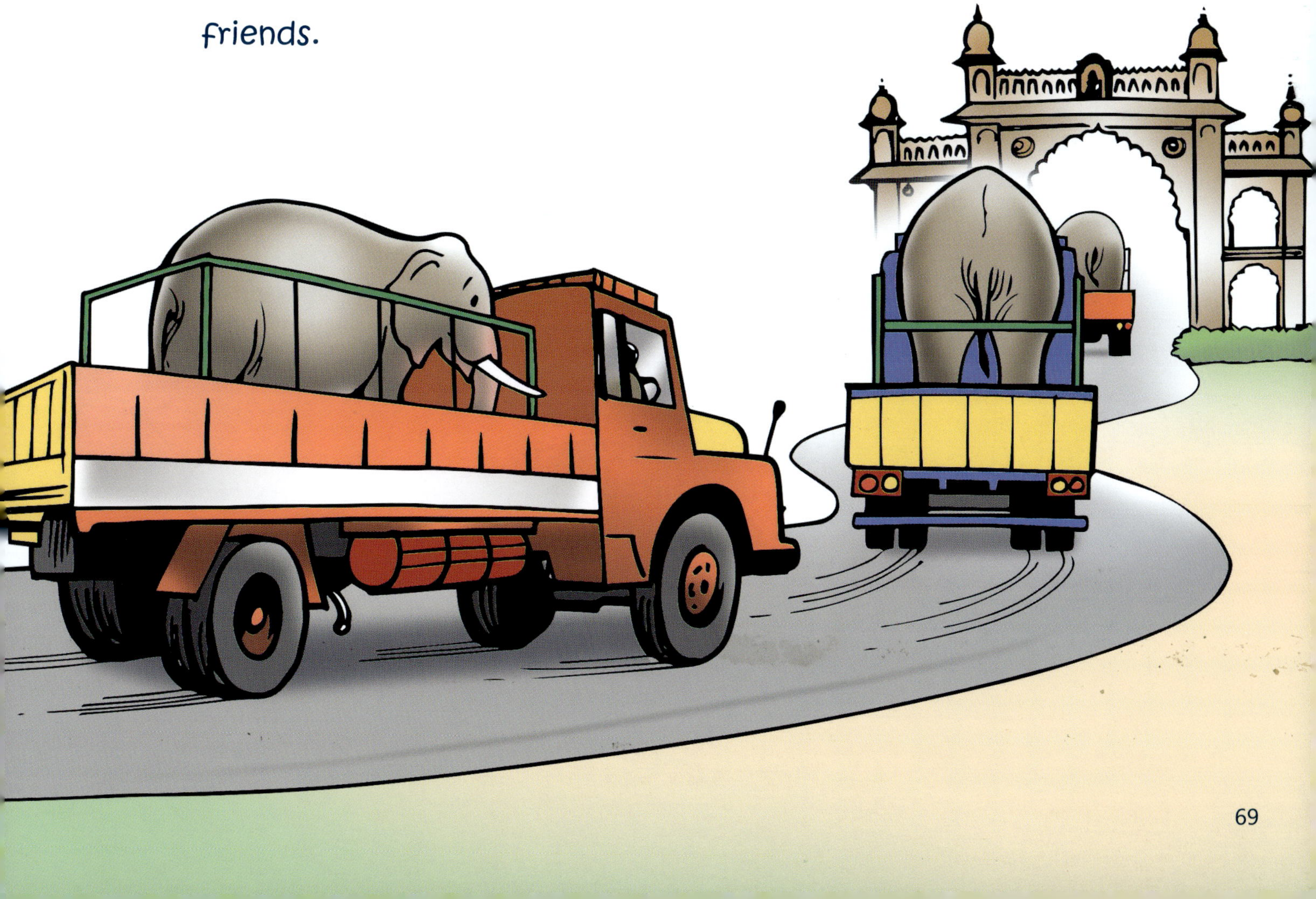

Drona had told him, and Arjuna that they must be very attentive. "Watch and learn," he told them.

The humans, who appeared to be important, came each morning to see how the elephants were doing. The mahouts reported to them. They would not come close to the elephants, but watched from a safe distance.

"Just as well,", Balarama said to Arjuna. "I would like to dig my tusk into their pot bellies and trample them. They are annoying."

A fortnight later, the elephants had all settled down to their new routine and Balarama was not apprehensive anymore.

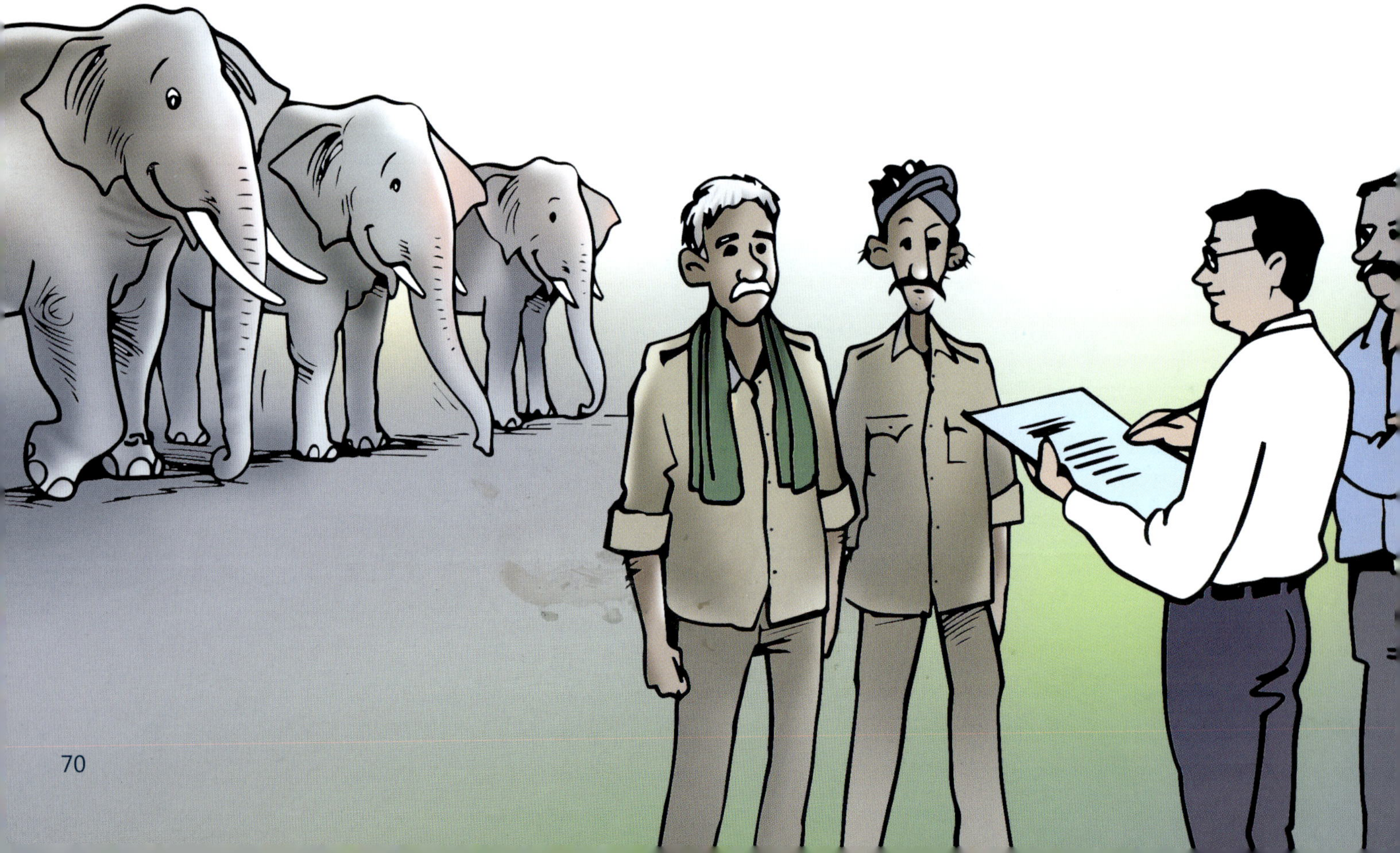

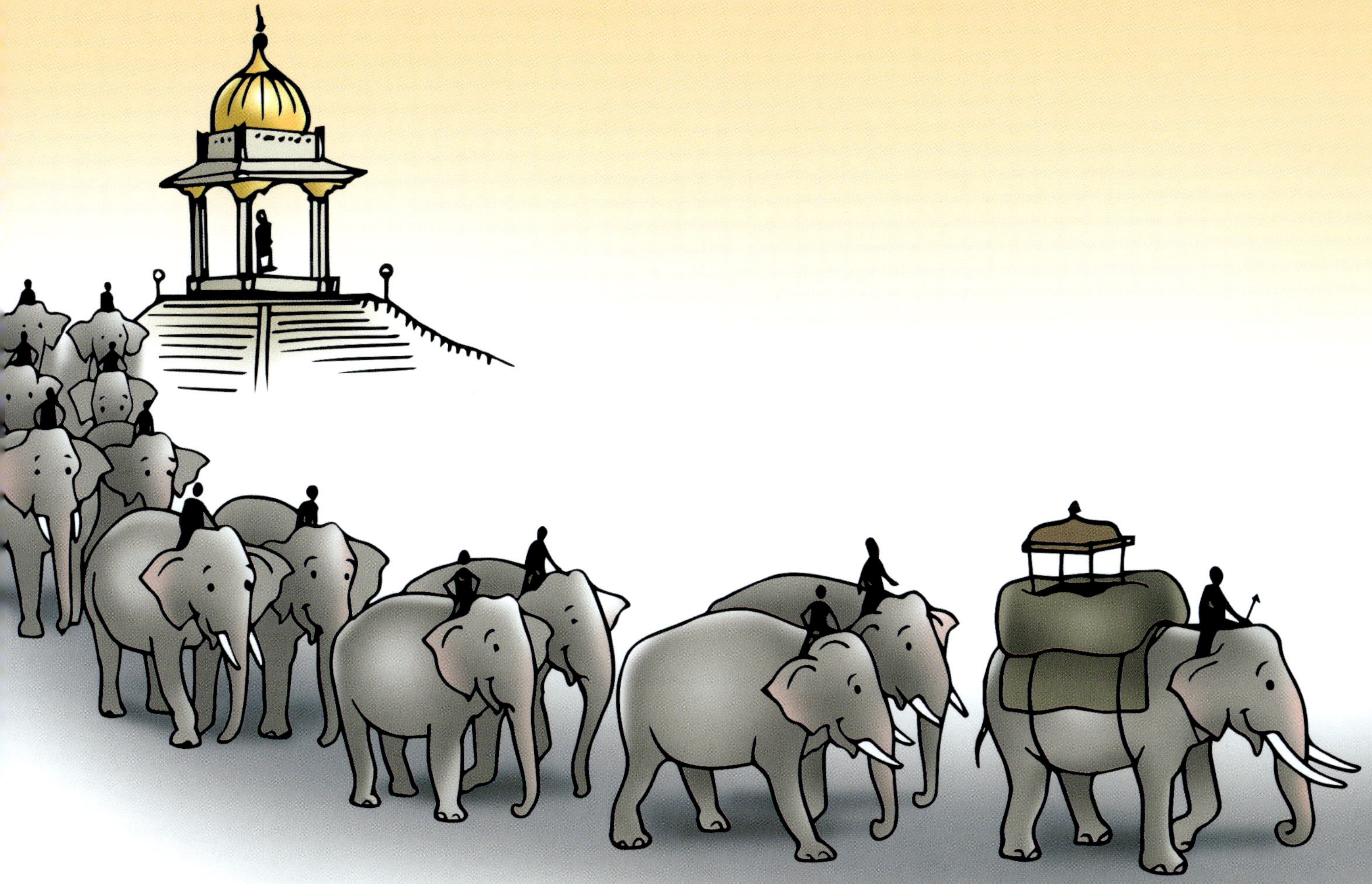

One morning, Sannappa took him out to the grounds where he found the other elephants standing in a row with their mahouts beside them.

When Balarama joined the others, Drona was brought forward. The others, including the new elephants were made to stand behind Drona in twos. Govinda, one of the new elephants, stood right behind Drona.

Balarama and Arjuna, he found to his relief was together, and they were the last pair of elephants in the procession.

They waited, with the mahouts on their backs. The musical band arrived with drums, flute, trumpet and bugles and the bandsmen stood in two neat little rows close by. When the conductor waved his baton, they begin playing.

Balarama was enchanted. This was the first time he heard a band playing music! He found it very soothing, and he was soon tapping his foot and nodding appreciatively. The others were doing the same!

When the song ended, the mahouts patted their elephants. Balarama heard Sannappa, who had hummed along, say, "very good Balarama! I'm so proud!"

The band struck up another song, and this time, Drona was goaded forward. Govinda followed behind, and the elephant pairs went after him. Balarama and Arjuna fell in step and marched bringing up the rear of the procession.

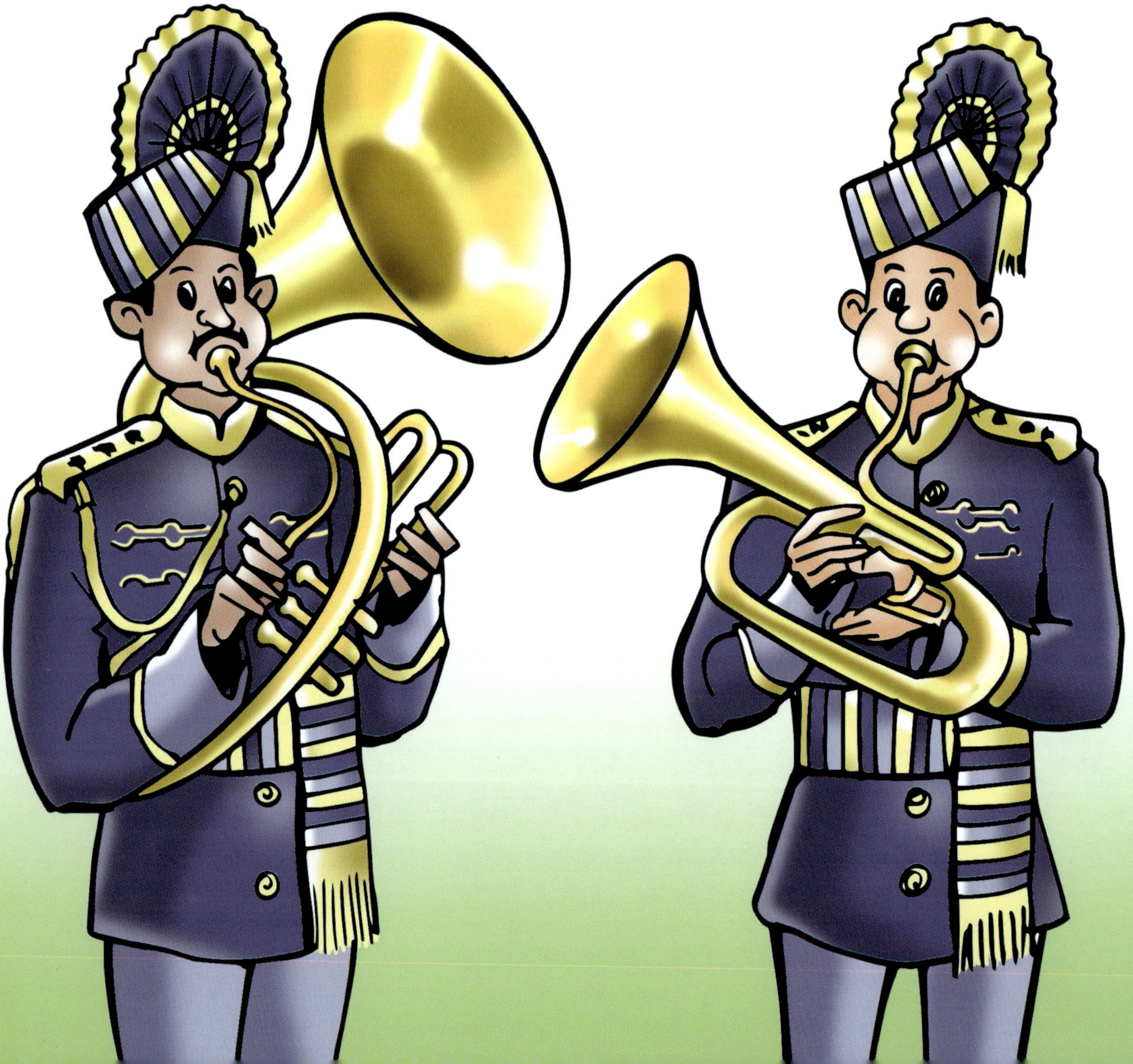

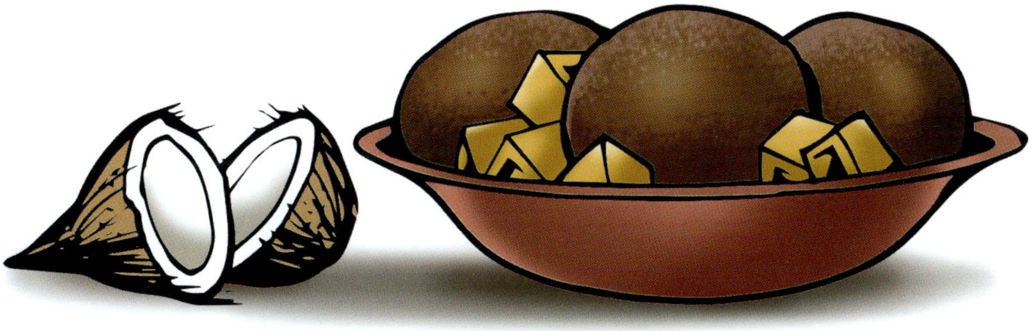

After circling the grounds several times, the elephants returned to their stables. Their first day at training was over.

Balarama and Arjuna were introduced to a new diet. They were given horse gram, plenty of jaggery, and ragi balls. "Eat up, Balarama, you will need all the energy for the big day"

As the days passed, the elephants practised keeping time with the music, walking in line and in tandem. Balarama soon learnt that Drona was the most important elephant. He would be festively caparisoned, his trunk and forehead painted in bright colors and designs.

More importantly, he would be carrying Devi Chamundeshwari, the goddess of Mysore on his majestic back. The Chamundeshwari idol would be seated in a golden ambari that weighed 800 kilos!

A long time ago, the Maharaja of Mysore would be seated in the ambari, which belong to the Royal house of Wadiyars. There would be a procession on the last day of Dasara, the Vijayadashami. It would start from the palace and end at the Banni Mantap.

This was the great Jamboo Savaari! All the jumbos, that was him and all the elephants, would walk in a procession to the Banni Mantap.

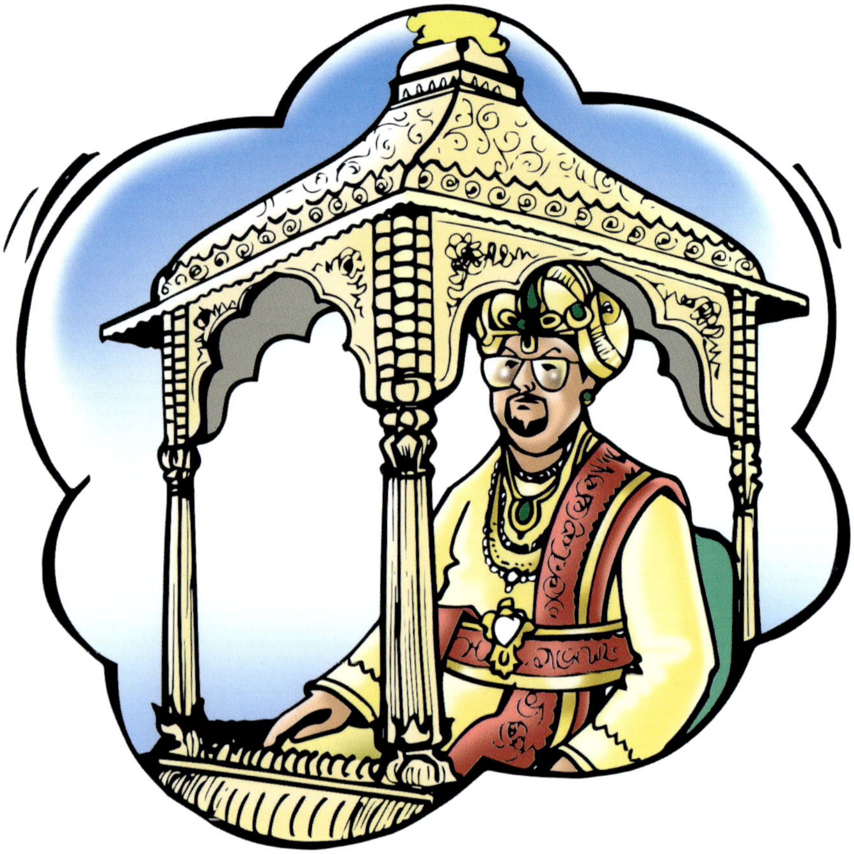

Drona had been doing this for nine years now. The other elephants would march behind. One or two would pull tableaux that told stories. There would be dancers, folk singers and stilts walkers.

The streets would be lined with people who cheered loudly as the procession passed.

Balarama wondered when his turn would come to carry the ambari. When Drona became too old, perhaps? Balarama began to dream....

He was carrying the ambari, the splendid golden seat on which the Devi was seated, and leading the train of elephants...people lining the streets shouted "Jai Chamundeshwari", and pointed at him.

"That's Balarama," the commentator was telling everyone, "he carries the Ambari. Look at his graceful gait..."

"What a fine elephant he is..."

Bhoom! Bhoom!

Balarama's reverie was suddenly broken. He froze in fright. And then he broke into a run. Sannappa who was sitting on his back, nearly fell off, and he began to shout "Balarama! Calm down! Stop!"

Balarama ran to the far corner of the grounds and stopped. He turned round, and saw all the other elephants were standing in their place, as if nothing had happened. Only Arjuna had run in the other direction.

Balarama allowed himself to be led back to his spot. "Balarama, you will get used to it. It's the canons being fired in honor of Devi", Sannappa said.

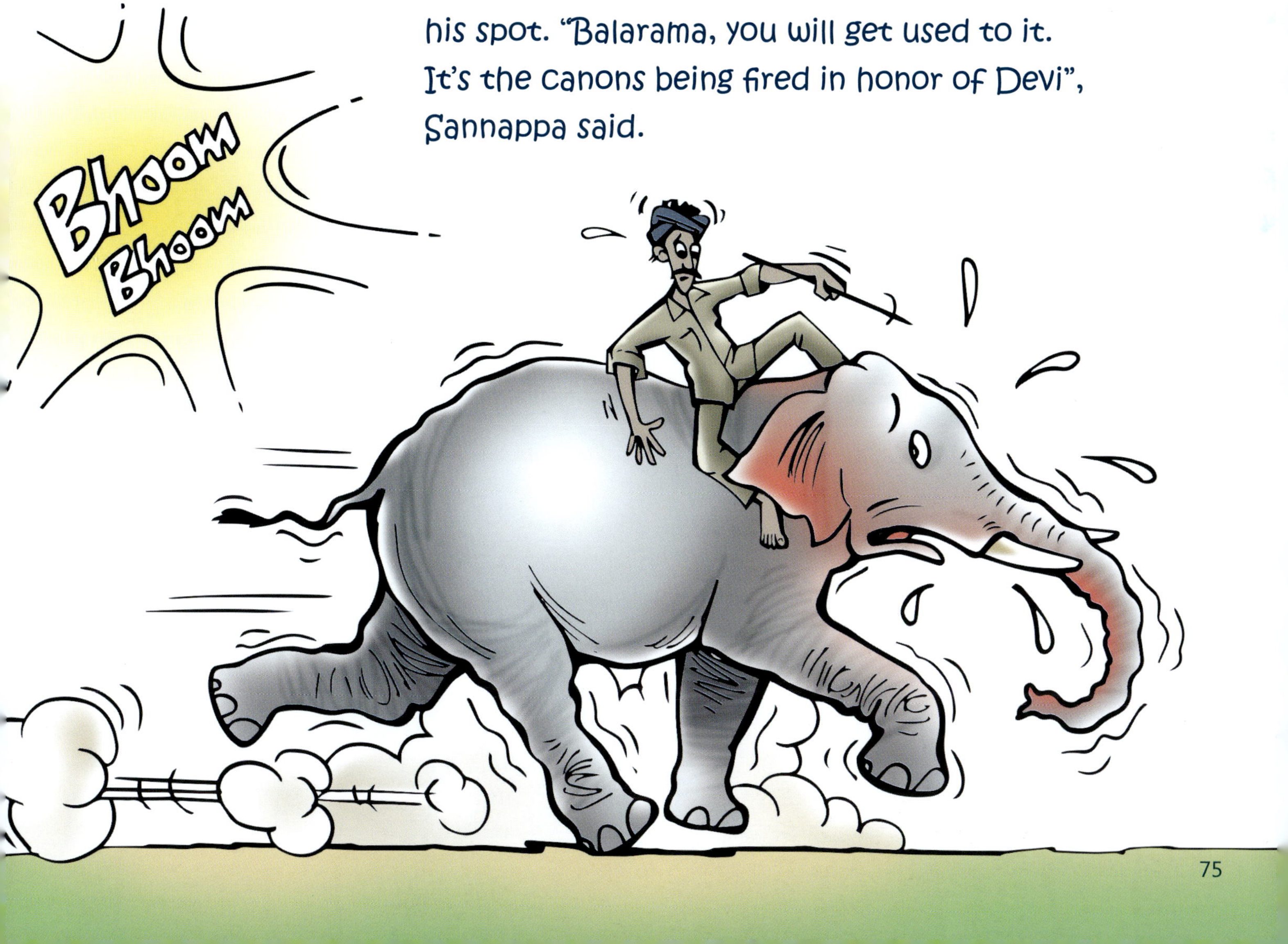

He was shaking like a leaf, and thought everyone could hear his bones rattle. Sannappa took him back to his stable, and fed him bananas and spoke softly till he calmed down.

That evening, he was taken to Drona. "Balarama" said Drona, "don't be afraid. You will get used to the canons. You have to be brave, and you must know the humans are more afraid of us. You will one day take my place and carry the ambari."

Balarama nodded. "Uncle Drona, I will do as you do, and learn to be the ambari elephant. But why are we doing this? Why are we not in the forest? We will never go back, will we?" he asked.

Drona said sadly, "I'm afraid not. We just have to make the best of what we have, don't we?" and nuzzled Balarama affectionately.

Balarama tried harder to get used to the canon blasts. The

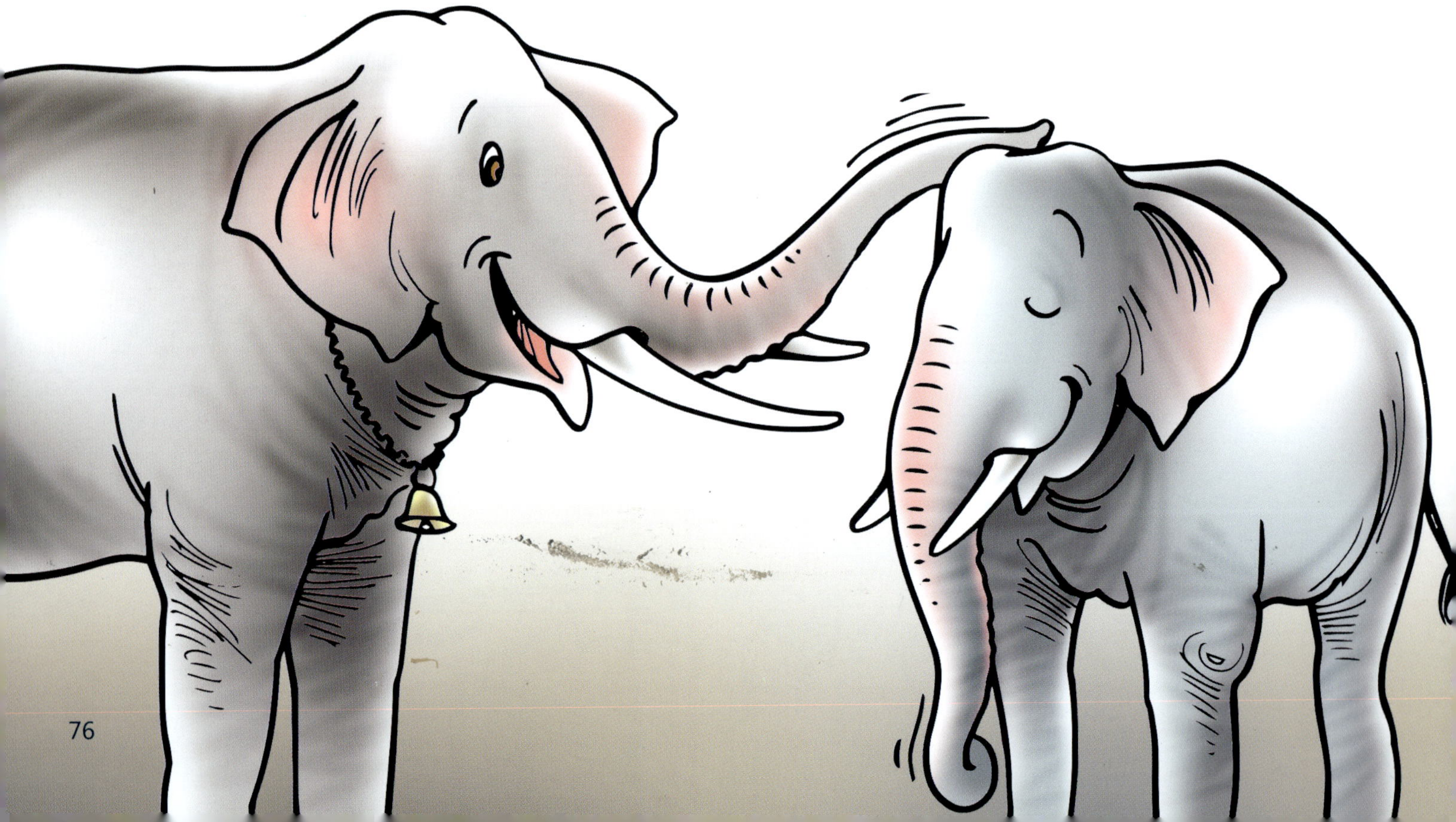

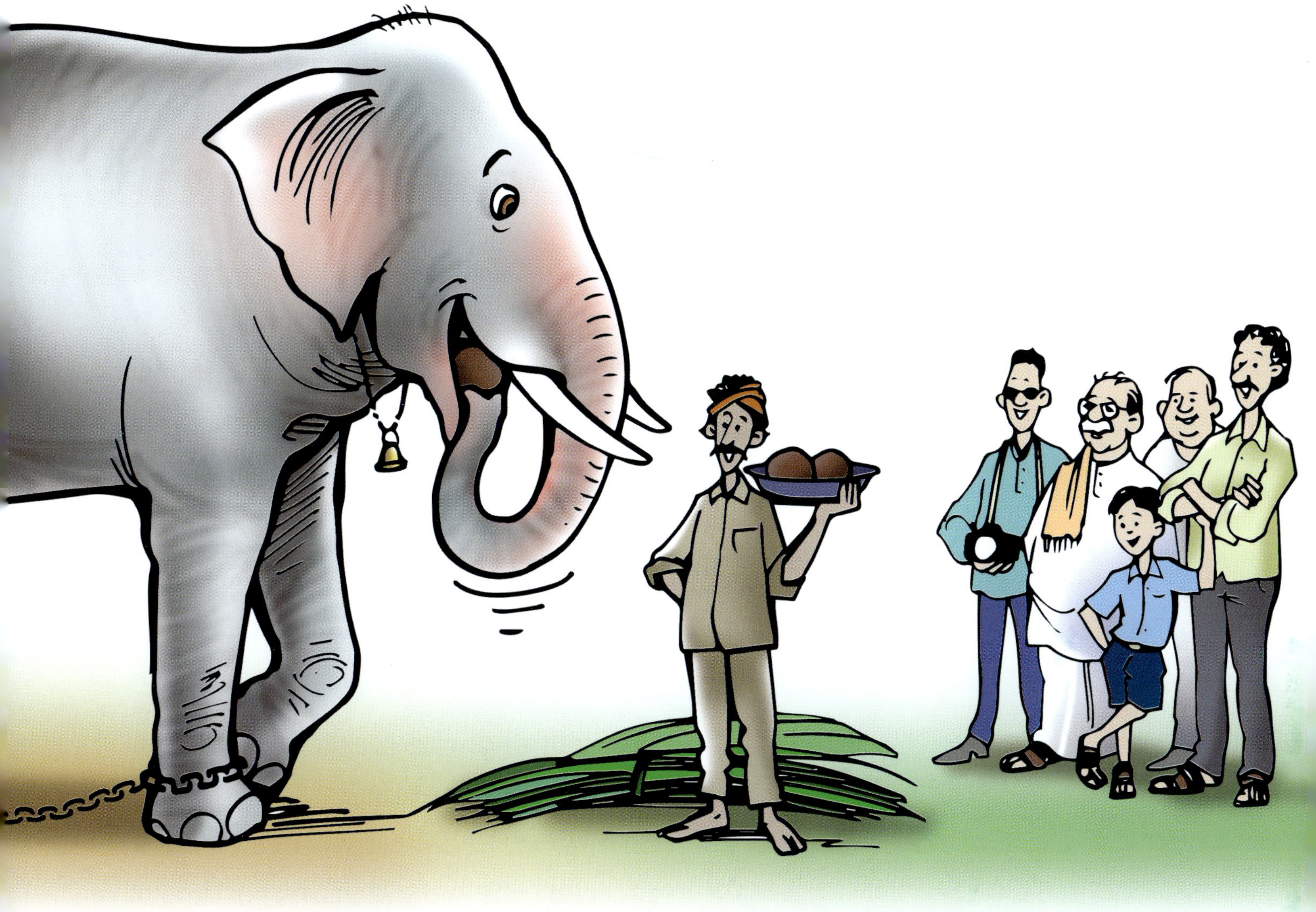

cannons boomed every day. Balarama and Arjuna got used to it. Fifteen days later, the two laughed till their sides ached, remembering their silliness over the cannons!

The weeks whizzed by, and in no time, it was Dasara. The elephants were dressed in finery, and grandly caparisoned. People gathered at the grounds to watch the elephants getting ready.

This annoyed Balarama a great deal, but he knew it would be a lot worse on Vijayadashami procession day. He could not let down the elephants. And Sannappa would be in trouble if he misbehaved!

Jamboo savaari

On the grand day of Vijayadashami, Drona was taken away to the Palace very early in the morning. Balarama and the others were woken up at dawn. They were all given a bath. Sannappa brought some men to him, who began painting floral and rangoli motifs on his trunk, ears and forehead. A yellow and purple satin robe was then thrown over him, and a jewelled forehead piece was placed on his head.

He looked at Arjuna, and found him dressed in red and green robes. They were then taken to the palace.

In the evening, the elephants were all rounded up. They waited in front of the palace. Important humans were seated in the palace front yard, and there were hundreds waiting to

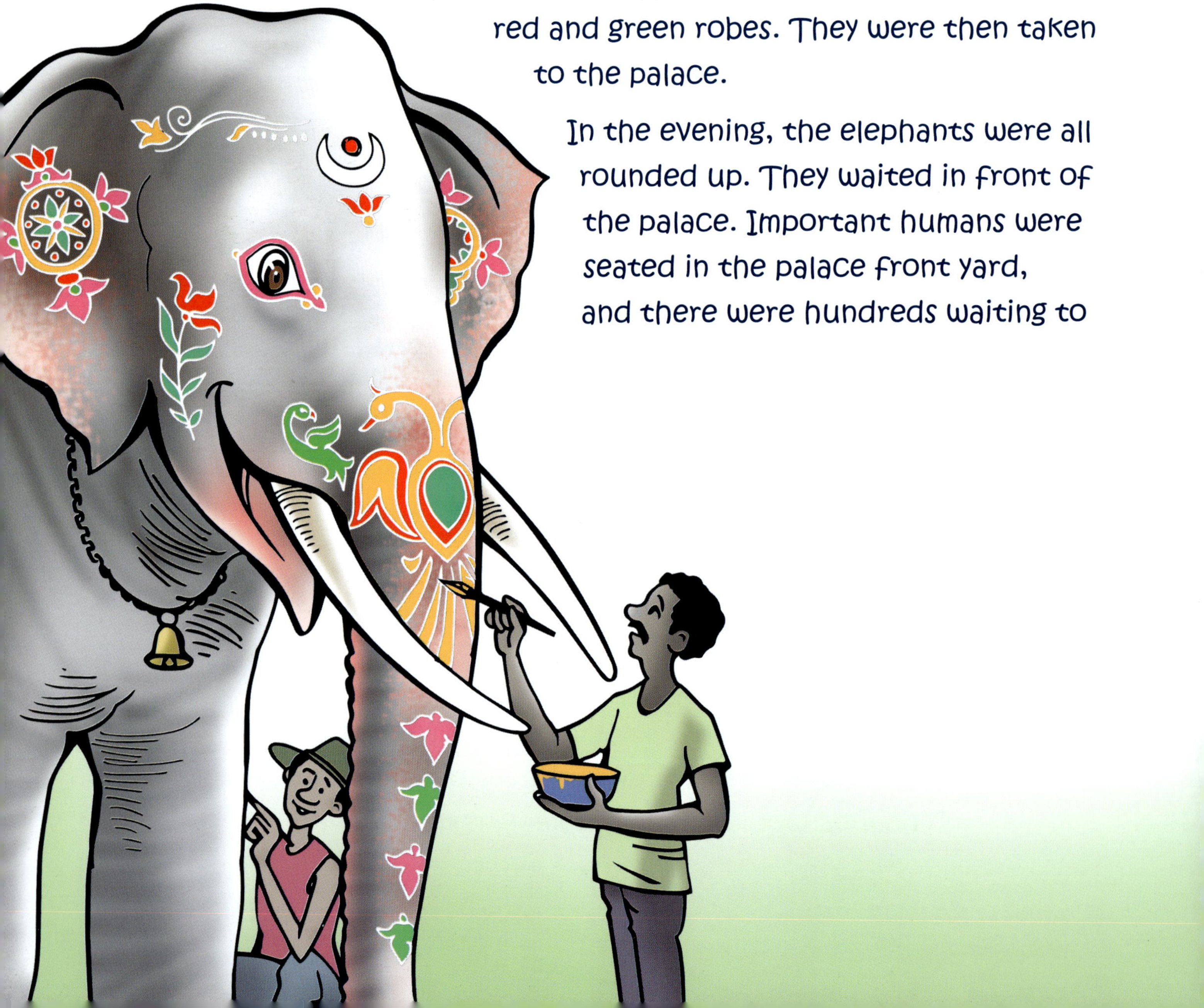

see these important people offer puja to the Devi, now mounted in the magnificent golden ambari that Drona was carrying.

One the sides there were men in colorful dress standing by the cannons. When the signal was given, all the cannons were fired. Balarama stood, without turning a hair, and was very proud.

Then Drona began the walk to Banni Mantap. The other elephants followed, Balarama and Arjuna bringing up the rear.

They reached Banni Mantap finally, with crowds cheering them all the way. Balarama felt both shy and pleased at all the attention. They were saying people came from all over the world to watch him and his friends! He was on TV!

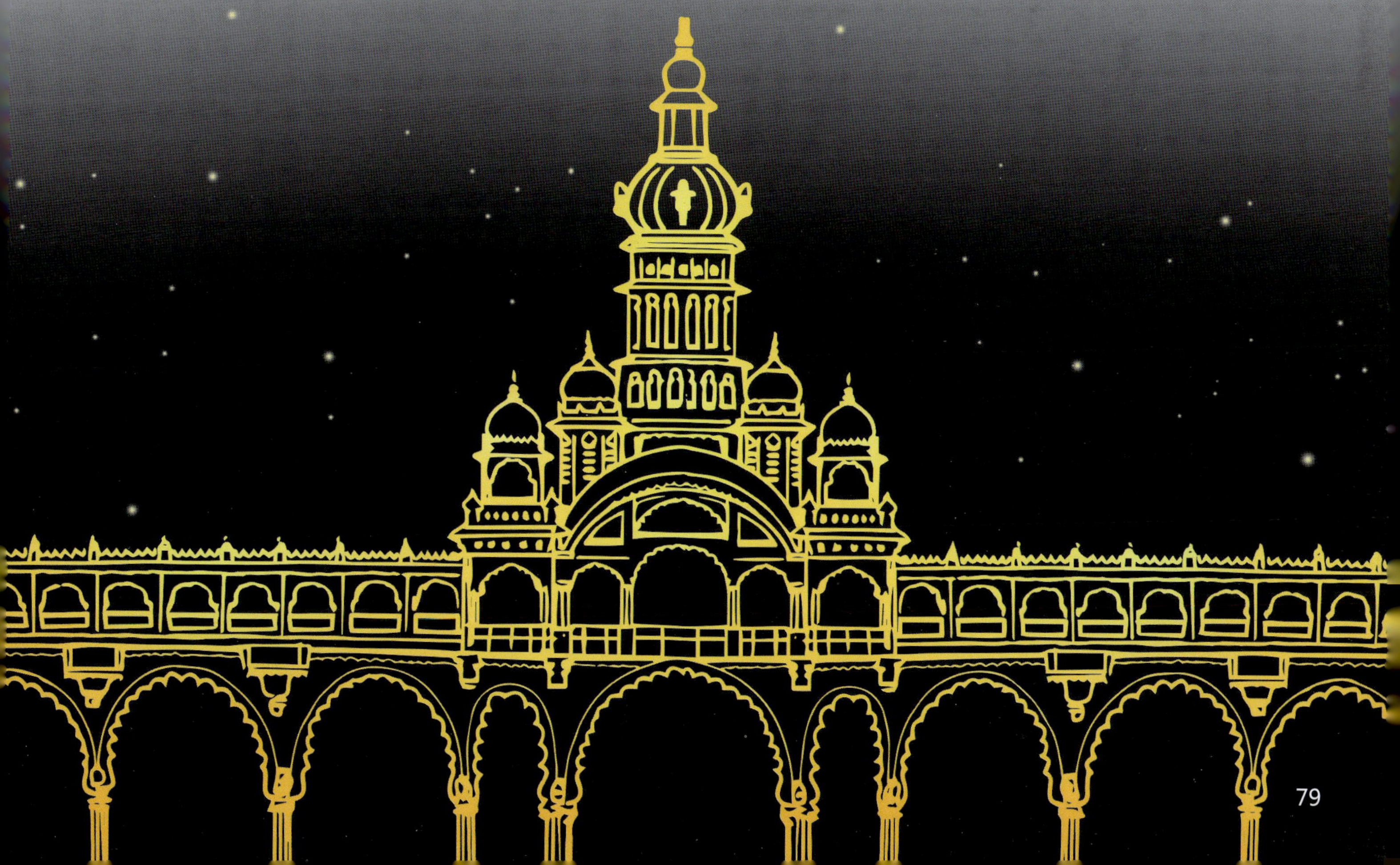

Though he wasn't quite sure what that meant.

It was a grand evening with fireworks. There was the Torchlight Parade. The night sky was lit up, as the flaming torches danced to music!

It was past midnight when the elephants returned to their stables. Their mahouts were very happy, and patted the elephants, nuzzled

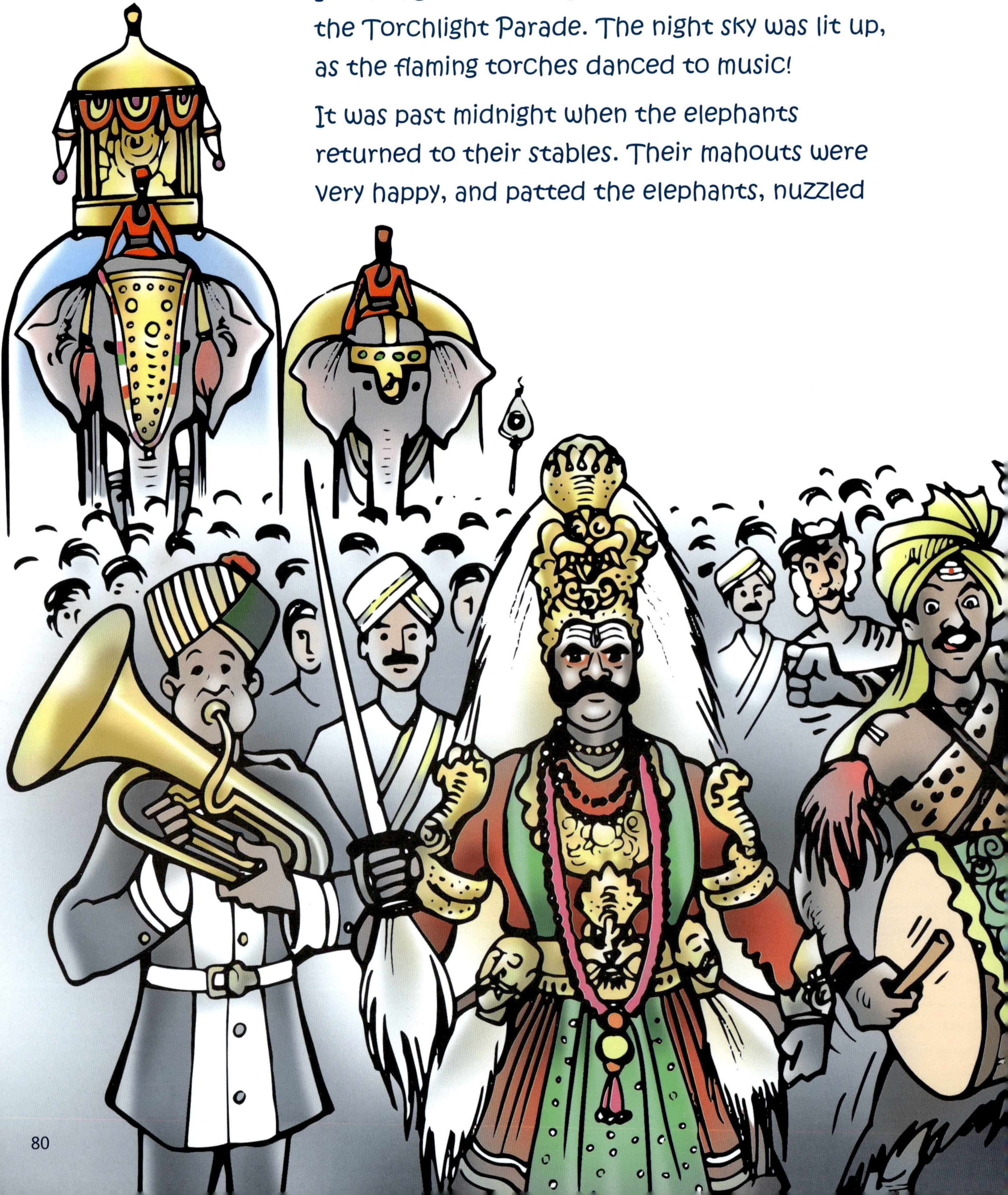

them and told them how proud they were. Balarama swung Sannappa high with his trunk, and ruffled his hair playfully.

A week later, Balarama returned to Dubare with the others. Balarama was happy to be back home. This was his home now. He must forget the forests, Mohini, and his friends. But he missed them all, and he tried his best not to!

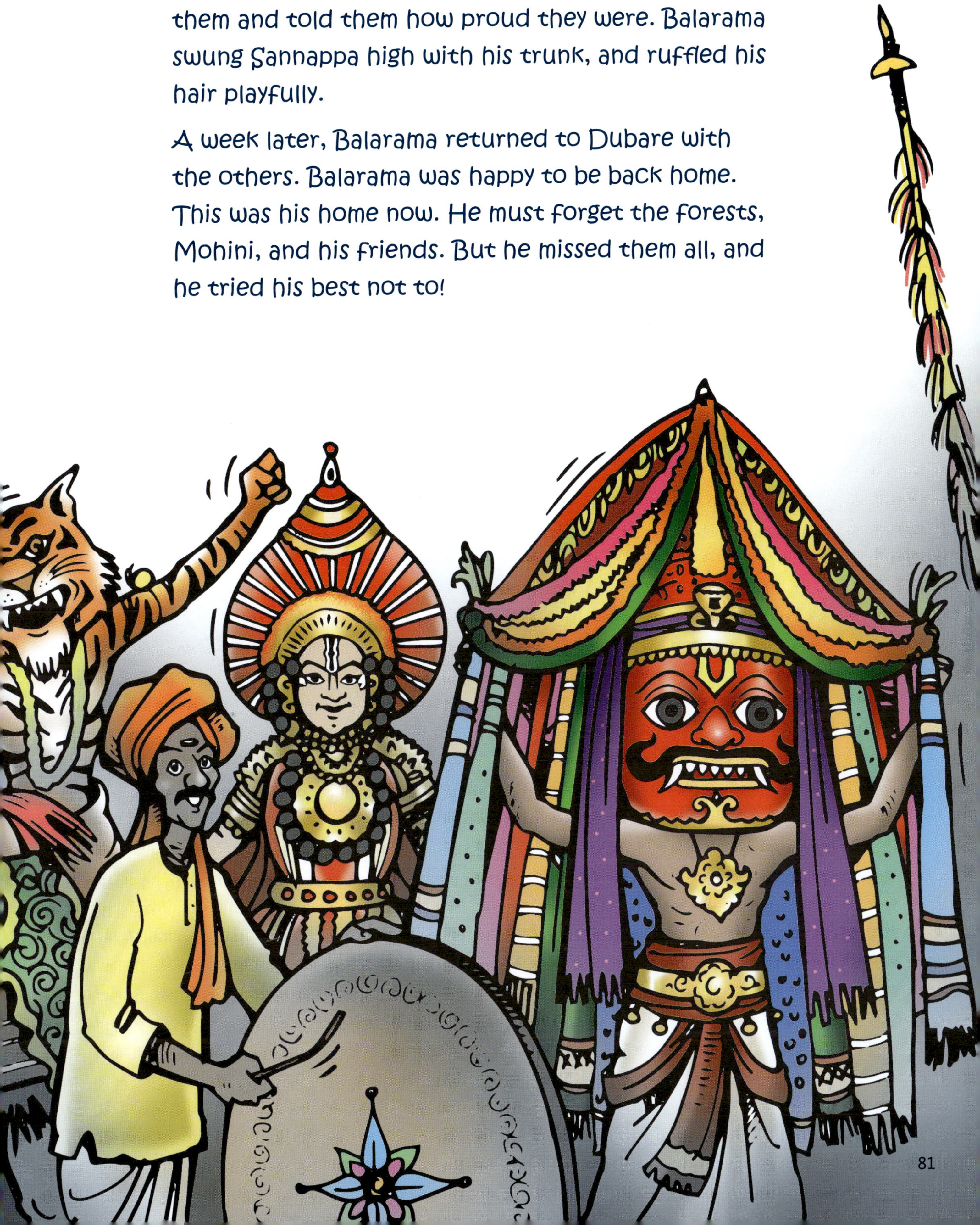

Balarama and son

It was a bright day at Dubare. Balarama had just finished sloshing about in the waters and was chewing on a sugarcane. Sannappa and his son Rajendra were attending to Balarama. Rajendra was very young, but Sannappa was teaching him to be a mahout. Balarama like him a lot, because he was kind, just like his father.

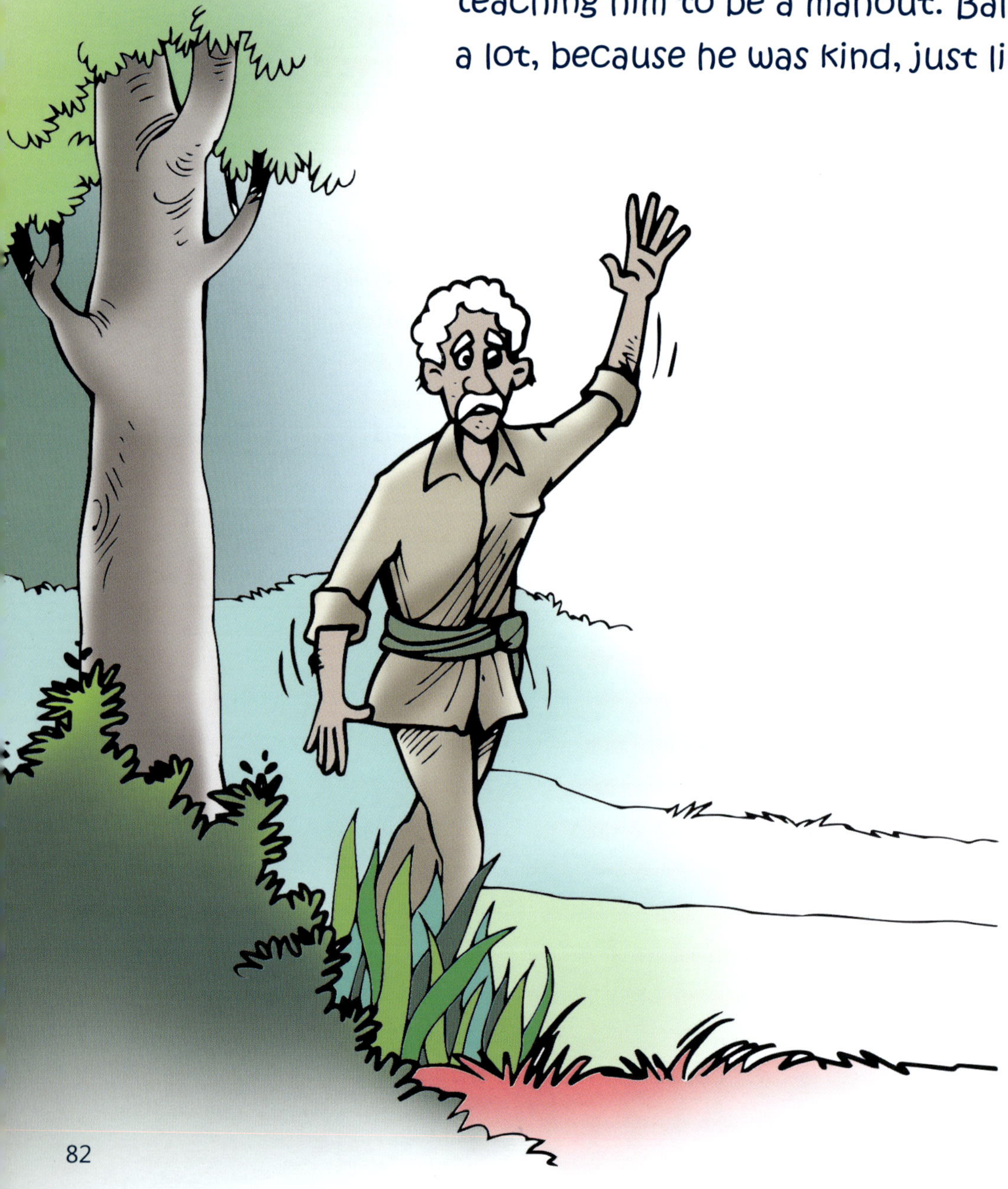

Basavaraju came to join them. He was looking worried. "I have bad news," he began… and Sannappa went over to him.

"It's Drona, isn't it? Sannappa said. Balarama perked up and listened.

"Yes," said Basavaraju, "he is not well. He is losing weight and gets weaker by the day…"

He will no longer be able to carry the ambari. They are retiring him, Basavaraju said.

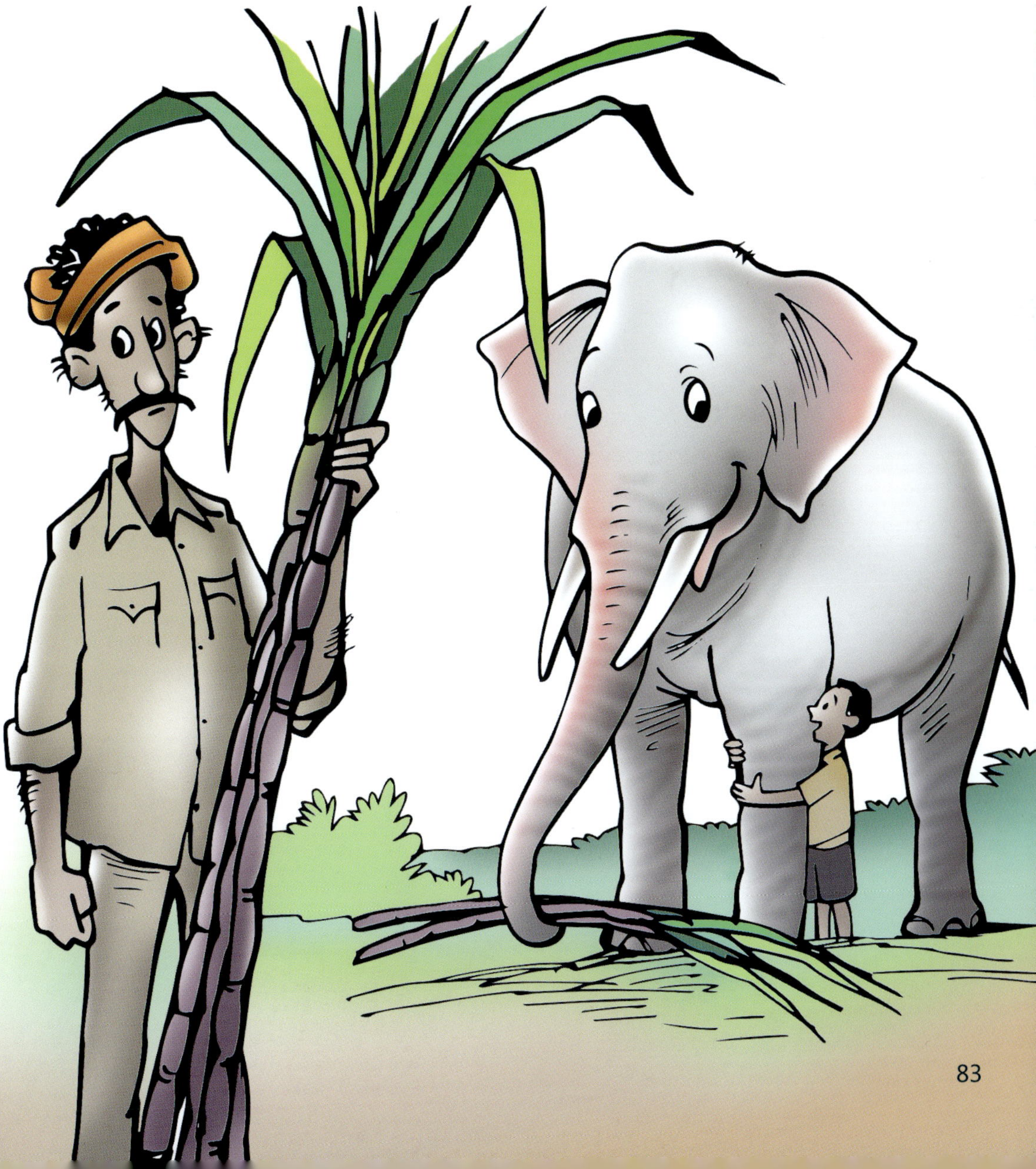

Poor Uncle Drona, Balarama thought. He was very sad. He wondered if Drona would die, just like Aunty Aaney had, all those years ago in Nagarahole forest.

Then he suddenly his name being mentioned...

"Do you think Balarama is ready? For the ambari?", Sannappa was asking.

Basavaraju said, yes, Balarama is ready. So is Arjuna. We have to wait and see...

Balarama wished they would pick him.

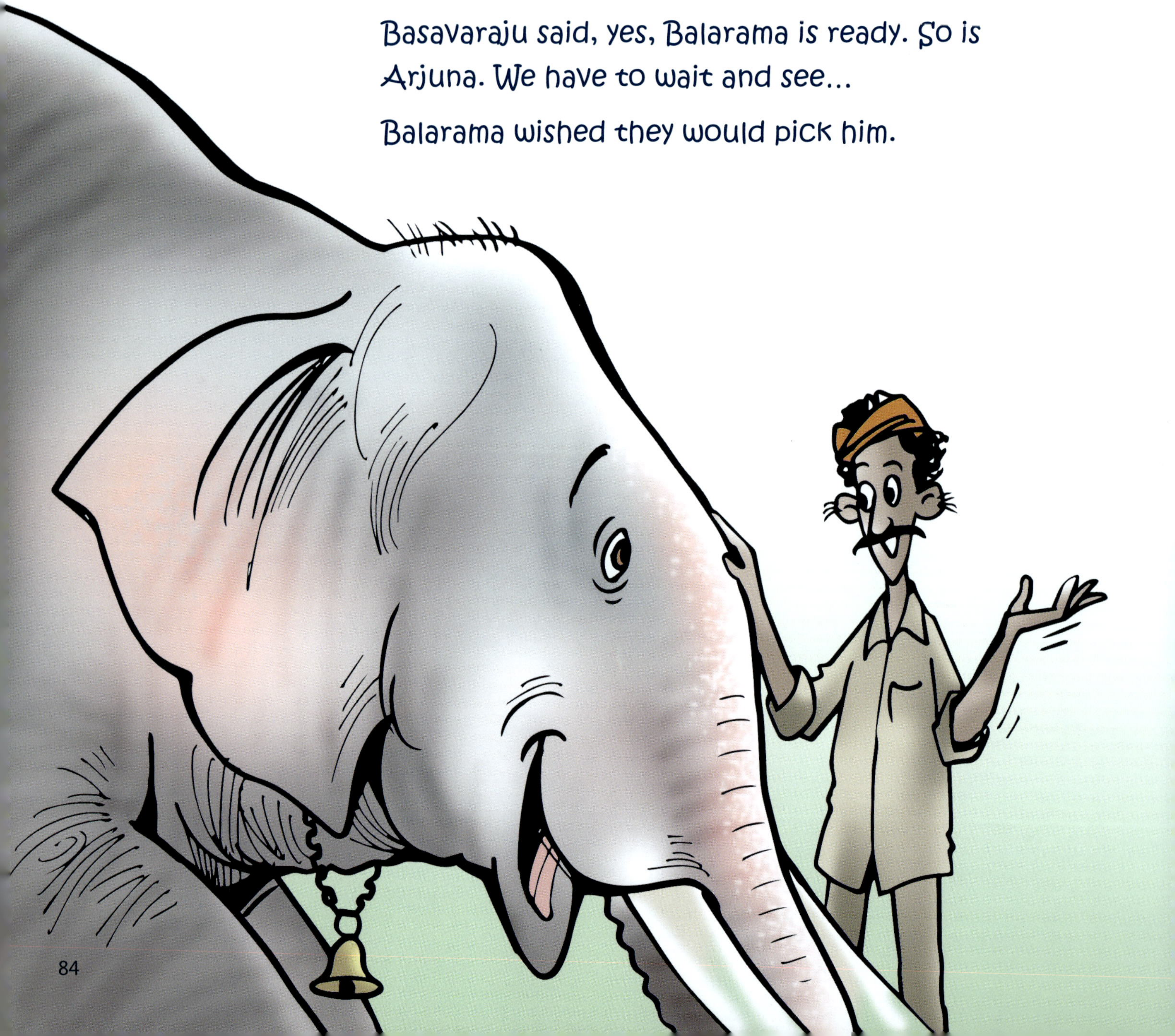

The next morning, Sannappa came to him. He was almost skipping joyfully. He said, "Balarama, you are the new ambari elephant!" and began to dance and laugh!

When he calmed down, Sannappa said, "Now Balarama, I want you to promise me, you'll make me proud. I will teach you to be the ambari elephant".

Balarama nodded vigorously. The bell round his neck peeled merrily, and he went forth, following Sannappa, to learn his new job.

Balarama became the ambari elephant. He was known all over the world. He was shown on television. Everyone cheered him, and clapped their hands joyfully when he ambled past them at the head of the procession to Banni Mantap.

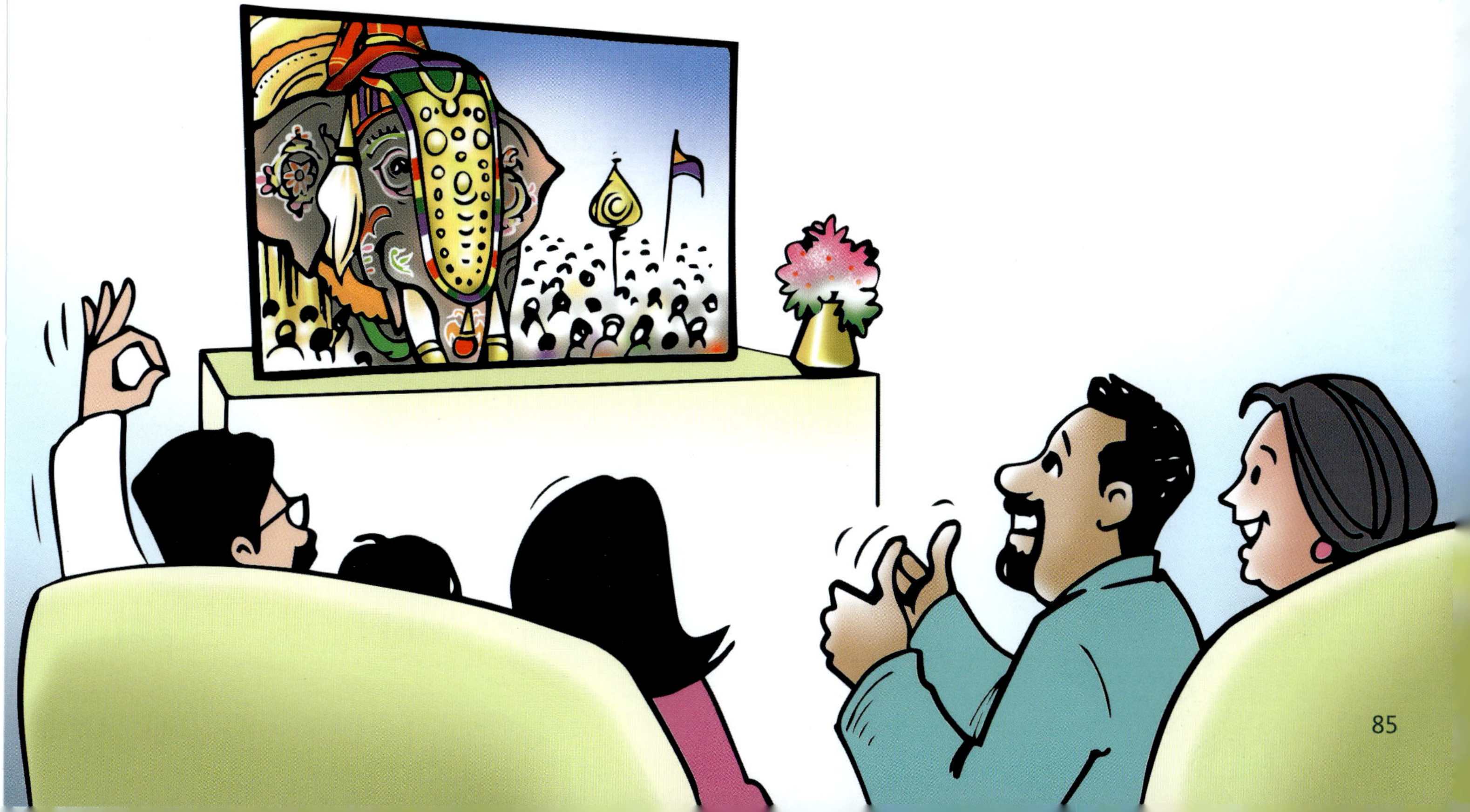

It was his first year at the head of the Jamboo Savaari. They had all returned to the camp, and Dasara had been declared a grand success. Balarama had been very popular. Everyone had welcomed him with cheering and clapping. People were throwing flowers at him... well not at him. Really, it was for the Devi, who sat in the grandest, golden ambari, which he was carrying! Walking gracefully and majestically, all the way to Banni Mantap. The streets were lined with thousands of humans! They couldn't take their eyes of him, and the other elephants in the procession!!

What a day it had been! Balarama had returned to the royal stables at midnight. Everyone had been so happy. Happy as elephants in the city can be, that is.

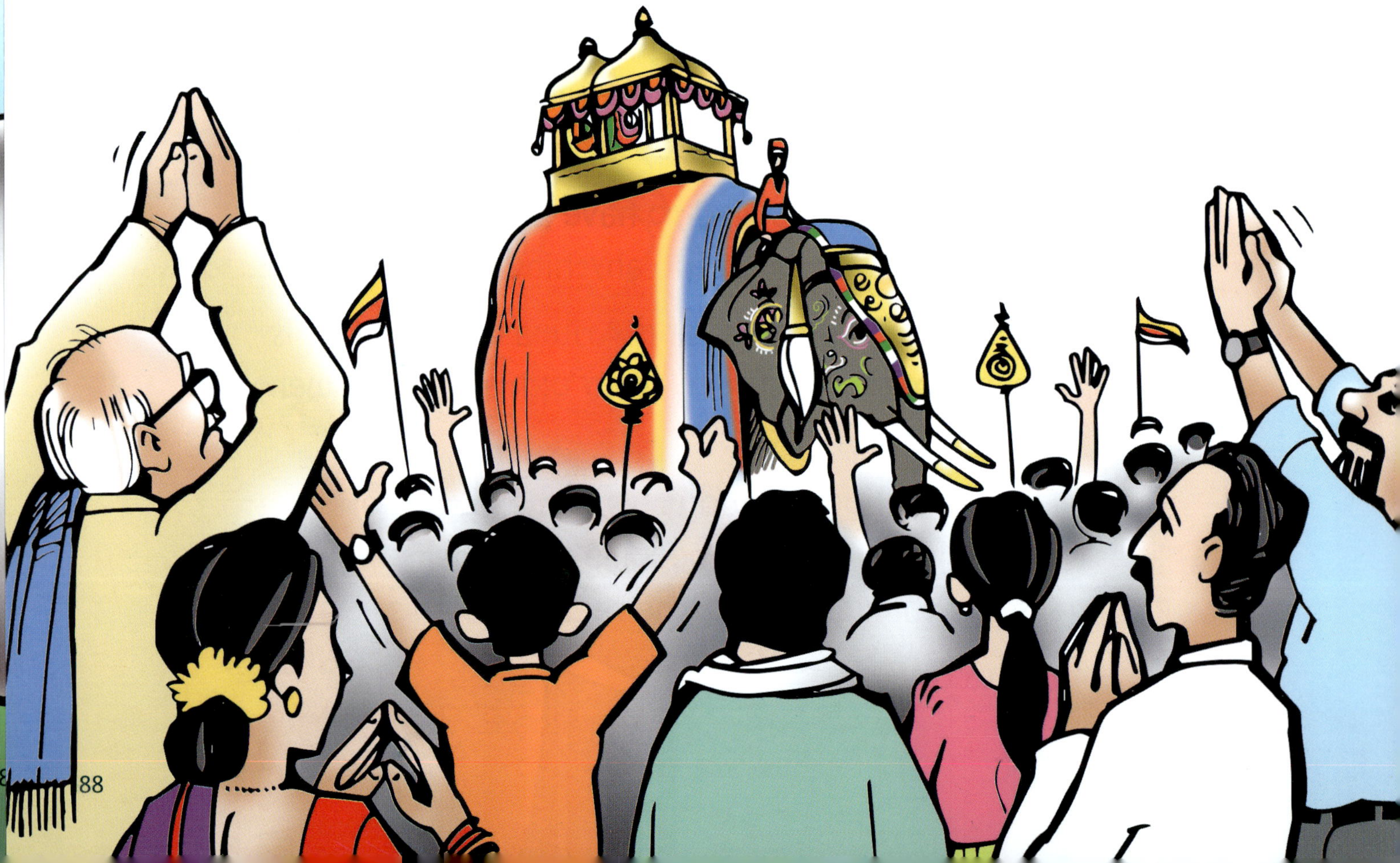

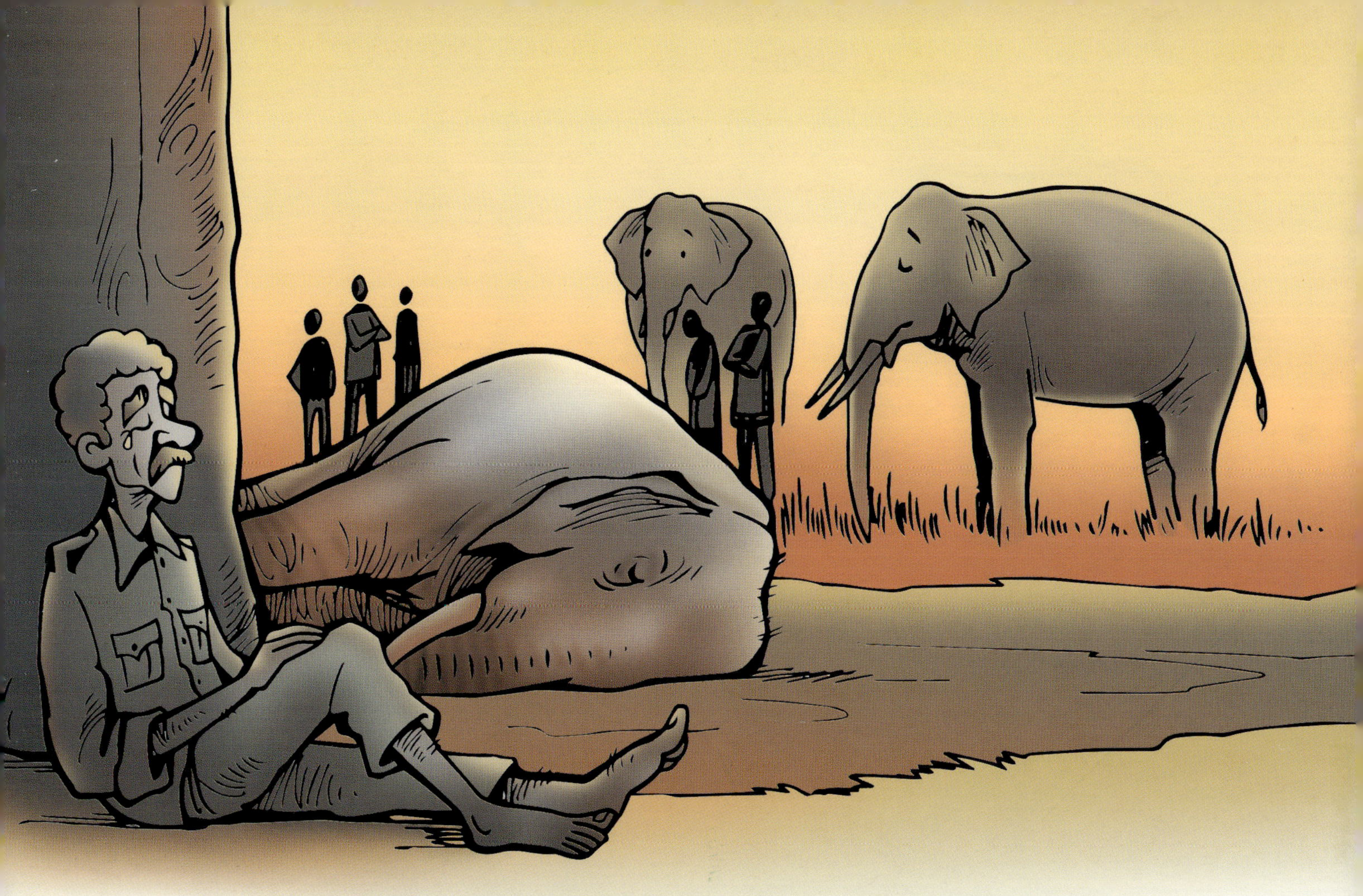

A week later they came home to camp at Dubare. Drona had not left the camp this time. He was too ill to be moved. Poor Uncle Drona! Balarama thought.

Drona had barely opened his eyes when Balarama went to tell him about the Dasara procession. He had died a few days later. All the elephants had wept. The mahouts too had been very sad. Basavaraju was inconsolable. Sannappa and Annayya did their best to cheer him up.

A few days later, when everyone had just stopped grieving for Drona, Sannappa walked up to Balarama and said, " Bala, here, I want you to meet someone. Be nice"

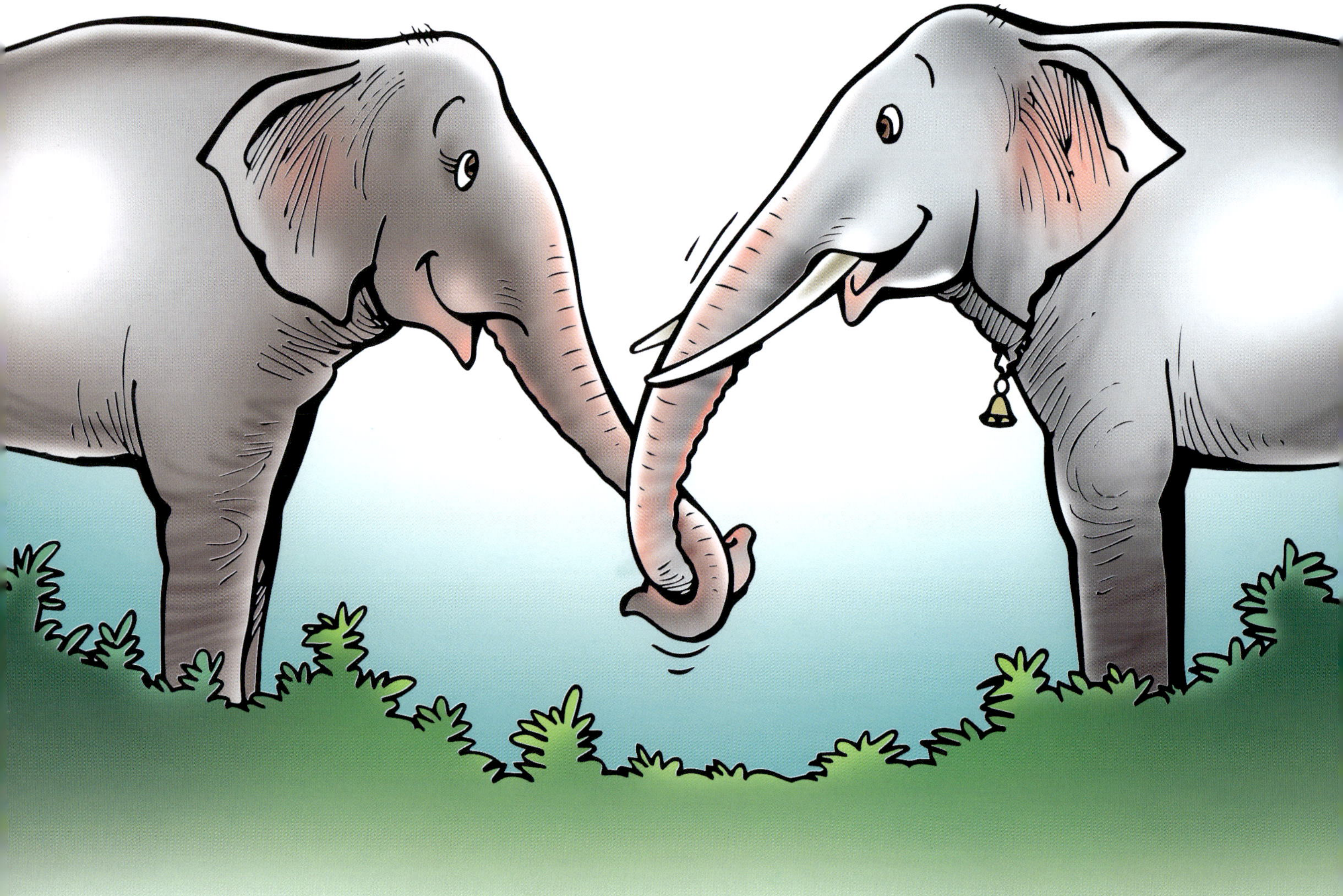

Balarama turned, smiling happily for he was always glad to see Sannappa.

"What are you smiling about?" said a sweet voice, and Balarama jumped out of his skin. He turned round and his "hellooo" froze in his throat at the vision before him. "I'm Indira," said the prettiest she elephant Balarama had ever set eyes on.

"B-b-b-balarama..."he stuttered, in great excitement, as Indira's mahout nudged her forward, and before they knew it, they were locking trunks and trumpeting joyously.

"You naughty fellow!" teased Sannappa, laughing at Balarama, who wasn't paying him any attention at all!

Ten years! It had been ten years since Indira had walked into his life, and made him the happiest elephant in the whole world. They played together, and romped about in the camp together. Indira's mahout was Venkatesha, a young man who was learning from Sannappa.

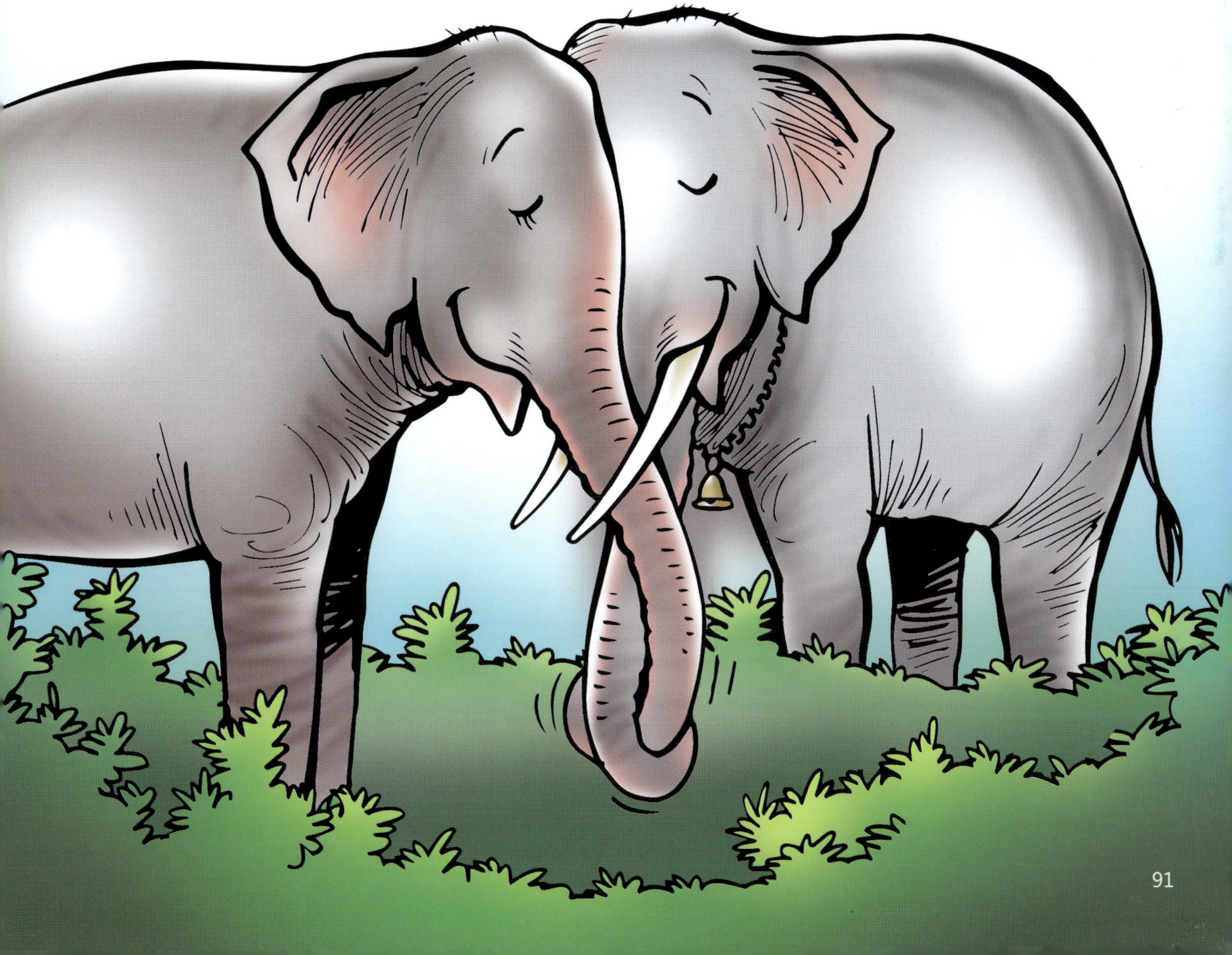

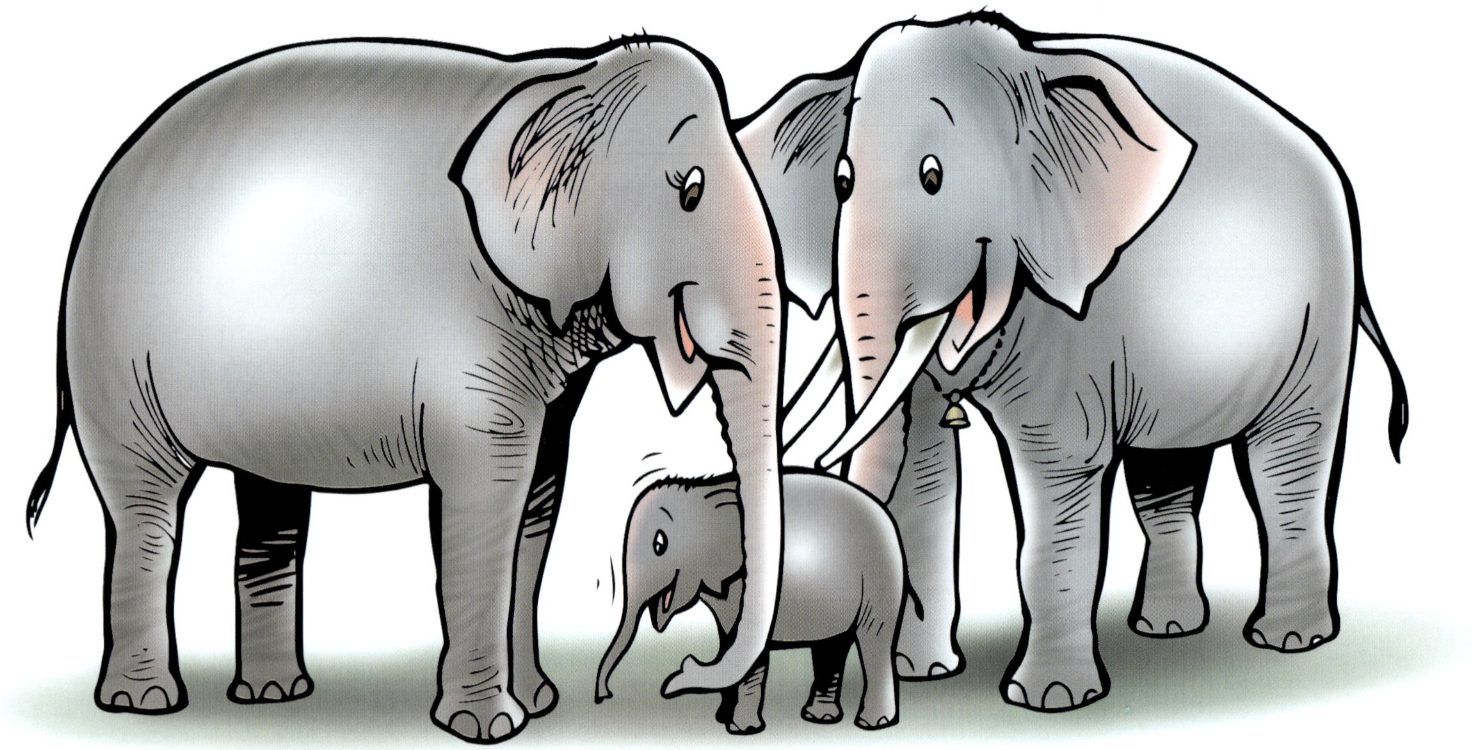

Two years later, Balarama and Indira became parents! The adorable little fellow was named Krishna. Everyone at Dubare fell in love with Baby Krishna instantly. He was the first baby elephant to be born there in 50 years! He soon became a spoilt brat, for the elephants and the mahouts vied with each other to give him little treats, and cuddle him.

Every year, when Dasara came, Indira stayed behind, while he and the other tuskers went off to Mysore. He missed her greatly. He missed baby Krishna too.

Sometimes Balarama would become sad. Krishna would never roam free in the jungle. He would grow up and become the ambari elephant, just like his Appa. It was never going to stop!

He told Krishna the story of Airavatha. When he heard the story of Ganesha, Krishna had been excited, just like Balarama all those years ago! He had sobbed loudly when he heard how Auntie Aaney had died. But when he told him about Nagarahole, and Kabini, he was puzzled. "And what is a tiger? Can you show me?" he asked. Indira would pull him close, and wind her trunk tight round him. She too did not understand why Krishna would never see the jungle.

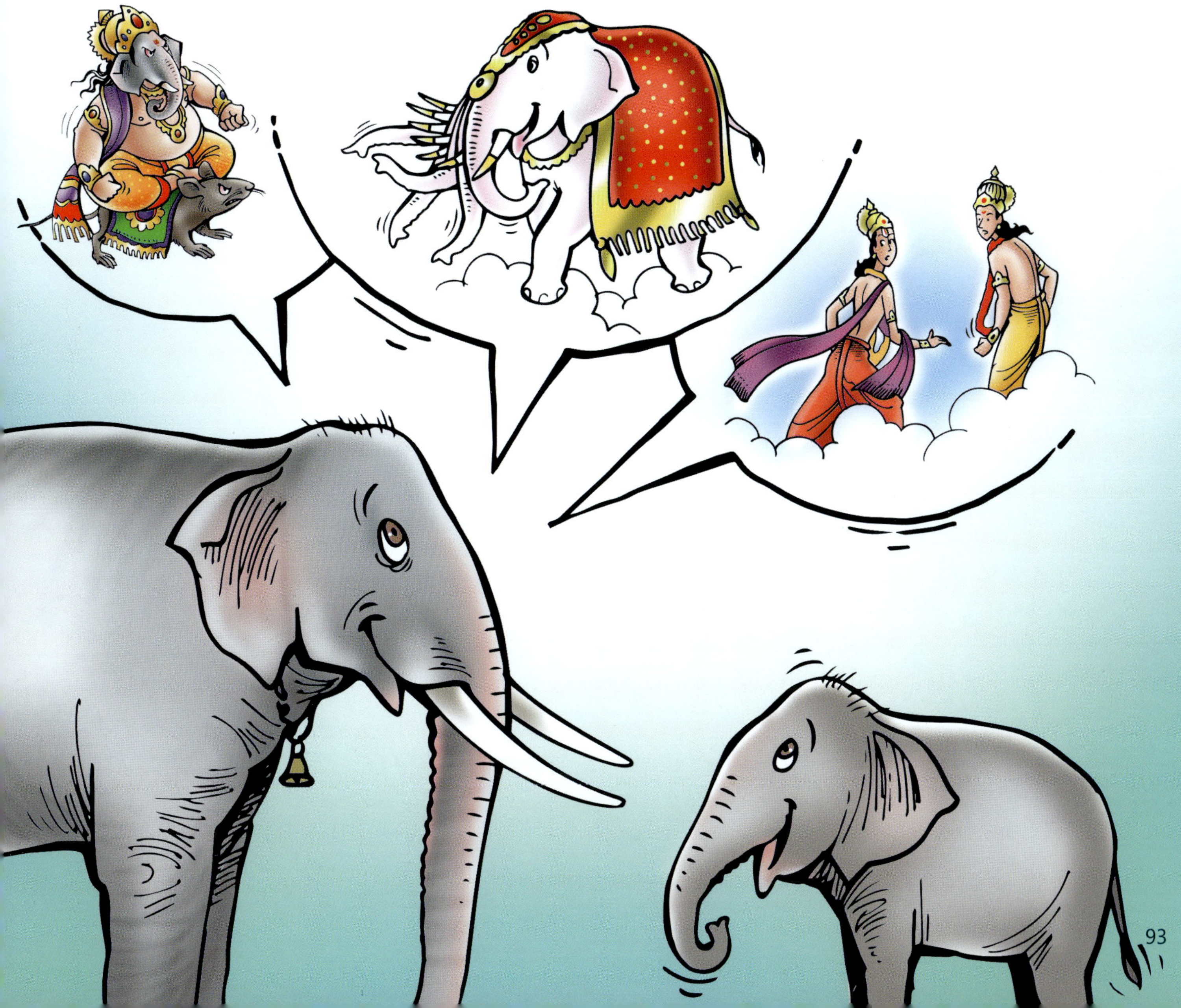

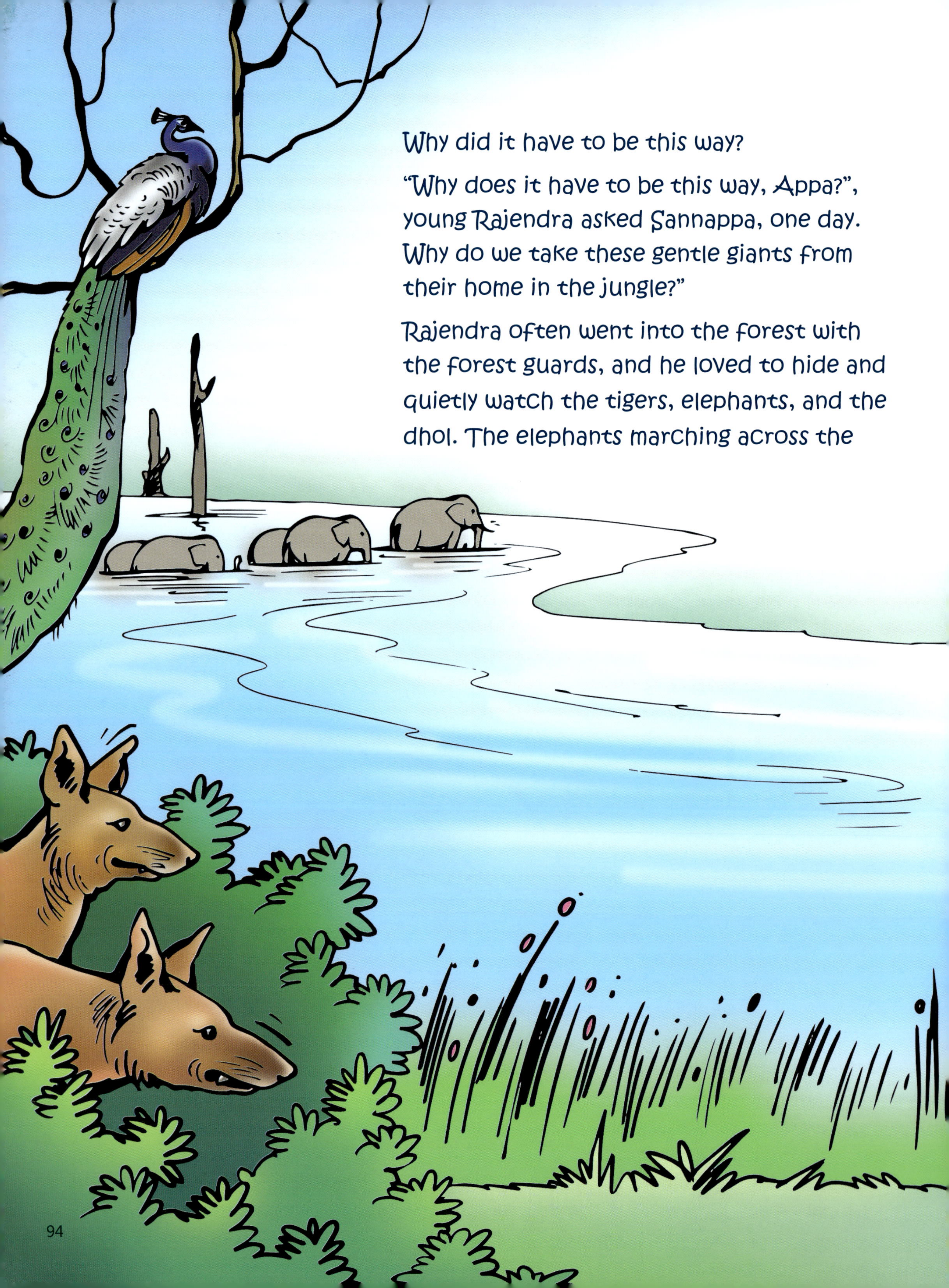

Why did it have to be this way?

"Why does it have to be this way, Appa?", young Rajendra asked Sannappa, one day. Why do we take these gentle giants from their home in the jungle?"

Rajendra often went into the forest with the forest guards, and he loved to hide and quietly watch the tigers, elephants, and the dhol. The elephants marching across the jungle and through the Kabini, was a spectacular sight. Peacocks danced, the koel and the neelakanta, flitted from tree to tree fearless. The crane and osprey posed prettily on the waters.

The forest was like heaven. The birds and beasts here had nothing to fear. Except the humans!

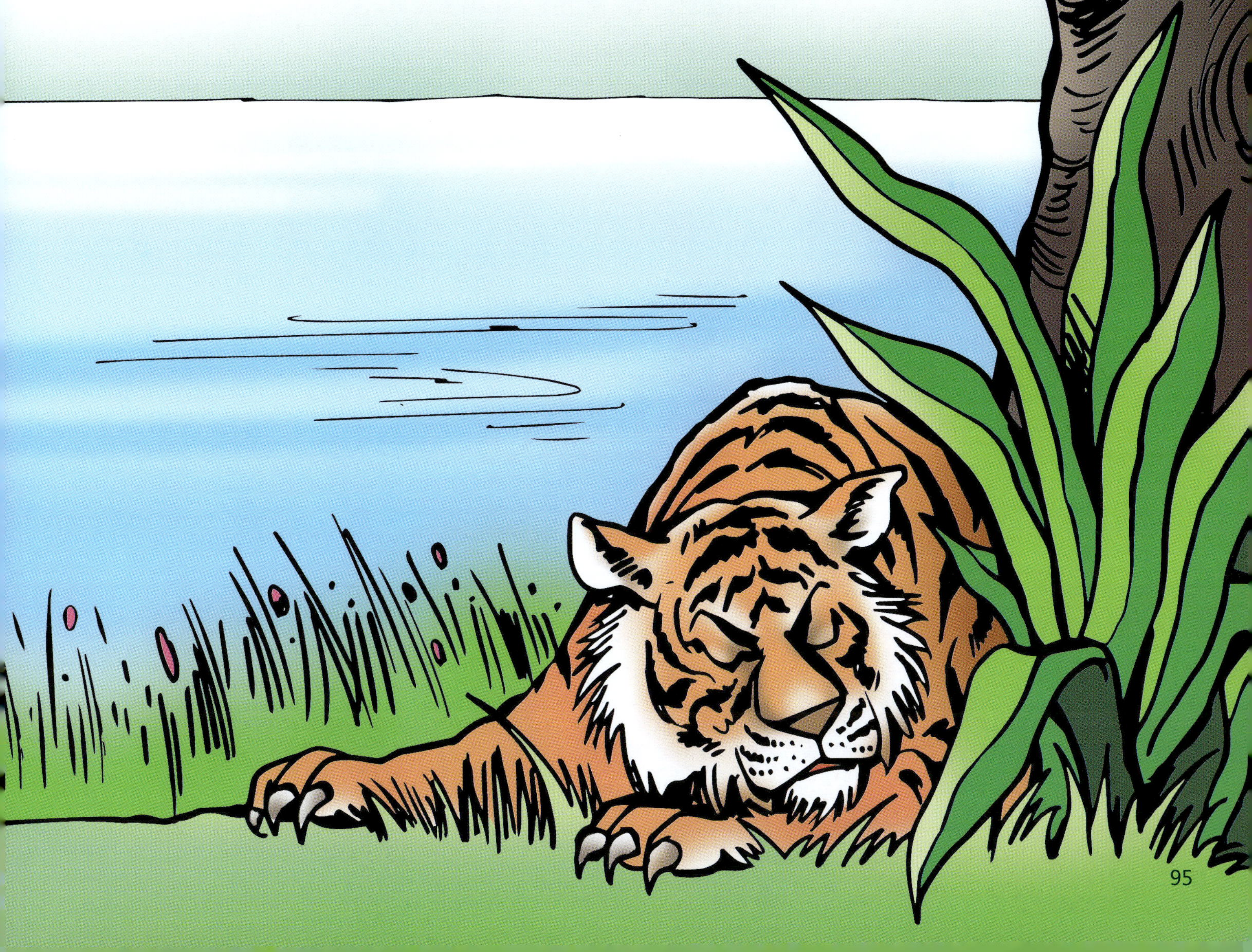

"That's the way it's been, Rajendra," said Sannappa , sadly.

It started 450 years ago. The Mysore Maharaja wanted a Nadahabba, a festival for all the people to enjoy. He chose Dasara, the festival of nine nights of the Devi. The Devi you know killed Mahishasura after a battle that lasted nine nights.

All the palace elephants were brought from their stables, and grandly decorated and on Vijayadashami, they all went in a procession to the Banni Mantap.

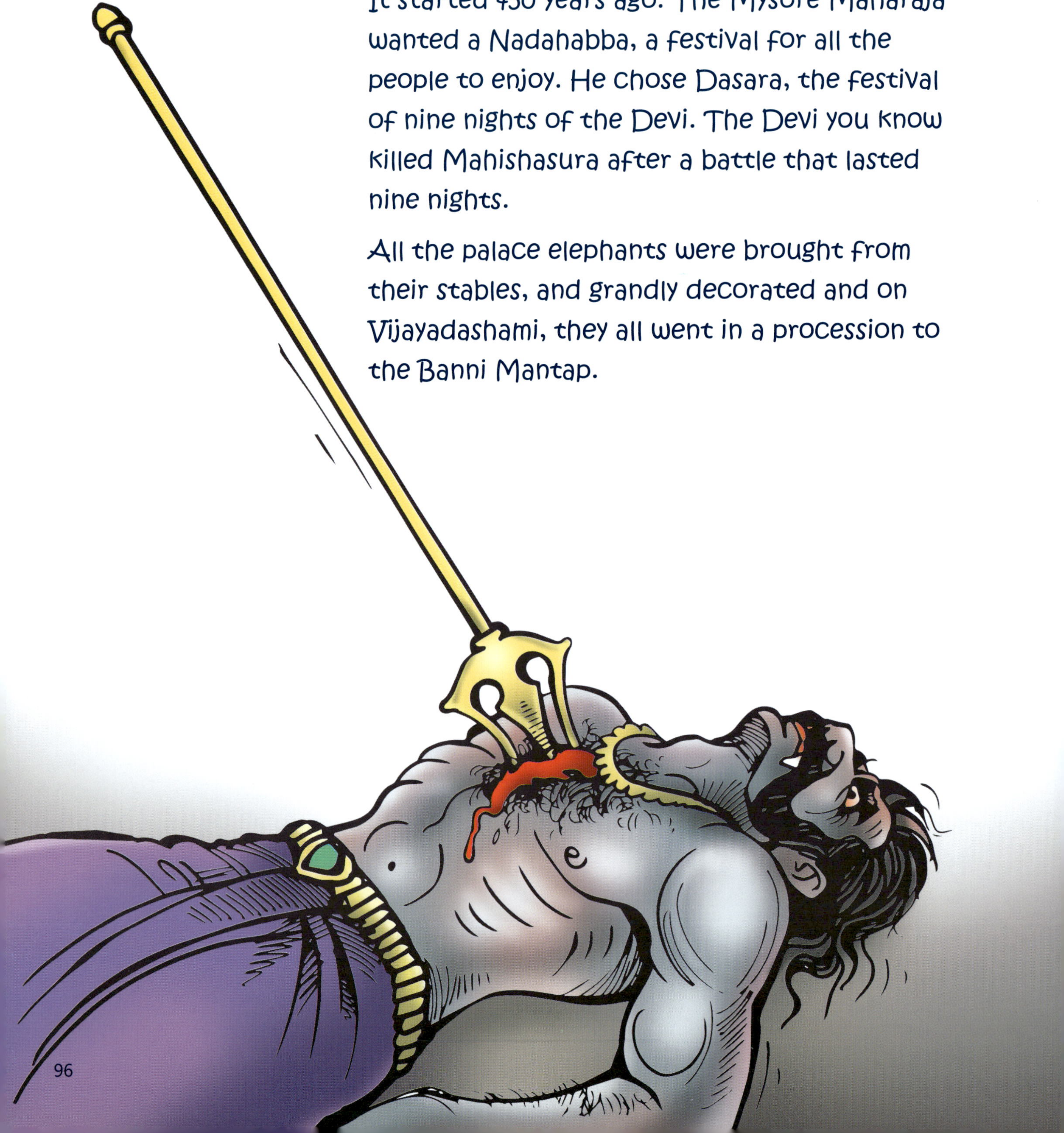

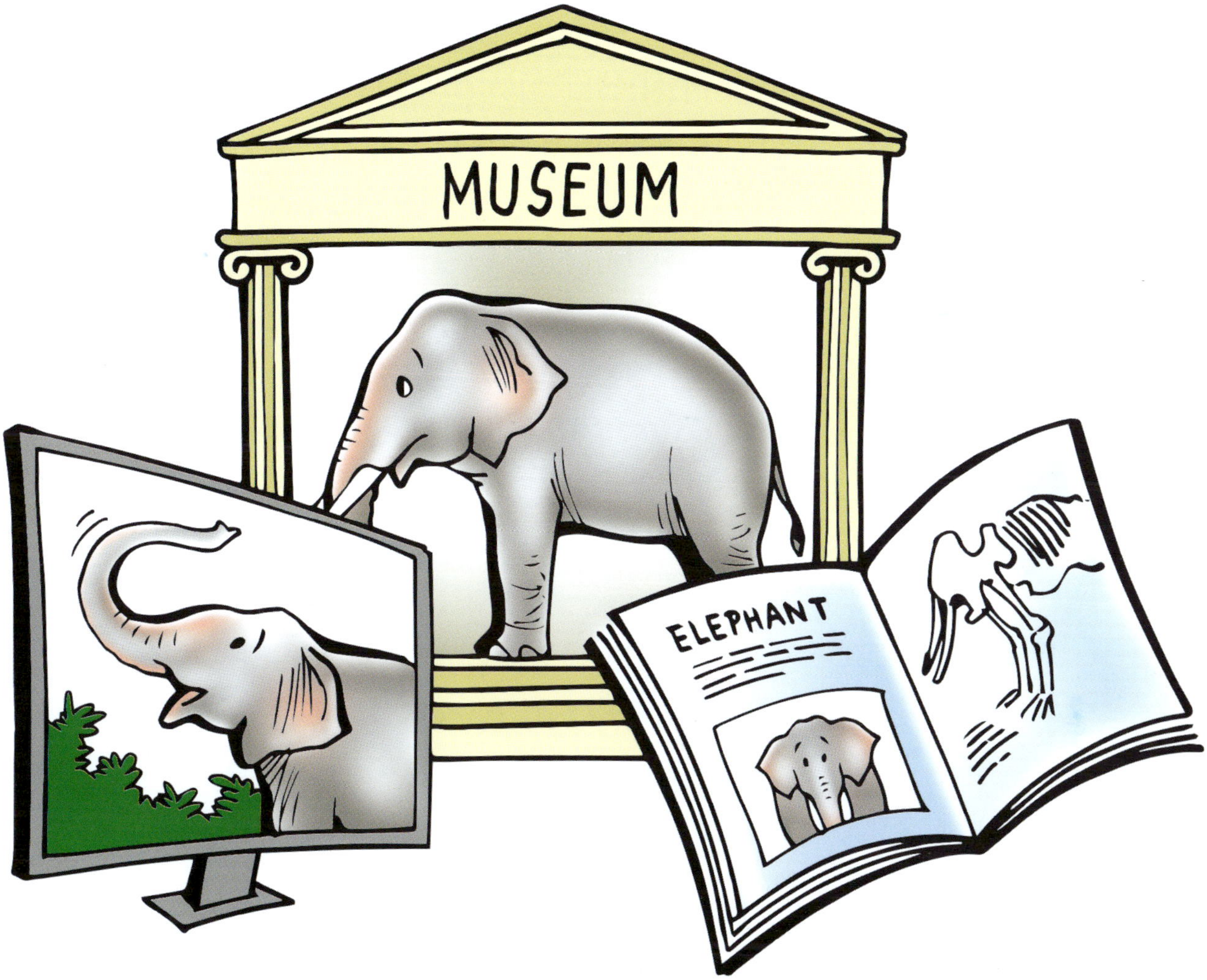

The King sat in the grand golden howdah, which was called Ambari, which was mounted on the best elephant.

Now we have no King. So the Devi's idol sits in the Ambari... One day it may all come to an end. The Government might decide to let the elephants go back to the forest.

Sannappa paused.

Speaking slowly, he said, "Or there may be no more elephants left in the jungle for us to trap."

A world without elephants! Rajendra was very angry. He went over to Baby Krishna, and hugged him tightly. He wished he could run away to the jungle. He would take Krishna, and leave him there, he said to Sannappa.

"No son!', Sannappa said quickly. "Come here, sit by me! We can't do that. When I was young, like you, I too wanted to take Devendra away from here. I had reached the Hemavathi, and was wondering how to go across. Your Tatha Ramappa caught up with me, and brought us right back.

"I was very scared. I thought he'd be very angry with me. But Tatha was not angry at all. He sat me down, and told me this wouldn't help Devendra."

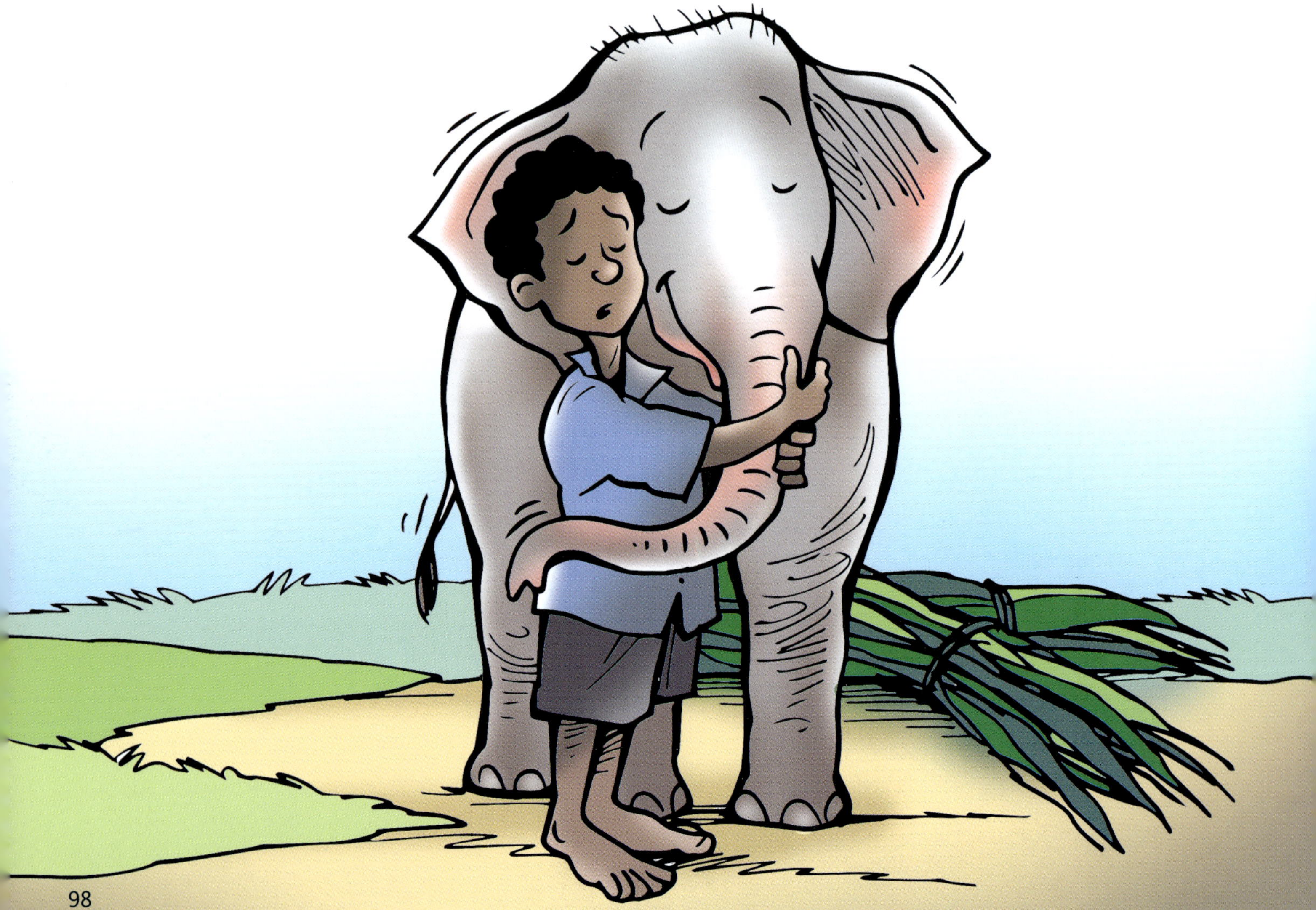

Devendra you see had become a city elephant. He would be very confused and scared in the jungle. Other elephants might fight him and he might die.

So you see, Rajendra, Krishna is just a baby. He needs his mother. He needs us. We must do the best we can with what we have.

Let's just love Krishna, Balarama Indira, Arjuna... and be kind to them."

It's time now to say goodbye to Balarama and his friends. Perhaps you will meet them all one day, if you happen to visit the Mysore Dasara. Now that you know the story of Balarama's life in the jungle, you will think kindly of him and hope that there will always be elephants in the forest, won't you?

Now everyone knows the story of Balarama, the Dasara Elephant. Wouldn't you like to meet him one day and say, "Hey! Balarama! I know all about you! and I love you!!

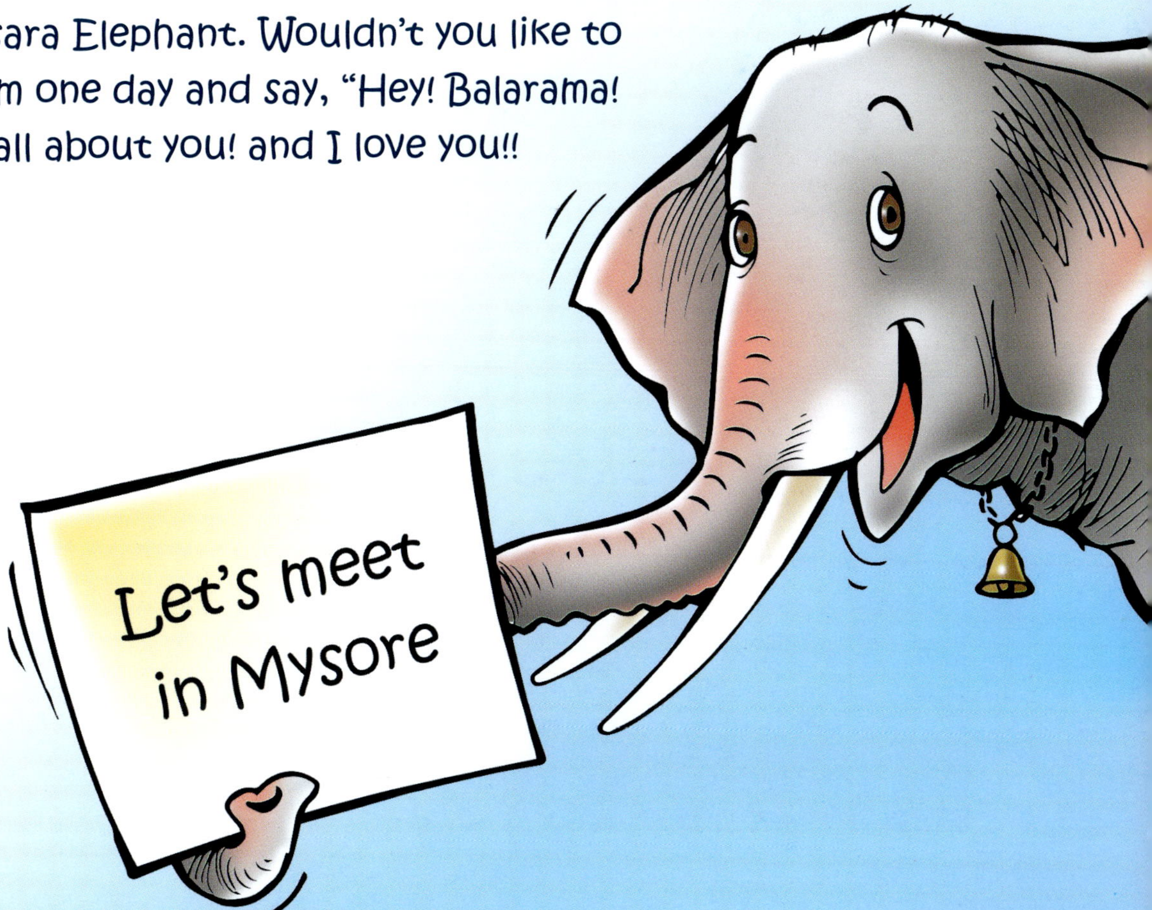

About Mysore Dasara

Dasara was celebrated by the kings of Vijayanagara Empire 500 years ago. The Italian traveler Niccolo de' Conti has descried the celebrations as a grand religious and martial event. Chamundeshwari, who battled Mahishasura for nine nights and killed him, was worshipped. Conti writes that singing, dancing, fireworks and a military parade (just like our Republic Day!) and sports competitions were organised!

When the Vijayanagar Empire came to an end, and Muslim rule began, Dasara was not celebrated. The Wadiyars of Mysore began celebrating Dasara in 1610! Exactly, 507 years ago, Raja Wadiyar I started the tradition of Dasara!

The King wanted a Nadahabba, a State festival, where the citizens could see the grandeur of the kingdom and know how the military protected. In 1805, Krishnaraja Wadiyar III began a new tradition. A special Durbar (Royal Court) was held in the Palace, and all the royal family, royal guests, and many citizens were invited to attend.

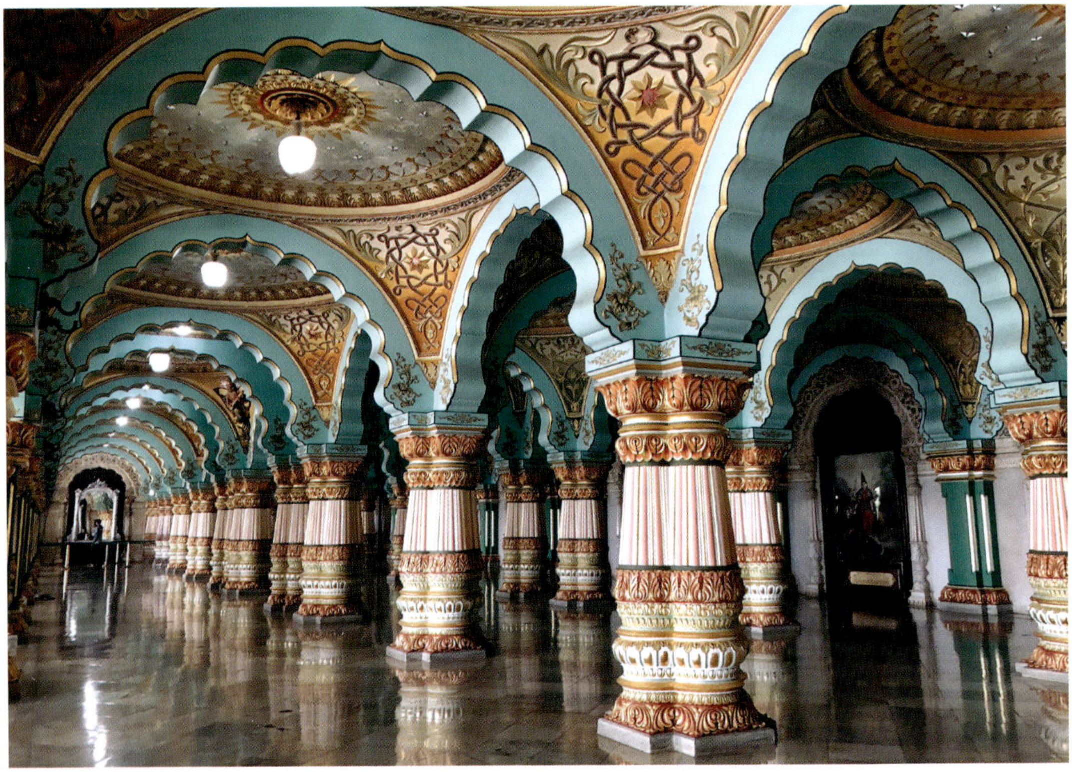

Photo: D. K. Bhaskar

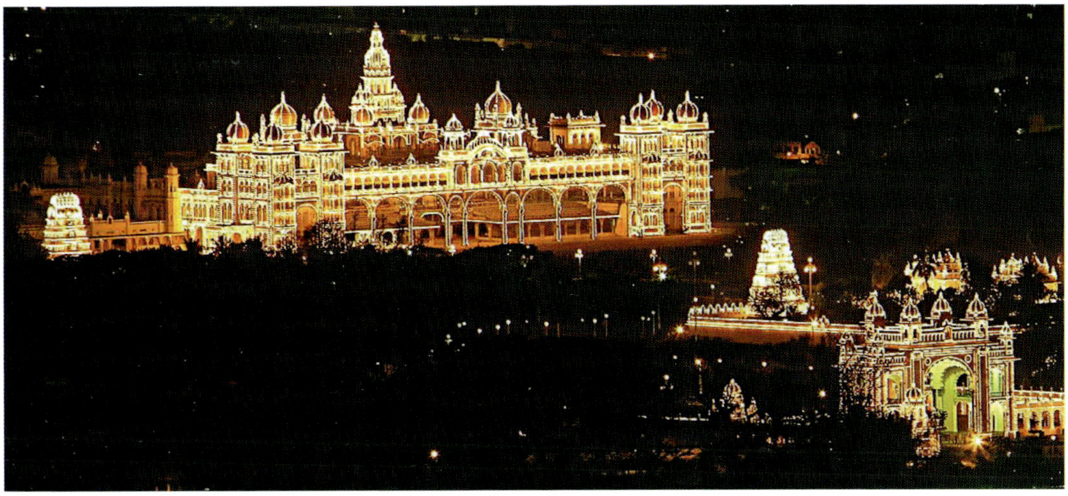

In 2013, when the King Srikanta Datta Narasimharaja Wadiyar died, there was no one to succeed him. The Durbar was held, by placing the Royal Sword -Pattada Katthi on the Golden Throne.

On Mahanavami Day, which was most auspicious, the Pattada Katthi is worshipped, and taken out in a procession of elephants, camels and horses.

During the ten days of Dasara, a 100, 000 light bulbs are used to illuminate the entire palace! Every evening from 7 pm to 10 pm, the Palace is grandly lit up, and resembles the palace of Indra in Swarga! The royal courtyard comes to life every evening, with music and dance and many religious programmes.

Vijayadashami, the tenth day, is the day Devi Chamundeswari slew Mahishasura. This is the grandest day, and its finale is the Jamboo Savaari. In the old days, the great Golden Ambari would be mounted on the best elephant in the palace stables. The elephant is grandly decorated in brightly coloured silk and satin. A jewelled headpiece that covers the forehead and trunk completes the elephant's attire. In the old days the Maharaja would sit in the ambari. Behind him the crown prince would be seated. Now it is the idol of Chamundeshwari that goes in a procession from the Palace to Banni Mantapa.

At the Banni Mantap the sacred Banni Tree is worshipped. When the Pandavas were exiled for 12 years, they had to spend the 13th year in Agnyatavasa (incognito) they hid their weapons in the Banni Tree. They retrieved their weapons when war became inevitable. They worshipped the Banni Tree, which had safeguarded their weapons, and prayed for victory. Since then, all kings of ancient India have worshipped the Banni Tree before going into battle.

The Wadiyar Kings worshipped the Banni Tree, and took a sapling back to the Palace.

Once the Jamboo Savaari reached the Banni Mantap, as the evening darkens, people are entertained by the magnificent Panjina Kavayatthu- the Torch light Parade. It's a dance of the flaming torches that lights up the skies.

The Ambari, or the Golden Howdah is the cynosure of all eyes. The Ambari is made from solid gold, and weighs 750 kilos (1654 lbs)! No one knows how old the howdah is, or which Wadiyar Raja was the first to sit in it and ride to the Banni Mantap.

It has two wide seats, one for the Maharaja, and another smaller seat behind

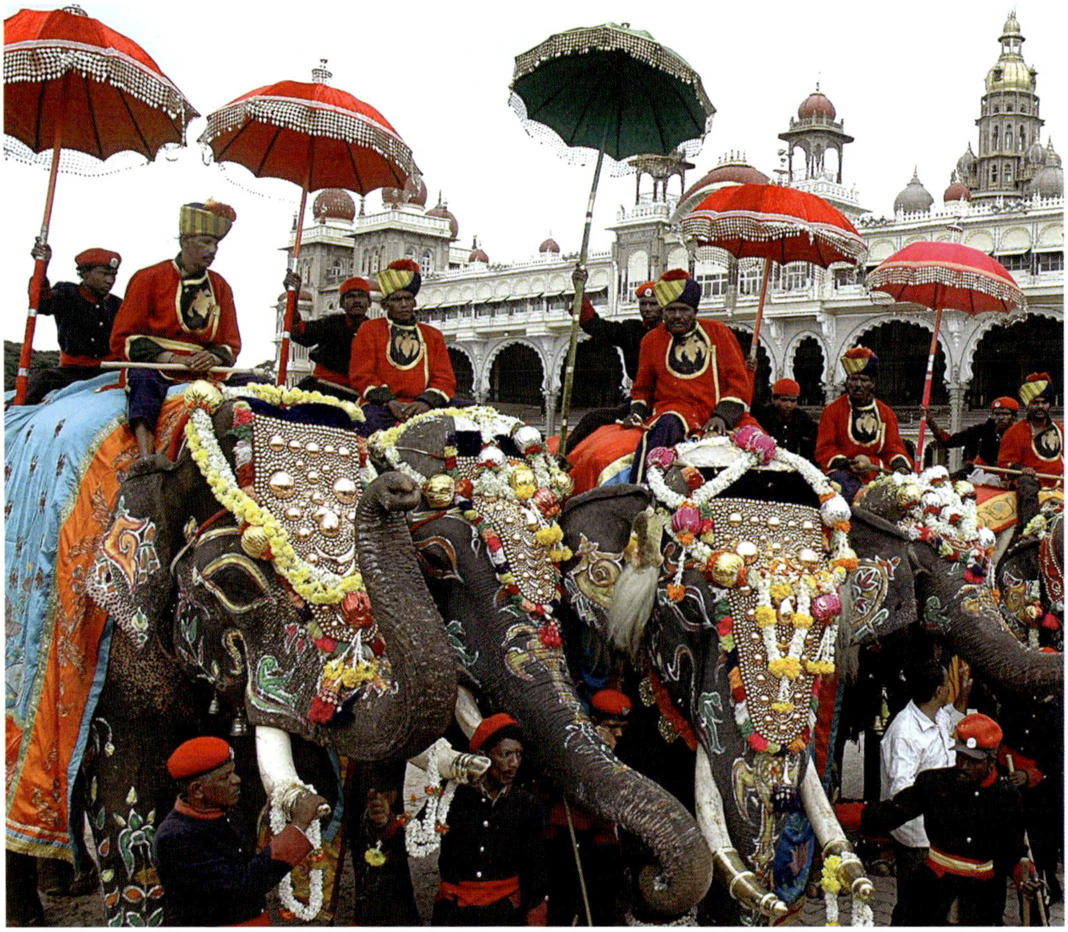

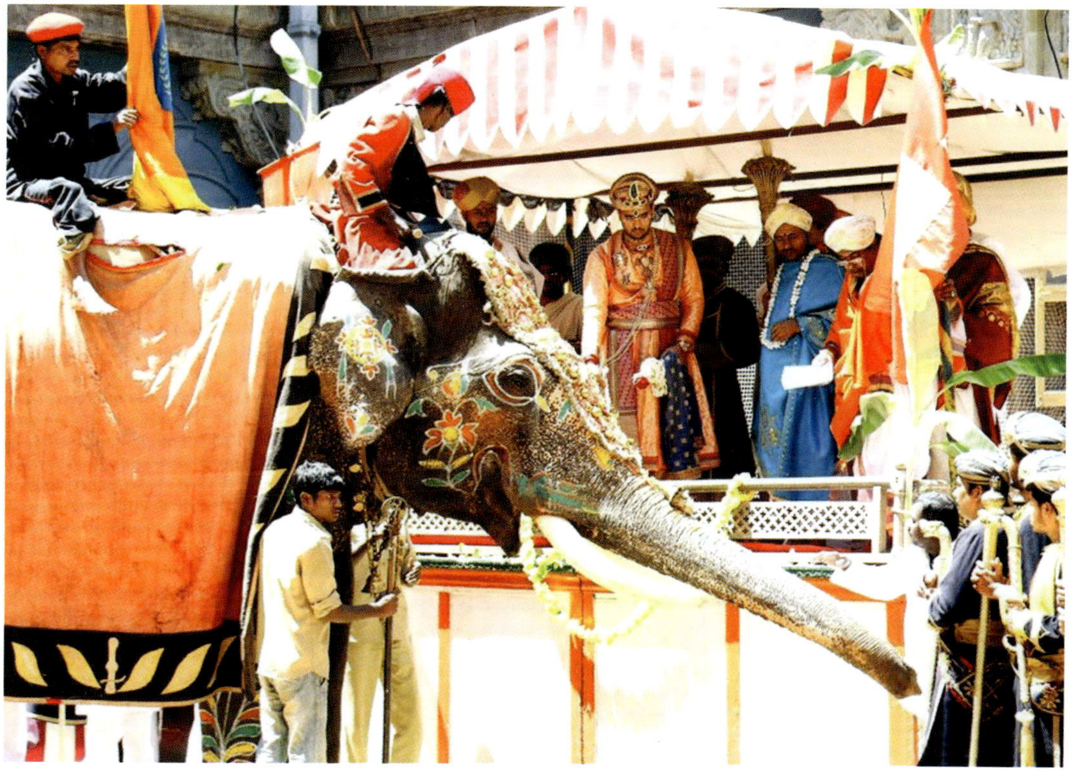

it for the Yuvaraja or the Crown Prince. After royalty was abolished, it is the Devi Chamundeshwari who rides in the howdah.

The Ambari elephant has to be strong, stable and regal in bearing. Once chosen, he must practice for weeks. Canon blasts, the crowds or the noises in the city must not distract the elephant!

The elephant chosen to carry the Ambari has to be strong, and stoic. Which means they must be unfazed by the noise of cannon blasts, crowds of people milling the streets. He must remember that he is carrying the sacred Ambari with the idol of the Goddess in it.

The elephant, in facts strides like a king. In the jungle, lions and tigers bow before the elephant! If elephants were human, they would all be royal- kings or queens!

In all these 500 years, no one has ever heard of the Ambari falling off!

Photo courtesy: Sri Yaduveer Krishnadatta Chamaraja Wadiyar

Glossary

Aarathi
Aarathi is a Hindu religious ritual of worship with burning camphor or an oil wick, symbolizing the removal of darkness.

Aaysa... Aaaisa
A chant that works in construction sites, or movers intone to keep the rhythm when pushing or lifting heavy weight.

Airavata
The mythological white elephant that is mount of the rain god Indra.

Ambari
A golden howdah that has been in use for centuries mounted on the lead elephant during the Dasara festivities.

Amma
Mother in Kannada.

Appa
Father in Kannada.

Ashoka
Was one of the successful emperors of India belonging to the Maurya dynasty between 262-238 BCE.

Auntie Aaney
An elderly elephant in the same herd that takes care of the younger elephants along with the Matriarch.

Brahma Vishnu Shiva
The Hindu Trinity of Gods.

Burray
Stripe in Kannada. Here, a name given to another tiger in the forest home of Balarama.

Chamundeshwari
Deity revered by the Hindus as the remover of evil over good and one that is characteristic of Dasara festivities.

Chiroo
Chirathe is the Kannada word for leopard. Here, Chiroo is the name of a leopard in the forest.

Dasara
A ten-day long festival celebrating the truth over evil.

Dubare
A reserve forest patch on the banks of River Kaveri where a temporary elephant camp is utilized as a tourism initiative.

Giduga
Eagle in Kannada.

Hemavathi
A river originating in the Western Ghats and a tributary to the mighty River Kaveri.

Heyday
The hood of a cobra in Kannada. Here, a name given to the cobra.

Hughlie
The Kannada word for tiger is huli. Here, it is the name given to a tiger, a fellow creature of Balarama in the forest.

Kabini
A River in the Western Ghats. It is a tributary of the mighty Kaveri River.

Kakankote
A forest patch in the Western Ghats famous for herds of wild elephants.

Kattepura
A little village in the southern state of Karnataka.

Khedda
A stockade trap method of elephant capture for 100 years (1873-1973) in the Kakankote forest patch.

Kumkum
A powder used for social and religious markings among Hindus. It is usually made from dried powdered turmeric.

Mahout
The trainer of elephants. Usually, each elephant has a personal mahout and they remain devoted to their mahout all their lives.

Motif
A decorative design or pattern.

Mysore
A city in Karnataka famous for silk, sandalwood and the Mysore palace, where the Dasara procession begins.

Mysore Palace
Once the official residence of the Wadiyars, erstwhile kings of Mysore. The palace is now the venue of Dasara festivities and a historical attraction.

Nada Habba
State Festival, in Kannada.

Nagarahole
Nagarahole is the 7th National park and tiger reserve in India, part of the Western Ghats and famous for the herds of elephants along the Kabini reservoir.

Polka
A reference given to Leopard in the jungle because of its characteristic spots on its body.

Vijayadashami
Tenth day of the Dasara festivities celebrated on the full moon day culminating in a grand procession in different parts of India.

Wadiyars
A successful dynasty that ruled the Mysore province from 1399 to 1950. In 1610, Raja Wadiyar I, started the first Dasara, while ruling from Srirangapatna, a town on the banks of River Kaveri.

Acknowledgement

A book of this nature can only see its light with wide-ranging support from diverse group of individuals and organizations. We thank CLIC Abroad Foundation for their generous support of many years for our initiatives in education innovation. Thanks to Abraham Baldwin Agricultural College for continued support on collaboration and exchange programs in India. Dr. Tom Grant has continued to believe in our ongoing efforts with storytelling and visual narration. Thanks to him for being a part of all of our efforts. We express our sincere thanks to Lori Sra and Frank Christian for being the source of strength in the pursuit of our passion.

We have continually sought guidance and support from Dr. Kamala Bawa from University of Massachusetts. We thank him for his unwavering support, generosity and inspiration and belief in the power of story telling in conservation. We remember the late, Manikandan Subbiah, Conservator of Forests, Government of Karnataka with whom we had many days and nights of conversation in the heart of the jungle. He helped move this story forward. It is ironic that when this manuscript was in the works, we received the tragic news of his death, trampled by a wild elephant. We remember him with deep respect, and hope that this book will serve as reminder of the dedication of forest officers who court death in the line of duty.

We fondly thank Prof. Ramesh from NLSIU for his support in the development of the manuscript. Our sincere and grateful thanks to Dr. Yellappa Reddy for his inspiration and forever providing a positive outreach with our pursuits. Ideas, conceptualization and thoughts often are given a structured direction in conversation with friends and we thank long time friend Rajesh Shrivana for helping with background information as we made progress with the book. We gratefully acknowledge the inspirational support and cheerful encouragement of Ramadas Kamath who kept the momentum going, and believed in our mission to tell compelling stories. We all need friends to keep up our cheer in the process of such complex work. Thanks to K.P. Nagaraj for being ever so supportive and hugely encouraging despite all adversities.

It takes a village to make a society. Creating an illustrated book is a complex process involving family and friends, near and far. Varchus Urs has been strong supporter and has been encouraging at many stages of production of this book. I fondly remember and thank talented Dr. Arun S.K. who has helped me every time I have reached out to him. In our creative pursuits and professional visual storytelling Jogi Franics of Nikon India has helped and supported on so many occasions. We sincerely acknowledge and thank him for encouragement and continued friendship.

We thank Satish and Bose Madappa, who has come along in our journey for many years, helping with fieldwork, logistics and fixing problems.

We greatly appreciate and thank Parthiv Parekh, Murali Kamma and Mehul Parekh who have stood with our passion for nearly a decade encouraging us to keep dreaming and pursuing our interests. Some friends stand and cheer you for your work and keep motivating in pursuit of excellence. We thank two wonderful friends, Ravi Sinha and Katherine Cleland for their cheer and support as we bring such stories into the world.

We have caused our loved ones much stress and frustration while growing this book. They have borne it with stoic love and boundless generosity. Our deepest gratitude to our spouses and parents for always being there! You make us better and bring out the best in us. Thank you.

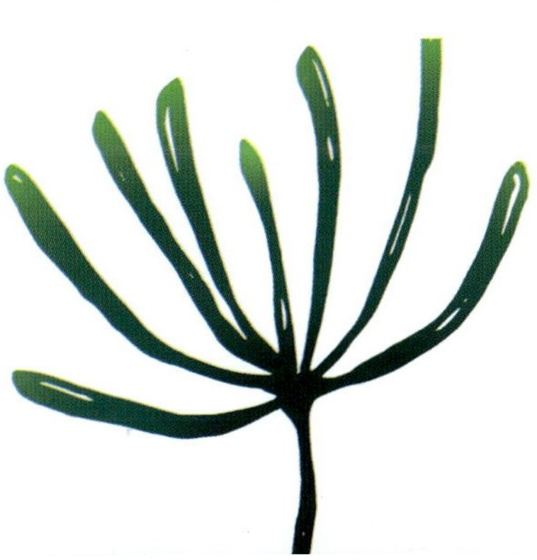

About the authors and illustrator

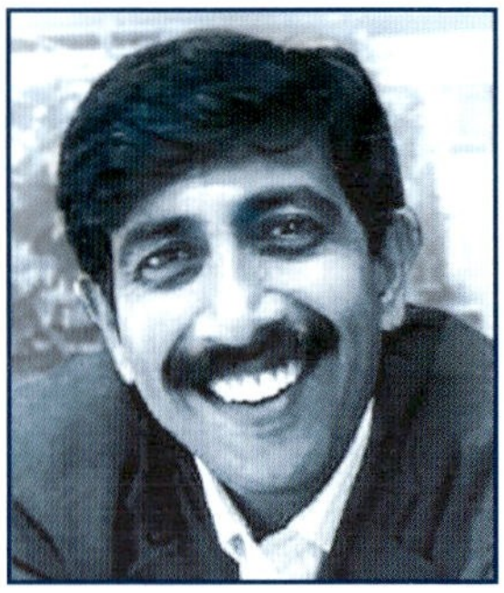

D. K. Bhaskar is an education innovator, visual storyteller & cultural explorer. He is the co-producer of the award-winning documentary "Elephants in the Coffee" and author of the popular book, "The Fragile Forest: Inside Brazilian Amazonia". Bhaskar is an international Fellow of the Explorer's Club, a Fulbright specialist and a finalist for the US Presidential Leadership Fellowship. At present he is the Managing Partner for based Choice Solar, LLC, a US based renewable portable energy company.

Based in Kansas City, Bhaskar is the founder of CLIC Abroad Foundation and Augusta International Photo Festival. He is passionate about elephants and lifelong supporter of its conservation efforts.

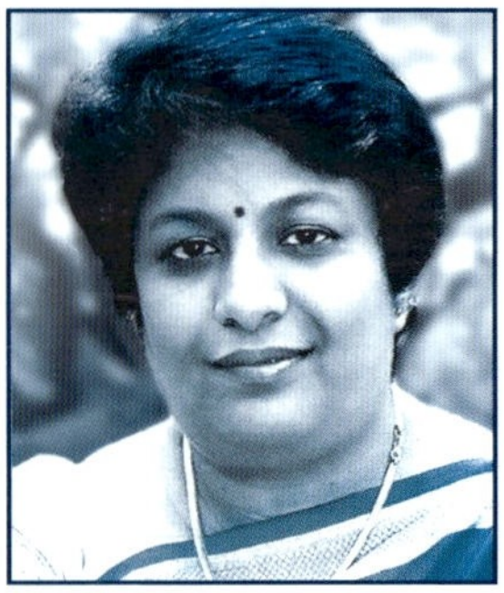

Alladi Jayasri is a journalist and writer. She has worked with leading newspapers The Hindu, The Times of India and Indian Express, writing and reporting extensively on the environment. She has been a Media Fellow of the National Foundation for India (1999) writing a series on "Success Stories in Women's Empowerment in Karnataka" and won the WISCOMP Scholar of Peace Media Fellowship in 2000, writing on "Empowerment of Women: Answers From Tibet".

Based in Virginia, Jayasri is currently chronicling the history of her family. She is passionate about The Ramayana, and deeply curious about the worlds within it, and all the ways in which it travels in our world.

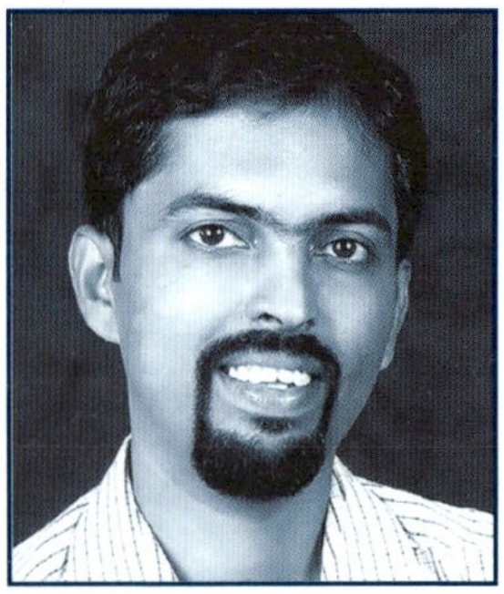

Yathi Siddakatte is an internationally recognized visual storyteller and illustrator whose work spans diverse mediums. A Master's in Fine Art from Karnataka Chitrakala Parishat, one of India's leading art schools, he began his career as an illustrator/ political cartoonist in the English daily, Deccan Herald. Yathish has constantly pursued his passion for creating nature art contributing his work in print and digital formats. His work today is an expression of his belief in education through art and lends support to campaigns, workshops, literature summits, and social causes.

Based in Bangalore and working for a software company, Yathish's illustrations and cartoons have been exhibited in Portugal, Spain, Italy, Peru, Brazil, Iran and India.

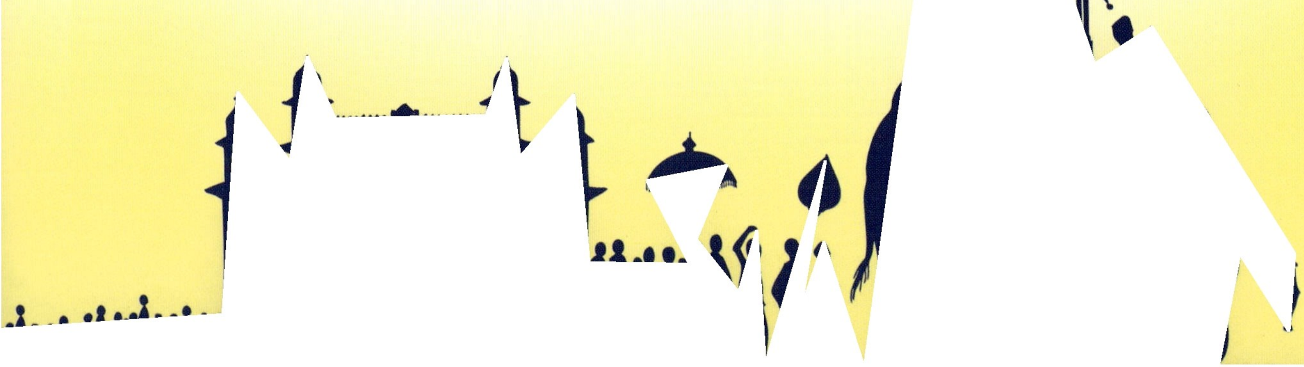